Web Designer's Reference
An Integrated Approach to Web Design with XHTML and CSS

Craig Grannell

friendsof

DESIGNER TO DESIGNER™

an Apress® company

Web Designer's Reference: An Integrated Approach to Web Design with XHTML and CSS

Credits

Lead Editors Steve Rycroft and Chris Mills	**Production Editor** Katie Stence
Technical Reviewer David Powers	**Compositor** Molly Sharp, ContentWorks
Editorial Board Steve Anglin, Dan Appleman, Ewan Buckingham, Gary Cornell, Tony Davis, Jason Gilmore, Chris Mills, Dominic Shakeshaft, Jim Sumser	**Proofreader** Elizabeth Berry
	Indexer Kevin Broccoli
Project Manager Beth Christmas	**Artist** Kinetic Publishing Services, LLC
Copy Edit Manager Nicole LeClerc	**Cover Designer** Kurt Krames
Copy Editors Nicole LeClerc and Damon Larson	**Cover Photography** Craig Grannell
Production Manager Kari Brooks-Copony	**Manufacturing Manager** Tom Debolski

CONTENTS AT A GLANCE

CONTENTS

Chapter 3: Working with Text 65

Chapter 4: Working with Images 105

CONTENTS

ABOUT THE AUTHOR

Craig Grannell is a well-known web designer who's been shouting about web standards at whoever will listen for the past few years, and now finally has this book he can throw at them instead.

Originally trained in the fine arts, Craig eventually became totally immersed in the world of digital media. Along the way, his creative projects encompassed everything from video and installation-based audio work, to strange live performances—sometimes with the aid of a computer, televisions, videos, and a PA system, and sometimes with a small bag of water above his head. His creative, playful work, which usually contained a dark, satirical edge, struck a chord with those who saw it, leading to successful appearances at a number of leading European media arts festivals.

Craig soon realized he'd actually have to make a proper living, however. Luckily in the mid 1990s the Web caught his attention, initially as a means to promote his art via an online portfolio, then as a creative medium in itself, and he's been working with it ever since. It was during this time that he founded Snub Communications (www.snubcommunications.com), a design and writing agency whose clients have since included the likes of 2000 AD, IDG UK, and Swim Records.

Along with writing the book you're holding right now, Craig recently co-authored *Foundation Dreamweaver MX 2004* (friends of ED, 2004) and *Dreamweaver MX 2004 Design Projects* (friends of ED, 2004). He's also written numerous articles for *Computer Arts*, *MacUser*, *Practical Web Projects*, *Macworld*, the dearly departed *Cre@te Online*, and many other publications besides.

When not designing websites, Craig can usually be found hard at work in his quest for global superstardom by way of his eclectic audio project, the delights of which you can sample at www.vmuonline.com.

ABOUT THE TECHNICAL REVIEWER

 **David Powers** has been a professional writer and journalist for more than 30 years, specializing in international affairs. A mild interest in computing was transformed almost overnight into a passion, when he was posted to Japan in 1987 as BBC correspondent in Tokyo. With no corporate IT department just down the corridor, he was forced to learn how to fix everything himself. When not tinkering with the innards of his computer, he was reporting for BBC TV and radio on the rise and collapse of the Japanese bubble economy.

It was back in the UK as editor for BBC Japanese TV that David started working with web design. He persuaded the IT department to let him have free run of a tiny corner of the BBC's Internet server, and built and maintained an 80-page Japanese and English website, first coding by hand, and then trying all variety of HTML editors, good and bad. He decided to set up his own independent company, Japan Interface (http://japan-interface.co.uk/), in 1999, and is actively involved in the development of an online bilingual database of economic and political analysis for Japanese clients of an international consultancy.

David applies to books about web design the same rigorous standards he did when reporting on world events. This is his second collaboration with Craig Grannell; both were co-authors of *Foundation Dreamweaver MX 2004* (friends of ED, 2004). David was also technical reviewer for the highly successful second edition of *Cascading Style Sheets: Separating Content from Presentation* (friends of ED, 2004) and co-author of *PHP Web Development with Dreamweaver MX 2004* (Apress, 2004). He is currently knee-deep in code for his latest book, *Foundation PHP 5 for Flash* (due to be published by friends of ED in March 2005).

ACKNOWLEDGMENTS

In many ways, this is the design book I've always wanted to write, and it's extremely satisfying seeing it finally come to fruition. But it couldn't have happened without those who supported me throughout. In particular, I'd like to thank Steve Rycroft, for getting on board at the beginning and then setting everything in motion; Chris Mills, for picking up the baton; and David Powers, whose excellent editing, reviewing, and insights were indispensable in the revision of the text. Thanks also to the entire team at Apress for their hard work and encouragement.

I also owe a debt of gratitude to those in the field of design whose work has affected mine along the way. Eric Meyer, Todd Fahrner, Tantek Çelik, Jeff Zeldman, and Eric Costello in particular warrant a special thank you. Thanks, too, go to those designers who pioneered and continue to advocate CSS-based, standards-compliant design. You are too many to mention, but you know who you are. Also, thanks to Drew McLellan for a timely nudge in the right direction.

And, finally, thanks to Kay for being there and supporting me throughout the writing of this book.

INTRODUCTION

I first got the idea for this book some time ago. Being both a designer and writer, I tend to see a lot of books on web design, and it struck me that although many are well written, few are truly integrated, modular resources that any designer can find useful in his day-to-day work. Instead, most web design books concentrate on a single technology or piece of software, leaving the designer to figure out how to put all the pieces together.

This book is different. *Web Designer's Reference* provides a modern, integrated approach to web design. Each of the dozen chapters looks at a specific aspect of creating a web page, such as typography, working with images, creating navigation, and crafting CSS layouts. In each case, relevant technologies are explored in context and at the appropriate times, just as in real-world projects—for example, XHTML elements are explored along with associated CSS, rather than them being placed in separate chapters, and visual design ideas are discussed so you can get a feel for how code affects page layouts. Dozens of practical examples are provided, which you can use to further your understanding of each subject. This highly modular and integrated approach means that you can dip in and out of the book as you need to, crafting along the way a number of web page elements that you can use on countless sites in the future.

Because the entire skills gamut is covered—from foundation to advanced—this book is ideal for those making their first moves into standards-based web design, experienced designers who want to move toward creating CSS layouts, and graphic designers who want to discover how to create cutting-edge web designs. This book's advocacy of web standards, usability, and accessibility with a strong eye toward visual design means it's of use to technologists and designers alike, enabling everyone to build better websites. And for those moments when a particular tag or property value slips your mind, this book provides a comprehensive reference guide that includes important and relevant XHTML elements and attributes, XHTML entities, web colors, and CSS 2.1 properties and values.

Remember that you can also visit the friends of ED support forums at www.friendsofed.com/forums to discuss aspects of this book, or just to chat with like-minded designers and developers. You can also download files associated with this book from www.friendsofed.com—just find the book in the friends of ED catalog located on the homepage, and then follow its link to access downloads and other associated resources.

CHAPTER 1
AN INTRODUCTION TO WEB DESIGN

In this chapter

- Introducing the Internet and web design
- Introducing HTML, XHTML, and web standards
- Working with CSS and understanding CSS rules
- Organizing web page content

A brief history of the Internet

Even in the wildest dreams of science fiction and fantasy writers, few envisioned anything that offers quite the level of potential that the Internet now provides for sharing information on a worldwide basis. For both businesses and individuals, the Internet has become the medium of choice, largely due to the ability it offers to present your wares to the entire world on a 24/7 basis. But the technology's origins were rather more ominous and somewhat different from the ever-growing, sprawling free-for-all that exists today.

Back in the 1960s, the American military was experimenting with methods by which the U.S. authorities might be able to communicate in the aftermath of a nuclear attack. The suggested solution was to replace point-to-point communication networks with one that was more akin to a net. This meant that information could find its way from place to place even if certain sections of the network were destroyed. Despite the project eventually being shelved by the Pentagon, the concept itself lived on, eventually influencing a network that connected several American universities.

During the following decade, this fledgling network went international and began opening itself up to the general public. The term *Internet* was coined in the 1980s, which also heralded the invention of Transmission Control Protocol/Internet Protocol (TCP/IP), the networking software that makes possible communication between computers running on different systems. For the first time, corporations began using the Internet as a means of communication, both with each other and also with those customers who were clued in to this exciting medium.

Despite the technology's healthy level of expansion, the general public remained largely unaware of the Internet until well into the 1990s, whereupon a combination of inexpensive hardware, the advent of highly usable web browsers such as Mosaic (see the following image), and improved communications technology saw an explosion of growth that continues to this day. Initially, only the largest brands dipped their toes into these new waters, but soon thousands of companies were online, enabling customers all over the globe access to information, and later even to shop online. Home users soon got in on the act, too, once it became clear that the basics of web design weren't rocket science, and that, in a sense, everyone could do it—all you needed was a text editor, an FTP client, and some web space. Therefore, unlike most media, the Web is truly a tool for *everyone*, and in many countries, the Internet has become ubiquitous. For those working in a related industry, it's hard to conceive that as recently as the mid 1990s relatively few people were even aware of the Internet's existence!

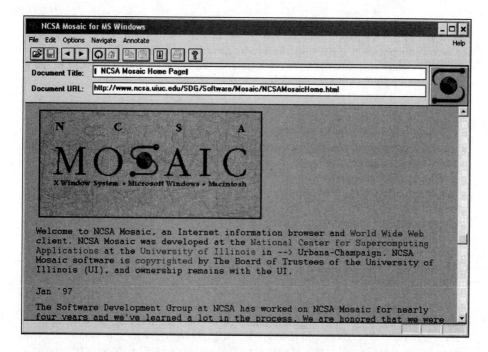

So, from relatively obscure roots as a concept for military communications, the Internet has evolved into an essential tool for millions of people, enabling them to communicate with each other, research and gather information, telecommute, shop, play games, and become involved in countless other activities on a worldwide basis.

Why create a website?

This is the question you need to ask yourself before putting pen to paper (and fingers to mouse and keyboard). There are already millions of sites online, so why do you need to create one yourself? Also, if you're working for a company, perhaps you already have plenty of marketing material, so why do you need a website as well?

I'm certainly not trying to put you off—far from it. Instead, I'm trying to get you to think about the *reason* for your site's existence. Planning is key in any web design project, and although some people swear that "winging it" is the best way to go, most such projects end up gathering virtual dust online. Therefore, before doing anything else, think through why you should build a website and what you're trying to achieve.

Companies and individuals alike have practical and commercial reasons for setting up a website. A website enables you to communicate with like-minded individuals or potential clients on a worldwide basis. Unlike printed media, a website exists online all day, every day (barring the odd hiccup with ISPs), and distribution is less expensive than sending out printed material. Likewise, development (particularly corrections and updates) is often significantly cheaper, too.

The Web is also ideal for reaching a small, loyal audience. This is perhaps why the paper fanzine has all but died, only to be reborn online, where development costs are negligible and worldwide distribution is a cinch. And for large companies, the ability to have relevant information online in a form that can often be updated in mere minutes, thereby keeping all customers up to date, is hard to resist.

Audience requirements

This book centers on the design and technology aspects of web design, but close attention must always be paid to your potential audience. It's no good forcing design ideas that result in inappropriate visuals, unusable navigation to all but the most technically minded of people, and huge download times on your site's unsuspecting visitors.

Prior to creating a site, you must ascertain what your audience wants and expects in terms of content, design, and how the site will work (by way of talking to the relevant people, and also, if your budget allows, by using surveys and focus groups). You don't have to take all of your audience's ideas into account (after all, many will be contradictory), but be mindful of common themes and ensure they're not ignored.

Technical considerations must be researched. If you're targeting designers, you can be fairly sure that a large proportion of the audience will be using monitors set to a high resolution and millions of colors, and you can design accordingly. If your site is aimed at business users, be mindful that much of your potential audience may be stuck using relatively obsolete equipment, with a screen resolution of 800×600.

Determining the web browsers your audience members use is another important consideration. Although use of web standards (used throughout this book) is more likely to result in a highly compatible site, browser quirks still cause many unforeseen problems; therefore, always check to see what browsers are popular with a site's visitors, and ensure you test in as many as you can. Sometimes you won't have access to such statistics, or you may just be after a "sanity check" regarding what's generally popular. A helpful place to go to research global web browser statistics is www.w3schools.com/browsers/browsers_stats.asp. Although not a definitive representation of the Web as a whole, such "global" statistics still provide a useful, sizeable sample that's indicative of current browser trends.

Although you might be used to checking browser usage and then, based on the results, designing for specific browsers, we'll be adhering closely to web standards throughout this book. When doing this, an "author once, work anywhere" approach is feasible, as long as you're aware of various browser quirks (which we explore fully in Chapter 12). Of course, you should still always ensure you test sites in as many browsers as possible, just to make sure everything works as intended.

Web design overview

Web design has evolved rapidly over the years. Initially, browsers were basic, and the early versions of HTML were fairly limited in what they enabled designers to do. Therefore,

1

many older sites on the Web are plain in appearance. Additionally, the Web was originally pretty much a technical repository, hence the boring layouts of many sites in the mid 1990s—after all, statistics, documentation, and papers rarely need to be jazzed up, and the audience didn't demand such things anyway.

As with any medium finding its feet, things soon changed, especially once the general public flocked to the Web. It was no longer enough for websites to be text-based information repositories. Users craved—demanded, even—color! Images! Excitement! Animation! Interaction! Even video and audio managed to get a foothold as compression techniques improved and connection speeds increased.

The danger of eye candy became all too apparent as the turn of the century approached: every site, it seemed, had a Flash intro, and the phrase skip intro became so common that it eventually spawned a parody website, which can still be accessed at www.skipintro.com.

These days, site designs tend to be more restrained, as designers have become more comfortable with using specific types of technologies for relevant and appropriate purposes. Therefore, you'll find beautifully designed XHTML- and CSS-based sites sitting alongside highly animated Flash efforts.

Of late, special emphasis is being placed on **usability** and **accessibility** (discussed later in the chapter) and, in the majority of cases, designers have cottoned to the fact that content must take precedence. Still, just because web *standards*, *usability*, and *accessibility* are the buzzwords of the moment doesn't mean design has to be thrown out the window. As we'll see in later chapters, web standards do not have to come at the expense of good design—far from it. In fact, a strong understanding of web standards helps to improve websites, making it easier for you to create cutting-edge layouts that work across platforms and are easy to update. It also provides you with a method of catering for obsolete devices.

Before we move on to those topics, though, in this section we'll examine the platforms, software, and tools used for modern-day web design.

The best platform for web design

A question commonly asked by web designers is, should you use a Mac or a Windows PC for web design? Some claim the former is superior for design, as evidenced by its dominance in the print industry, but others reckon because the Mac is a minority platform, you should avoid it and author sites on the platform used by the majority of your potential audience—the PC. **The truth is, it really doesn't matter what platform you use.**

I put that last sentence in bold type, because I really want to get this message across loud and clear. The majority of web design and graphic design applications exist for both the Mac *and* Windows, and for those that don't, alternatives usually exist. With regard to everything we'll be doing in this book, it doesn't matter what you use, largely because we'll be dealing with concepts that are platform- and software-agnostic (see the section "Why we don't use WYSIWYG tools in this book" later in this chapter).

When it comes to *testing* your web pages, though, ensure you have a good selection of web browsers on hand. This is one area where Windows users are fortunate—after all, well over 90% of the Web's users favor Windows, therefore any Mac-based web designer not testing sites in Windows-based browsers is taking a massive risk and running headlong toward commercial suicide (or, at the very least, the creation of websites that may only function as intended on a minority of clients).

I'm sure there are at least a few Windows users out there now struggling to contain a smug grin, but the reverse of the situation just described needs to be considered too. Although non-Windows users *may* account for less than 10% of your potential visitors, do you want to create a site that forbids one in ten people entrance? What if those people are the ones that were going to spend the most money? The thing is, you never know who's going to visit, and as you head toward clients specializing in design and media, the number of Mac users increases considerably.

Although we'll explore this in more depth in Chapter 12, it's worth getting acquainted with (and installing) a number of browsers on your computer. If you're using a Mac, get yourself a cheap PC or invest in Microsoft's Virtual PC application (see www.microsoft.com/mac). If you're using a Windows PC, invest in a cheap Mac that's able to run Mac OS X—even many old CRT iMacs are capable of doing so.

At the very least, a test suite should consist of the following:

- Internet Explorer for Windows
- Mozilla/Firefox
- Opera
- Internet Explorer for Mac
- Safari

That's not even the end of it: Internet Explorer for Windows changed considerably during versions 5, 5.5, and 6, and you really need to test in all of these (despite Internet Explorer 6 superceding 5 and 5.5, the earlier releases are still in common usage). There are various methods for getting around Microsoft's limitation of one version of Internet Explorer on a PC, one of which is explored in Chapter 12.

Software overview

As with any mainstream design activity, many tools are available for web design. In the upcoming sections, we'll briefly look at Dreamweaver, GoLive, Freeway, FrontPage, and other tools.

Macromedia Dreamweaver

Dreamweaver (www.macromedia.com/software/dreamweaver) is the current market leader for web design software on both Windows and Mac platforms. This is largely due to its excellent interface and the fact that it enables designers to take either a code-based or a layout-based approach to web page design. As of Dreamweaver MX 2004, the application's workflow is centered on Cascading Style Sheets (CSS), keeping it at the cutting edge. As with previous versions of the application, designers can use Dreamweaver MX 2004 to create dynamic websites, using a number of different technologies.

> *To learn more about Dreamweaver, check out* Foundation Dreamweaver MX 2004 *(friends of ED, ISBN: 1-59059-308-1) and* Dreamweaver MX 2004 Design Projects *(friends of ED, ISBN: 1-59059-409-6).*

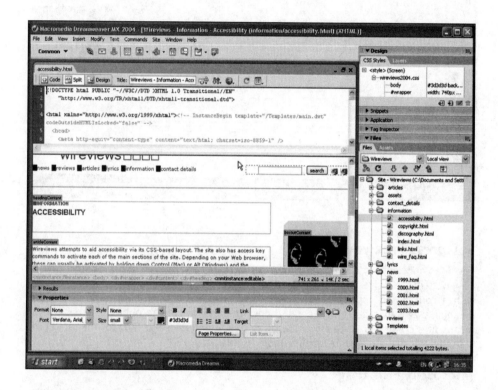

Adobe GoLive

Also available for Windows and Mac platforms, GoLive (www.adobe.com/products/golive/ main.html) is Dreamweaver's closest challenger in terms of enabling designers and developers to take various approaches in their work, although it's noticeably geared more toward graphic designers (as evidenced by its interface, which borrows from other Adobe applications such as Photoshop). In this area it excels, but unfortunately it pales beside Dreamweaver when it comes to working with CSS-based sites and web standards.

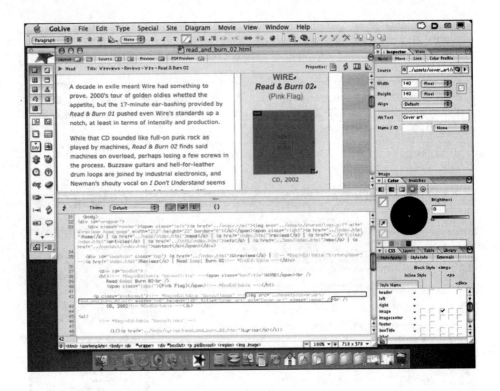

Softpress Freeway

The Mac-only application Freeway (www.softpress.com) is even more geared toward designers than GoLive, and it has an interface akin to QuarkXPress. Dispensing entirely with a code-based approach, Freeway instead relies on a publishing workflow model, meaning that web page code is created once the user decides to publish the pages. This means sites created in Freeway can be tricky to edit and fine-tune, but for the rapid prototyping of visual designs, the application is useful.

Microsoft FrontPage

An application many novice designers start with is Microsoft's Windows-only FrontPage (www.microsoft.com/frontpage)—something professional designers wouldn't touch with a ten-foot pole. But is FrontPage really as bad as some people claim? Can it not kick out decent code, even if provided with some counseling and a really good book on web standards? The answers to these questions are "No" and "Sort of," in that order.

To be fair (and read all of this before flaming us), FrontPage is a fairly capable web page editor. Its organization tools are worthy, and it has the sort of interface that beginners can readily adapt to. However, it stumbles badly when it comes to web standards. Despite improvements, the FrontPage-produced code is full of errors and geared toward Internet Explorer. For a total beginner creating a personal site or an intranet for a small company that has employees only using Internet Explorer on Windows PCs, FrontPage can be ideal, but it simply doesn't cut it as a professional web design tool. (Then again, that's not really what it's supposed to be, despite what middle managers the world over seem to think.)

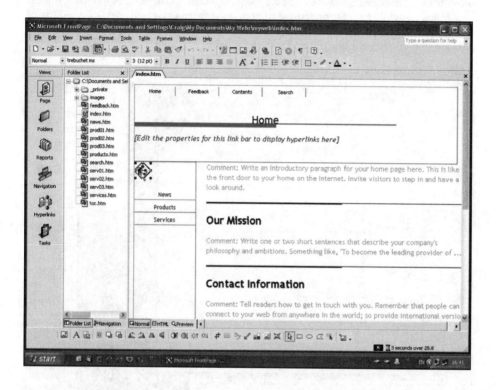

Tools for hand-coders

The applications mentioned in this chapter so far have one major thing in common: they provide the user with a way of working visually with web pages, via a WYSIWYG (What You See Is What You Get) interface. (Although one suspects this type of interface should be renamed WYHFINNWYEUW—What You Hope For Is Not Necessarily What You End Up With—even if the acronym is impossible to pronounce.)

A different approach is available through hand-coding. "Why the hell would you want to hand-code these days?" you might be asking. "After all, aren't web design applications supposed to do that for us?" Well, yes, but they're not always successful. And, in the hands of a skilled, knowledgeable designer, using a text-based editor is much faster than using a WYSIWYG editor. After all, it's quicker to edit a rule directly in a style sheet than it is to wade through dialog boxes.

Understandably, this approach isn't for everyone. If you don't know your way around the relevant technologies, you'll be in trouble, and there's no way of dragging elements around your web page. But if you have the time, patience, and inclination to learn, you may find it a good way of working.

Although Dreamweaver and GoLive both have excellent code views and additional tools that enable you to code at speed, dedicated applications tend to be superior. Mac users often favor Bare Bones Software's **BBEdit** (www.barebones.com; see the following image) or Optima System's **PageSpinner** (www.optima-system.com/pagespinner). The editor of choice for Windows users is usually Macromedia **HomeSite** (www.macromedia.com/homesite). If you're on a budget, any text editor will do, though.

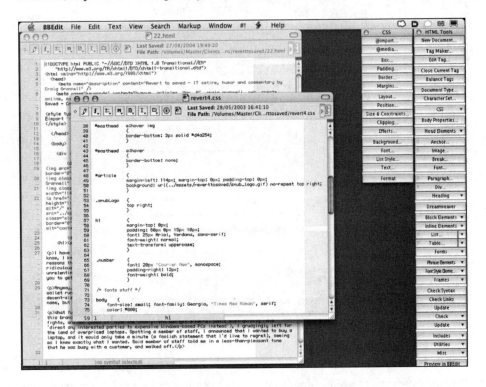

Graphic design tools

For working on layout visuals, most professionals typically use applications from Adobe and Macromedia. Macromedia's **Fireworks** (www.macromedia.com/fireworks) was the first major graphics application aimed solely at the Web, and it has many useful tools to aid web designers, along with powerful export functions. Adobe heavyweights **Illustrator** (www.adobe.com/illustrator) and **Photoshop** (www.adobe.com/photoshop) are typically geared toward print work, but they're more than capable of providing enough scope for web designers (and most *graphic* designers will already own these tools anyway). In order to combat Fireworks' increasing popularity, Adobe began bundling **ImageReady** with Photoshop, because of Fireworks' web-specific functions; however, most designers avoid using it, largely because many of its most important features (such as Save For Web, shown in the following image) are available in Photoshop. If you're on a restricted budget, you might like to check out Jasc Software's **Paint Shop Pro** (www.jasc.com).

Why we don't use WYSIWYG tools in this book

With all that software available, you might be surprised to discover that we *won't* be using WYSIWYG web design tools in this book. This isn't because I shun such tools or because I had a bad experience with them in my childhood. The reason is far simpler: in order to best learn how to do something, you need to start from scratch, with the foundations. Many web design applications make it tempting to "hide" the underlying code from you, and most users end up relying on the graphical interface. This is fine until something goes wrong and you don't know how to fix it. Also, web design applications are littered with proprietary elements, so if you make the odd mistake here or there, it can be pricey. However, as I've said, it's feasible to create web pages using affordable shareware (in fact, many noted web design gurus, such as Jeffrey Zeldman, do just that) or the free default text editor that comes with your operating system.

Removing software from the equation means we concentrate on the underlying technology that drives web pages, without the distraction of working out which button does what. Therefore, I suggest you install a quality text editor to work through the exercises in this book, or set your web design application to use its code view. Once you're familiar with the concepts outlined in this book, you can apply them to your work, whatever your chosen application for web design. This level of flexibility is important, because you never know when you might have to switch applications—something that's relatively painless if you know how to design for the Web and understand technologies like CSS and HTML. Speaking of which . . .

Introducing HTML and XHTML

The foundation of the majority of web pages is **HyperText Markup Language**, commonly known by its initials, **HTML**. A curious facet of the language is that it's easy to pick up the basics—anyone who's computer literate should be able to piece together a basic page after learning some tags—but it has enough flexibility and scope to keep designers interested and experimenting, especially when HTML is combined with Cascading Style Sheets (CSS), which we'll discuss later in this chapter. This section presents an overview of HTML tags and elements, and how HTML and XHTML relate to web standards.

Introducing the concept of HTML tags and elements

HTML documents are text files that contain **tags**, which are used to mark up HTML **elements**. These documents are usually saved with the .html file extension, although some prefer .htm, which is a hangover from 8.3 DOS file name limitations.

The aforementioned tags are what web browsers use to display pages and, assuming the browser is well behaved (most modern ones are), the display should conform to standards as laid out by the **World Wide Web Consortium (W3C)**, the organization that develops guidelines and specifications for many web technologies.

> The W3C website is found at www.w3.org. The site offers numerous useful tools, including validation services against which you can check your web pages. We'll be using these later on in the book.

HTML tags are surrounded by angle brackets—for instance, <p> is a paragraph tag. It's good practice to close tags once the element content or intended display effect concludes, and this is done with an **end tag**. End tags are identical to the opening start tags, but with an added forward slash, /. A complete HTML element looks like this:

```
<p>Here is a paragraph.</p>
```

This element consists of the following:

- **Start tag**: <p>
- **Content**: Here is a paragraph.
- **End tag**: </p>

> HTML doesn't have a hard and fast rule regarding the case of tags, unlike XHTML, which we'll shortly be talking about and which we'll use throughout the book. If you look at the source code of HTML pages on the Web, you may see lowercase tags, uppercase tags or, in the case of pages put together over a period of time, a mixture of the two.

Nesting tags

There are many occasions when tags must be placed inside each other, a process that's called **nesting**. One reason for nesting is to apply basic styles to text-based elements. Earlier, you saw the code for a paragraph element. We can now make the text bold by surrounding the element content with a strong element:

```
<p><strong>Here is a paragraph.</strong></p>
```

> You might be used to using the bold element to make text bold, but it is a **physical** element that only amends the look of text rather than also conveying semantic meaning. Therefore, we prefer **logical** elements, such as strong. You can find out more about both types of elements in Chapter 3.

Note that the strong tags are nested within the paragraph tags (<p></p>), not the other way around. That's because the paragraph is the parent element, to which formatting is being applied. The paragraph could be made bold *and* italic by adding another element, emphasis (<em></em>), as follows:

```
<p><strong><em>Here is a paragraph.</em></strong></p>
```

In this case, the strong and em tags could be in the opposite order, as they're at the same level in the hierarchy. However, you must always close nested tags in the reverse order to that in which they're opened, otherwise some browsers may not display your work as intended. For instance, the following should be avoided:

```
<p><strong><em>Here is a paragraph.</strong></em></p>
```

As previously mentioned, it's good practice to close tags. Take a look at the following:

```
<p><strong><em>Here is a paragraph.</strong></p>
```

Here, the emphasis element isn't closed, meaning subsequent text-based content on the page is likely to be displayed in italics—so take care to close all your tags.

Web standards and XHTML

As I said earlier, we'll be working with **Extensible HyperText Markup Language (XHTML)** in this book, rather than HTML. The differences between HTML and XHTML are few, but important, and largely came about because of the inconsistent way that browsers displayed HTML. XHTML is stricter than HTML and has additional rules; oddly, this actually makes it *easier* to learn, because you don't have to worry about things like which case to use for tags and whether they require closing. You have hard and fast rules in each case. XHTML-specific rules are as follows:

All tags must be in *lowercase* and they must *always* be closed. Therefore, the following is *incorrect*:

```
<P>This is a paragraph.
<P>This is another paragraph.
```

The preceding lines should be written like this:

```
<p>This is a paragraph.</p>
<p>This is another paragraph.</p>
```

Unlike HTML, all XHTML elements require an end tag, including empty tags and those with no content, such as br, img, and hr. The HTML for a carriage return is br. In XHTML, this must be written
</br> or, more usually, in a combination form that looks like this: <br />. The trailing slash is placed at the end of the start tag, with a space prior to it, ensuring that obsolete browsers don't ignore the tag. Writing <br/> means Netscape 4 will ignore the tag and not display the carriage return.

Tags often have **attributes** that modify them in some way. For instance, two attributes for the table cell tag td are nowrap (to stop content wrapping) and colspan (which states how many columns this cell should span). In XHTML, attributes must be quoted and always have a value. If necessary, the attribute name itself is repeated for the value. Therefore, the following is *incorrect*:

```
<td colspan=2 nowrap>
```

Instead, in XHTML, we write this:

```
<td colspan="2" nowrap="nowrap">
```

Evolution is another aspect that we have to deal with. Just as the survival of the fittest removes some species from nature, so too are tags (and attributes) unceremoniously dumped from the W3C specifications. Such tags are referred to as **deprecated**, meaning they are marked for removal from the standard and may not be supported in future browsers. In the rare cases when deprecated tags are used in this book, this will be highlighted (and likewise in the reference section); in most cases, these tags can be avoided, often by replacing them with CSS properties and values, but some still have uses.

Web standards in action

If there's any doubt in your mind about using current web design practices and web standards, this section highlights the benefits of modern working methods with regard to web design. We'll look at a small web page that's been created by a web design application geared toward the old way of working, in HTML, with many deprecated tags, and then we'll strip out the content and restyle it in a modern manner.

> *Don't worry about understanding everything at this stage—all relevant information will be explained later in the book.*

1

The original page

The original HTML web page is shown in the following image. As you can see, it's pretty simple, containing a few paragraphs of text, one of which is a pull quote, and some simple styling.

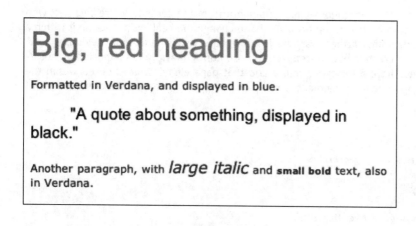

Here's the mess of code that it's composed of:

```
<html>
<head>
<title>A Web page</title>
</head>
<body bgcolor="white">

<p><font face="Arial" color="red"><big><big><big><big><big>Big, red heading
➥</big></big></big></big></big></font>

<p><font face="Verdana" color="blue"><small>Formatted in Verdana, and displayed
➥in blue.</small></font></p>

<p>           
➥<font face="Arial" color="black"><big>"A quote about something, displayed in
➥black."</big></font></p>

<p><small><font face="Verdana" color="blue">Another paragraph, with
<big><big><em>large italic</em></big></big> and <small><strong>small
➥bold</strong></small>text, also in Verdana.</font></small></p>

</body>
</html>
```

There's plenty of redundancy here. In some cases, big tags have been used to overpower small ones. The pull quote is pushed to the right by nonbreaking spaces ( ), and each paragraph is styled by a font element, even if its styling is the same as a previous one.

Removing the junk

First, let's clear the superfluous junk, stripping it from the content. We're then left with clean HTML, with basic markup only. We'll also change the heading by placing it within a heading element (h1) rather than the inappropriate styled paragraph previously used. This method of creating pages—referred to as **semantic markup**—is important in ensuring web pages have a logical structure and that page elements are housed within the most appropriate markup element. This is something we'll return to in later sections of the book.

```
<html>
<head>
<title>A web page</title>
</head>
<body>

<h1>A big, red heading</h1>

<p>Formatted in Verdana, displayed in blue.</p>

<p>"A quote about something displayed in black."</p>

<p>Another paragraph with <em>large italic</em> and <strong>small bold</strong>
➡text, also in Verdana.</p>

</body>
</html>
```

Here's how the page looks now, devoid of its colors and font sizes:

Big, red heading

Formatted in Verdana, and displayed in blue.

"A quote about something, displayed in black."

Another paragraph, with *large italic* and **small bold** text, also in Verdana.

Because the heading element was used, the web browser displays the heading more prominently than text housed within paragraph elements. This means that even when using non-CSS-savvy browsers, you can still make sense of the logical structure of the page.

Reformatting the web page

Next, we add a style element to the head of our document and define styles for the various page elements. This is an embedded style sheet. As mentioned earlier, **Cascading Style Sheets (CSS)** is the W3C standard for controlling the visual presentation of web pages, and it's something we'll use extensively throughout this book. We've added some other elements to our page, such as a **document type definition (DTD)** at the beginning, which tells web browsers what version of XHTML is being used, so the browser can render the page accordingly. Again, don't worry about understanding all this just yet—we'll look at CSS in a little while and DTDs later in the book.

```
<!DOCTYPE html PUBLIC "-//W3C//DTD XHTML 1.0 Strict//EN"
        "http://www.w3.org/TR/xhtml1/DTD/xhtml1-strict.dtd">
<html xmlns="http://www.w3.org/1999/xhtml">
<head>
  <title>A Web page</title>

<style type="text/css" media="Screen">
/* <![CDATA[ */

body {
background-color: white;
font-family: Verdana, sans-serif;
}

h1 {
font-family: Arial, sans-serif;
font-size: 40px;
color: red;
font-weight: normal;
}

p {
font-family: Verdana, sans-serif;
font-size: 13px;
color: blue;
}

.quote {
font-family: Arial, sans-serif;
color: black;
font-size: 20px;
```

```
padding-left: 50px;
}

.large {
font-size: 140%;
}

.small {
font-size: 85%;
}

/* ]]> */
</style>

  </head>

<body>
  <h1>Big, red heading</h1>

  <p>Formatted in Verdana, and displayed in blue.</p>

  <p class="quote">"A quote about something, displayed in black."</p>

  <p>Another paragraph, with <span class="large"><em>large italic</em></span>
➡and <span class="small"><strong>small bold</strong></span> text, also in
➡Verdana.</p>
  </body>
</html>
```

Here's the resulting page, which looks very similar to the earlier document:

Big, red heading

Formatted in Verdana, and displayed in blue.

"A quote about something, displayed in black."

Another paragraph, with *large italic* and **small bold** text, also in Verdana.

Though it appears similar to the earlier version, this web page was created in a far more modern manner. Looking at the code, you may be thinking that it's as heavy as the outdated markup, but bear in mind that CSS style sheets can be (and usually are) external documents attached to web pages by a single XHTML element. This means that, for instance, you can control how *every* paragraph tag on your site looks by defining a style for paragraphs in one external document and then attaching that document to your XHTML pages. The old method requires that you add the style definition to each individual font tag. Not only is this time consuming, but it also makes it a headache to make the website consistent.

Also, this web page's elements can be controlled with more precision. For instance, the quote has now been indented an exact number of pixels to the right with a CSS declaration (and the entire quote moves, rather than just the first line). Previously, this was achieved by using nonbreaking spaces, the size of which varies from browser to browser.

Rapid restyling

Another advantage of using CSS is the ability to rapidly alter the look of an entire page, just by editing the style sheet. For example, replace the style element of the page with the following:

```
<style type="text/css" media="Screen">
/* <![CDATA[ */

body {
background-color: black;
font-family: Georgia, serif;
}

h1 {
font-family: "Trebuchet MS", sans-serif;
font-size: 40px;
color: red;
font-weight: normal;
}

p {
font-family: Georgia, serif;
font-size: 13px;
color: white;
padding-left: 25px;
}

.quote {
width: 100px;
font-family: Arial, sans-serif;
color: white;
font-size: 18px;
```

```
    padding: 5px 15px;
    margin-left: 70px;
    border-left: 5px solid white;
    border-right: 5px solid white;
    }

    .large {
    font-size: 130%;
    border: 1px dotted white;
    padding: 5px;
    }

    .small {
    font-size: 90%;
    border: 2px dashed #555;
    padding: 10px;
    }

    /* ]]> */
    </style>
```

The following image shows the updated web page:

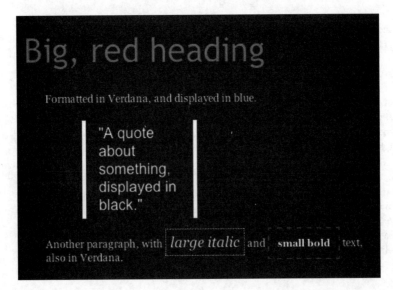

We didn't touch a single XHTML tag, yet we managed to totally alter the look of the page just by editing the style sheet. We also added additional design elements, such as the borders flanking the quote to make it stand out, and dotted lines around the large italic and small bold text.

Introducing CSS

We've been working with a bit of CSS, so it could do with a proper introduction. CSS is the W3C standard for defining the visual presentation for web pages. HTML was designed as a structural markup language, but the demands of users and designers encouraged browser manufacturers to support and develop presentation-oriented tags. These tags "polluted" HTML, pushing the language toward one of decorative style rather than logical structure. Its increasing complexity made life hard for web designers, and source code began to balloon for even basic presentation-oriented tasks. Along with creating needlessly large HTML files, things like font tags created web pages that weren't consistent across browsers and platforms, and styles had to be applied to individual elements—a time-consuming process.

The concept behind CSS was simple, yet revolutionary: remove the presentation and separate design from content. Let HTML (and later XHTML) deal with structure, and use a separate CSS document for the application of visual presentation.

The idea caught on, albeit slowly. The initial problem was browser support. At first, most browsers supported only a few aspects of CSS—and badly at that. But Internet Explorer 5 for Mac made great strides with regard to CSS support, and it was soon joined by other browsers fighting for the crown of standards king. These days, every up-to-date browser supports the majority of commonly used CSS properties and values, and more besides.

Another problem has been educating designers and encouraging them to switch from old to new methods. Benefits constantly need to be outlined and proven, and the new methods taught. Many designers style text with CSS, but relatively few use CSS for entire web page layouts, despite the inherent advantages in doing so. This, of course, is one of the main reasons for this book: to show you, the designer, how CSS can be beneficial to you, and to provide examples for various areas of web page design and development that you can use in your sites.

To that end, in this section we'll look at separating content from design, CSS rules, CSS selectors and how to use them, and how to add styles to a web page.

Separating content from design

Do you ever do any of the following?

- Use tables for website layout?
- Use invisible GIFs to "push" elements around your web page?
- Get frustrated when the combination of the above leads to unwieldy web pages that are a pain to edit?

If so, the idea of separating content from design should appeal to you. On one hand, you have your HTML documents, which house content marked up in a logical and semantic manner. On the other hand, you have your CSS documents, giving you sitewide control of the presentation of your web page elements from a single source. Instead of messing around with stretching transparent GIFs, and combining and splitting table cells, you can edit CSS rules to amend the look of your site, which is great for not only those times when things just need subtle tweaking, but also when you decide everything needs a visual over-haul. After all, if presentation is taken care of externally, you can replace the CSS to provide your site with a totally new design. (Also, using JavaScript, you can do this on the fly, providing visitors with a number of visual designs to choose from.)

Designers (and clients paying for their time) aren't the only ones to benefit from CSS. Visitors will, too, in terms of faster download times, but also with regard to **accessibility**. For instance, people with poor vision often use screen readers to surf the Web. If a site's layout is composed of complex nested tables, it might visually make sense; however, the underlying structure may not be logical. View the source of a document and look at the order of the content. A screen reader reads from the top to the bottom of the *code* and doesn't care what the page looks like in a visual web browser. Therefore, if the code compromises the logical order of the content (as complex tables often do), the site is compromised for all those using screen readers.

Accessibility is becoming increasingly important in the field of web design. Legislation is slowly being passed to strongly encourage designers to make sites accessible for web users with disabilities. It's likely that this trend will continue, encompassing just about everything except personal web pages. (However, even personal websites shouldn't be inaccessible.)

The rules of CSS

Style sheets consist of a number of **rules** that define how various web page elements should be displayed. Although sometimes bewildering to newcomers, CSS rules are simple to break down. Each rule consists of a **selector** and a **declaration**. The selector begins a CSS rule and specifies which part of the HTML document the rule will be applied to. The declaration consists of a number of property/value pairs that set specific properties and determine how the relevant element will look. In the following example, p is the selector and everything thereafter is the declaration:

```
p {
color: blue;
}
```

As you probably know, p is the HTML tag for a paragraph. Therefore, if we attach this rule to a web page (see the section "Adding styles to a web page" later on in this chapter for how to do so), the declaration will be applied to any HTML marked up as a paragraph, thereby setting the color of said paragraphs to blue.

> *CSS property names are not case sensitive, but it's good to be consistent in web design—it's highly recommended to always use lowercase.*

When you write CSS rules, you place the declaration within curly brackets {}. Properties and values are separated by a colon (:), and property/value pairs are terminated by a semicolon (;). Technically, you don't have to include the final semicolon in a CSS rule, but most designers consider it good practice to do so. This makes sense—you may add property/value pairs to a rule at a later date, and if the semicolon is already there, you don't have to remember to add it.

If we want to amend our paragraph declaration and define paragraphs as bold, we can do so like this:

```
p {
color: blue;
font-weight:bold;
}
```

> You don't have to lay out CSS rules as done in this section; rather, you can add rules as one long string. However, the formatting we're using here proves to be highly readable, both on- and offscreen.

Types of CSS selectors

In the previous example, we used the most basic style of selector, known as an **element selector**. This defines the visual appearance of the relevant HTML tag. In the sections that follow, we'll examine some other types of CSS selectors: class, ID, grouped, and contextual.

Class selectors

In some cases, you may wish to modify an element or a group of elements. For instance, you may wish for your general website text to be blue, as in the examples so far, but some portions of it to be red. The simplest way of doing this is by using a **class selector**.

In CSS, a class selector's name is prefixed by a period (.), like this:

```
.redText {
color: red;
}
```

This style is applied to HTML elements in any web page the style sheet is attached to using the class attribute, as follows:

```
<p class="redText">This text is red.</p>

<h2 class="redText">This heading is red, too.</h2>
```

If you want a class to apply to only a specific element, then place the relevant HTML tag before the period in the CSS rule:

```
p.redText {
color: red;
}
```

From our previous example, this results in the paragraph remaining red, but not the heading, because the redText class is now tied to the paragraph selector only.

ID selectors

ID selectors can be used only once on each web page. In HTML, you apply a unique identifier to an HTML element with the id attribute:

```
<div id="navigation">(Links would go here)</div>
```

To style this element in CSS, precede the ID name with a hash mark (#):

```
#navigation {
padding: 20px;
}
```

In this case, the navigation div would have 20 pixels of padding on all sides.

Essentially, then, classes can be used multiple times on a web page, but IDs cannot. Typically, IDs are used to define one-off page elements, such as structural divisions, whereas classes are used to define the style for multiple items.

Grouped selectors

Should you wish to set a property value for a number of different selectors, you can use **grouped selectors**, which take the form of a comma-separated list:

```
h1, h2, h3, h4, h5, h6 {
color: green;
}
```

In the preceding example, we've set all our website's headings to be green. (Not particularly tasteful, granted, but hey, this is CSS, and we can easily change it later!)

You're not restricted to a single rule for each element—you can use grouped selectors for common definitions and separate ones for specific property values, as follows:

```
h1, h2, h3, h4, h5, h6 {
color: green;
}

h1 {
font-size: 150%;
}

h2 {
font-size: 120%;
}
```

If you define a property value twice, browsers render your web element depending on each rule's position in the cascade. See later in the chapter (in the section "The cascade") for more information.

Contextual selectors

This selector type is handy when working with advanced CSS. As the name suggests, **contextual selectors** define property values for HTML elements depending on context. Take, for instance, the following example:

```
<p>I am a paragraph.</p>
<p>So am I.</p>

<div id="navigation">
<p>I am a paragraph within the navigation div.</p>
<p>Another paragraph within the navigation div.</p>
</div>
```

We can style the page's paragraphs and then set some specific values for those within the navigation div by using a standard element selector for the former and a contextual selector for the latter:

```
 p {
color: black;
}

#navigation p {
color: blue;
font-weight: bold;
font-size: 120%;
}
```

As shown, syntax for contextual selectors (#navigation p) is simple—you just separate the individual selectors with some white space.

The result of this is as follows, although I also put a border around the navigation div, using an ID selector, to make everything more obvious. This was done using the following CSS:

```
#navigation {
border: 1px solid #000;
}
```

I am a paragraph.

So am I.

I am a paragraph within the navigation div.

Another paragraph within the navigation div.

By working with contextual selectors, it's possible to get very specific with regard to styling things on your website, and we'll be using these selectors regularly.

> There are some other types of selectors used for specific tasks. These will be covered as relevant later in the book.

Adding styles to a web page

The most common (and useful) method of applying CSS rules to a web page is by using **external style sheets**. CSS rules are defined in a text document, which is saved with the file suffix .css. This document is attached to an HTML document in one of two ways, both of which require the addition of HTML elements to the head section.

The first method of attaching a CSS file is to use a link tag:

```
<link rel="stylesheet" type="text/css"
href="mystylesheet.css" />
```

> Remember that we're working with XHTML in this book, hence the trailing slash on the link tag, a tag that has no content.

Alternatively, we can import the style sheet into the style element:

```
<style type="text/css">
@import url(mystylesheet.css);
</style>
```

Each method has its advantages in particular scenarios. For instance, the @import method is commonly used by web designers who want to hide CSS rules from noncompliant browsers, thereby giving users of such devices access to the website's content, if not its design.

The style tag can also be used to embed CSS directly into the head section of a specific HTML document, like this:

```
<head>
<style type="text/css">

p {
color: black;
}

#navigation p {
color: blue;
font-weight: bold;
font-size: 120%;
```

```
        }

    </style>
    </head>
```

This is only worth doing if you have a one-page website, or you want to affect tags on a specific page, overriding those in an attached style sheet (see the next section for more information).

The third method of applying CSS is to do so as an **inline style**, directly in an element's HTML tag:

```
<p style="color: blue;">This paragraph will be
displayed in blue.</p>
```

As you can see, this method involves using the `style` attribute, and it's only of use in very specific, one-off situations. There's no point in using inline styles for all styling on your website—to do so would give few benefits over the likes of font tags. Inline styles also happen to be deprecated in XHTML 1.1, so they're eventually destined for the chop!

The cascade

It's possible to define the rule for a given element multiple times: you can do so in the same style sheet, and several style sheets can be attached to an HTML document. On top of that, you may be using embedded style sheets and inline styles. The **cascade** is a way of dealing with conflicts, and its simple rule is this:

> *The value closest to the element in question is the one that is applied.*

In the following example, the second `font-size` setting for paragraphs takes precedence because it's closest to paragraphs in the HTML:

```
p {
font-size: 100%;
}

p {
font-size: 120%;
}
```

Subsequently, paragraphs on pages the preceding rule is attached to are rendered at 120%. If a similar rule was placed as an embedded style sheet below the linked style sheet, that rule would take precedence, and if one was applied as an inline style (directly in the relevant element), then that would take precedence over all others.

CSS uses the concept of **inheritance**. A document's HTML elements form a strict hierarchy, beginning with html, then branching into head and body, each of which has numerous descendant elements (such as title and meta for head and p, and img for body). When a style is applied to an element, its descendants—those elements nested within it—often take on CSS property values, unless a more specific style has been applied. However, not all CSS style properties are inherited. See the CSS reference section of this book for more details.

Working with website content

Before we explore how to create the various aspects of a web page, we're going to briefly discuss working with website content and what you need to consider prior to creating your site. Technology and design aren't the only factors that affect the success of a website. The human element must also be considered. Most of the time, people use the Web to get information of some sort, whether for research purposes or entertainment. Typically, people want to be able to access this information quickly; therefore, a site must be structured in a logical manner. It's imperative that a visitor doesn't spend a great deal of time looking for information that should be easy to find. Remember, there are millions of sites out there, and if yours isn't up to scratch, it's easy for someone to go elsewhere.

> There are exceptions to the general rule of a website having a structured and logical design—notably sites that are experimental in nature or the equivalent of online art, thereby requiring exploration. In these cases, it may actually be detrimental to present a straightforward and totally logical site, but these cases are strictly a minority.

In this section, we'll look specifically at information architecture and site maps, page layout, design limitations, and usability.

Information architecture and site maps

Before you begin designing a website, you need to collate and logically organize the information it's going to contain. A **site map** usually forms the basis of a site's navigation, and you should aim to have the most important links immediately visible. What these links actually are depends on the nature of your website, but it's safe to say that prominent links to contact details are a common requirement across all sites. A corporate website may also need prominent links to products, services, and a press area. The resulting site map for a corporate site might resemble the following:

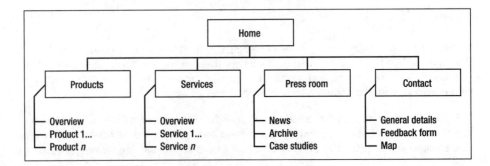

Here, the boxed links serve as the primary navigation and are effectively sections of the website. Underneath each boxed link is a list of subcategories or pages housed within that section. With this structure, it's easy for a newcomer to the site to work out where information is located. When working on site maps, try talking to people who might be interested in the site to get their reaction to your organization of the content. When working for a client, ensure you get sign-off on the site map, and that you get feedback on the site map from people at all levels in the company and, if possible, from the company's customers. In all cases, seek the opinions of both the technically minded and relative computer novices, because each may have different ideas about how information should be structured. After all, most web designers are technically minded (or at least well versed in using a computer), and they often forget that most people don't use the Web as regularly as they do. In other words, what seems obvious to you might not be to the general public.

For larger sites, or those with many categories, site maps can be complex. You may have to create several versions before your site map is acceptable. Always avoid burying content too deep. If you end up with a structure in which a visitor has to click several times to access information, it may be worth reworking your site's structure.

Basic web page structure and layout

Once you've sorted out the site map, avoid firing up your graphics package. It's a good idea to sketch out page layout ideas on paper before working on your PC or Mac. Not only is this quicker than using graphics software, but also you can compare many ideas side by side. At this stage, you shouldn't be too precious about the design—work quickly and try to get down as many ideas as possible. From there, you can then refine your ideas, combine the most successful elements of each, and then begin working on the computer.

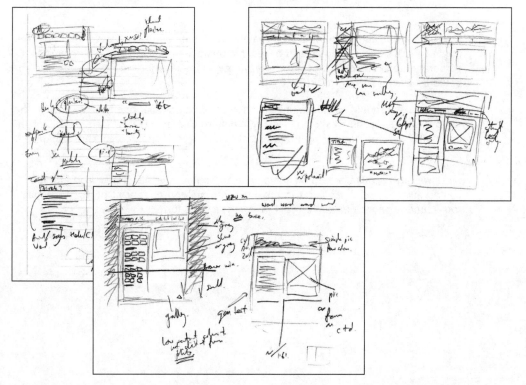

Although the Web has no hard and fast conventions, themes run throughout successful websites, many of which are evident in the following image of the Snub Communications homepage:

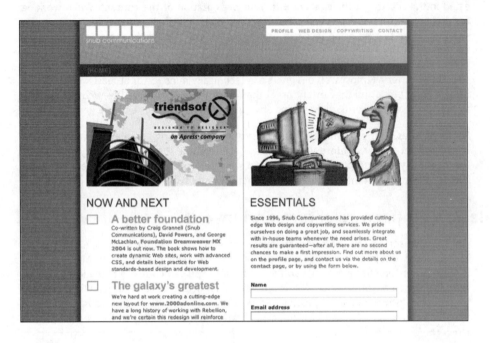

A website's navigation should be immediately accessible—you should never have to scroll to get to it. It's also a good idea to have a masthead area that displays the organization's corporate brand (or, if it's a personal site, whatever logo/identity you wish to be remembered by, even if it's only a URL).

The homepage should include an introduction of some sort that briefly explains what the site owner is about, and it should have some pull-ins to other areas of the site. These pull-ins could be in the form of news items that link to recent product launches, completed projects, and so on.

Most websites require a method for people to contact the site owner, and although a contact page is useful, it's good to provide some method of contact on the homepage, too—either a phone number, e-mail address, or a small form.

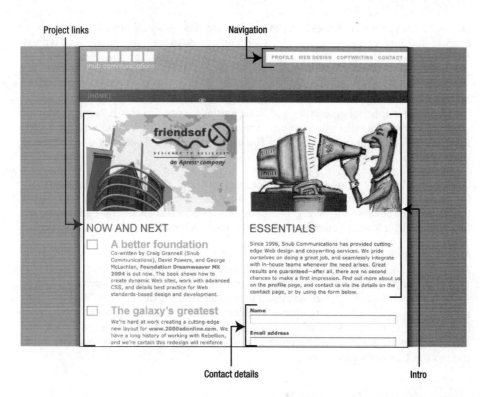

Project links

Navigation

Contact details

Intro

Avoid constantly changing the design throughout the site. In print, this sometimes works well and provides variation within a book or magazine. Online, people expect certain things to be in certain places. Constantly changing the position of your navigation, the links themselves, and even the general design and color scheme often creates the impression of an unprofessional site and makes it harder to use.

Limitations of web design

Depending on your viewpoint, the inherent limitations of the Web are either a challenge or a frustration. Print designers often feel the latter, and consider themselves hampered by the Web when compared to the relative freedom of print design. Resolution is low, and you can't place whopping great images everywhere, because if you did download speeds would slow to a crawl and all your visitors would go elsewhere.

Columns take on a different role online compared to in print, as they're primarily used to display several areas of content with the same level of prominence (as shown in the Snub Communications homepage image earlier). You don't use columns online to display continuous copy, unless you use just one column. If you use several columns, the visitor has to constantly scroll up and down to read everything.

Text becomes problematic elsewhere, too. There are few web-standard fonts (detailed in Chapter 3); serifs, which work well on paper, don't work so well online; and reading text onscreen is already harder than reading print, so complex page backgrounds should be avoided.

And then there are issues like not knowing what an end user's setup is, and therefore having to consider monitor resolution and color settings, what browser is being used, and even the various potential setups of web browsers. Do you go for a **liquid** design, which stretches with the browser window, or a **fixed** design, which is flanked by blank space at larger monitor resolutions?

Don't worry, this isn't a pop quiz. These are questions that will be answered in this book, but I mention them now to get you thinking and realizing that planning is key with regard to web design. Because this is largely a book about concepts, ideas, and techniques, we won't return to talk about planning very much, hence drumming it in at this early stage.

Also, don't get disheartened by the previous limitations spiel. The Web is a truly magnificent medium, and for every downside there's something amazing to counter it. So what if the resolution's low? Nowhere else can you so effortlessly combine photography, video, sound, and text. Sure, it's all well and good to read a magazine, but the Web enables interaction, and navigation can be nonlinear, enabling you to link words within specific pieces to other articles on your website or elsewhere on the Internet. Don't get me wrong: the Web is a great thing. If it wasn't, I wouldn't be interested in it, wouldn't be designing for it, and wouldn't be writing this book!

The magic word: Usability

Although the "a" word (accessibility) has been used in this chapter, the "u" word (usability) has not really been discussed. However, if you've been paying close attention, you'll be aware that we've covered a lot of usability concerns during this chapter. Depending on whom you speak to, you may get various responses regarding what this word actually means. As far as we're concerned, it simply means making things usable to the visitors to your website, and therefore taking into account many of the things we've already covered:

- Ensuring content can be easily found
- Making the site highly navigable
- Keeping download times to a minimum
- Designing for the target audience
- Using familiar conventions

Some people go further on this path, pointing out things like default link colors are blue, and so all your links should always be blue. I think that's sweet and rather quaint, but ultimately an archaic way of thinking. So long as links are obvious, that's what matters. In many ways, website usability, like many areas of creating a website, is about common sense. Sometimes, though, a guiding hand is needed, and this book can be of help there.

Anyway, after swallowing all this theory, you're probably itching to get started exploring some actual web design. Fortunately, you'll begin doing so in the very next chapter.

CHAPTER 2
WEB PAGE ESSENTIALS

In this chapter

- Creating XHTML documents
- Understanding document type definitions
- Using meta tags
- Attaching external documents
- Working with the body section
- Examining CSS web page backgrounds
- Commenting your work

Starting with the essentials

You might be wondering what I mean by the title of this chapter: web page essentials. This chapter will run through everything you need to do with a web page prior to working on the layout and content, including creating the initial documents, attaching external documents to HTML files, dealing with the head section of the web page, and so on. Little of this is particularly exciting with regard to visual design, which is why many designers ignore the topics we'll cover, or stick their fingers in their ears, hum loudly, and wish it would all go away (and then probably get rather odd looks from nearby colleagues). However, as the chapter's title states, everything we'll be talking about is *essential* for any quality web page, even if you don't see exciting things happening visually.

This chapter will also explore web page backgrounds, which, although they should be used sparingly and with caution, can nonetheless come in handy. It's worth bearing in mind that some aspects discussed here will crop up later. For example, the techniques used to attach backgrounds to a web page can be used to attach a background to *any* web page element (be that a div, table, heading, or paragraph)—such is the power of CSS. But before we get into any CSS shenanigans, we'll put our CSS cheerleading team on hold and look at how to properly construct an XHTML document.

Document defaults

As mentioned in Chapter 1, we'll be working with XHTML in this book rather than HTML. Although XHTML markup differs slightly from HTML, the file suffix for XHTML web pages remains .html (or .htm if you swear by archaic 8.3 DOS naming techniques).

Although XHTML's stricter rules make it easier to work with than HTML, you need to be aware of the differences in the basic document structure. In HTML, many designers are used to starting out with something like the following code:

```
<html>
  <head>
    <title></title>
  </head>
  <body>
  </body>
</html>
```

But in XHTML, a basic, blank document awaiting content may well look like this (although there are variations):

```
<!DOCTYPE html PUBLIC "-//W3C//DTD XHTML 1.0 Transitional//EN"
    "http://www.w3.org/TR/xhtml1/DTD/xhtml1-transitional.dtd">
<html xmlns="http://www.w3.org/1999/xhtml" xml:lang="en" lang="en">
  <head>
    <meta http-equiv="content-type" content="text/html; charset=iso-8859-1" />
    <title></title>
  </head>
```

```
<body>
</body>
</html>
```

This is similar to the minimal HTML document, but there are important differences. The most obvious is found at the beginning of the document: a **DOCTYPE declaration** that states what **document type definition** (**DTD**) you are following (and no, I'm not shouting—DOCTYPE is spelled in all caps according to the W3C).

```
<!DOCTYPE html PUBLIC "-//W3C//DTD XHTML 1.0 Transitional//EN"
    "http://www.w3.org/TR/xhtml1/DTD/xhtml1-transitional.dtd">
```

The DTD indicates to a web browser what markup you're using, thereby enabling the browser to accurately display the document in question (or at least as accurately as it can—as we'll see later in the book, browsers have various quirks, even when you're using 100% tested and validated markup).

Next is the html start tag, which contains both a **namespace** and a **language declaration**. The first of those is intended to reduce the ambiguity of defined elements within the web page. In XML, elements can mean different things, depending on what technology is being used. The following namespace therefore ensures a browser interprets elements as XHTML unless otherwise overridden elsewhere within the document:

```
<html xmlns="http://www.w3.org/1999/xhtml" xml:lang="en" lang="en">
```

You'll also notice that a meta tag appears in the head section of the document:

```
<meta http-equiv="content-type" content="text/html; charset=iso-8859-1" />
```

To pass validation tests and ensure browsers correctly format content, you must always declare your content type. The most reliable way to do this is by using this meta tag. Here, the defined character set is the default in most English HTML editors: ISO-8859-1, sometimes referred to as Latin-1. There are other sets in use, too, for the likes of Hebrew, Nordic, and Eastern European languages, and if you're using them, the charset value would be changed accordingly. You can also define your charset as utf-8 to specify Unicode. Although www.iana.org/assignments/character-sets provides a thorough character set listing, and wwwwbs.cs.tu-berlin.de/user/czyborra/charsets contains useful character set diagrams, it's tricky to wade through it all, so listed here are some common values and their associated languages:

- **ISO-8859-1 (Latin-1)**: Western European and American, including Afrikaans, Albanian, Basque, Catalan, Danish, Dutch, English, Faeroese, Finnish, French, Galician, German, Icelandic, Irish, Italian, Norwegian, Portuguese, Spanish, and Swedish.

- **ISO-8859-2 (Latin-2)**: Central and Eastern European, including Croatian, Czech, Hungarian, Polish, Romanian, Slovak, Slovene, and Sorbian.

- **ISO-8859-3 (Latin-3)**: Southern European, including Esperanto, Galician, Maltese, and Turkish. (See also ISO-8859-9.)

- **ISO-8859-4 (Latin-4)**: Northern European, including Estonian, Greenlandic, Lappish, Latvian, and Lithuanian. (See also ISO-8859-6.)

- **ISO-8859-5**: Cyrillic, including Bulgarian, Byelorussian, Macedonian, Russian, Serbian, and Ukrainian.

- **ISO-8859-6**: Arabic.

- **ISO-8859-7**: Modern Greek.

- **ISO-8859-8**: Hebrew.

- **ISO-8859-9 (Latin-5)**: European. Replaces Icelandic-specific characters with Turkish ones.

- **ISO-8859-10 (Latin-6)**: Nordic, including Icelandic, Inuit, and Lappish.

For an overview of the ISO-8859 standard, see http://en.wikipedia.org/wiki/ISO_8859.

DOCTYPE declarations explained

XHTML 1.0 offers you three tempting choices of DOCTYPE declaration: XHTML Strict, XHTML Transitional, and XHTML Frameset. In the initial example, the DOCTYPE declaration is the first thing in the web page. This is always how it should be—you should *never* have *any* content or HTML elements prior to the DOCTYPE declaration. (An exception is the XML declaration; see the section "What about the XML Declaration?" later in this chapter.)

XHTML Strict

For extreme XHTML purists and masochists only, this is the DTD that screams blue murder if you dare use any presentational markup or deprecated elements:

```
<!DOCTYPE html PUBLIC "-//W3C//DTD XHTML 1.0 Strict//EN"
    "http://www.w3.org/TR/xhtml1/DTD/xhtml1-strict.dtd">
```

"Hang on," you might say. "You've been rambling on about 'doing things properly' and now you're saying to avoid using a strict DTD? I don't understand."

It's a fair point. However, sometimes it's useful to be able to use the odd deprecated element, and by declaring your document as XHTML 1.0 Strict, you cannot do so. In some cases, browsers will ignore such elements, and in all cases, the page will not pass validation tests.

XHTML Transitional

This is a friendly DTD for web designers who don't like banging their heads against a brick wall, trying to work out how to get around using one of those few still-useful old tags:

```
<!DOCTYPE html PUBLIC "-//W3C//DTD XHTML 1.0 Transitional//EN"
    "http://www.w3.org/TR/xhtml1/DTD/xhtml1-transitional.dtd">
```

This is what most designers tend to use, as it provides the greatest degree of freedom and doesn't make validation tools have a hissy fit if the odd deprecated element sneaks through. Also, most of you reading this book will be making the transition from older methods to newer ones, so this is the best choice (and the one with a sensible, friendly name). And even if you end up solely using strict markup, the transitional DTD still ensures browsers render elements correctly.

XHTML Frameset

Some people still swear by frames (and to appease them, there is a short chapter about frames later on in the book). Although the individual pages within the frames require one of the aforementioned DTDs, the frameset itself requires the following:

```
<!DOCTYPE html PUBLIC "-//W3C//DTD XHTML 1.0 Frameset//EN"
    "http://www.w3.org/TR/xhtml1/DTD/xhtml1-frameset.dtd">
```

Partial DTDs

Always include the full DTDs. Some web design packages and online resources provide incomplete or outdated ones that often switch browsers into "quirks" mode, displaying your site as though it were written with browser-specific, old-fashioned markup. An example of an incomplete DTD looks like this:

```
<!DOCTYPE html PUBLIC "-//W3C//DTD XHTML 1.0 Transitional//EN"
    "/DTD/xhtml1-transitional.dtd">
```

In this case, the URI (web address) is relative. Unless you have the DTD in the relevant place on your own website, the browser will display the page this DTD is included on in quirks mode. (And, quite frankly, if you do have the DTD on your website instead of using the one on the W3C's site, you are very odd indeed.) The same thing happens if you leave out DTDs entirely. Therefore, *always* include a DTD and *always* ensure it's complete.

What about the XML declaration?

As stated earlier, there is an exception to the DTD being the first thing on a web page. The one thing that can precede it is an XML declaration (often referred to as the **XML prolog**). This unassuming piece of markup looks like this (assuming you're using Latin-1 encoding):

```
<?xml version="1.0" encoding="ISO-8859-1"?>
```

The tag tells the browser which version of XML is being used and that the character encoding is ISO-8859-1.

> *For an overview of character sets, see the following URLs:* www.w3.org/International/0-charset.html, www.w3.org/International/0-charset-lang.html, *and* www.w3.org/International/0-charset-list.html.

Some web design applications add this tag by default when creating new XHTML documents, and the W3C recommends using it to declare the character encoding used within your document. *I don't.* This is because some browsers take one look at the XML declaration, recoil in horror, and then spit out your site in a way rather different from how you intended, either by not displaying it at all or by displaying it inaccurately—we're looking at *you*, Internet Explorer 6 for Windows. Although this is a browser bug, if such a small piece of code can cause such huge problems with the web browser used by the majority of people, it's cause for concern. However, as mentioned earlier, there's an alternative, compliant, totally safe option that you can use instead:

```
<meta http-equiv="content-type" content="text/html; charset=iso-8859-1" />
```

Using the preceding meta tag works fine, does the same job as one of the main roles of the XML declaration (stating the page's character encoding), and no browsers choke on it. The net result is that everyone goes home happy, and we can finally start talking about the next part of a web page.

> Although the content-type meta *tag can be placed anywhere in the head of a web page, it's worth noting that some browsers don't get the right encoding unless this tag is the first element within the* head *section.*

The head section

The head section of a web page contains information about the document, the majority of which is invisible to the end user. Essentially, it acts as a container for the tags outlined in this section (which should generally be added in the same order that we run through them).

Page titles

Many designers are so keen to get pages online that they forget to provide a title for each page. Titles are added using the title element, as follows:

```
<title>A title for a Web page</title>
```

The title is usually shown at the top of the browser window (and sometimes within the active tab, if you're using a browser that has a tabbed interface), as shown in the following image.

By default, web design packages usually do one of the following things with regard to the title element:

- Add no content.
- Set the title element's content as "Untitled Document."
- Set the title element's content as the application's name.

The first of these results in no title being displayed for the web page and is invalid XHTML, while the second means your page joins the legions online that have no title. The third option is just as bad: using your web page to advertise the application you used to create it. Therefore, add a title to every web page you create—in fact, make it one of the first things you do, so you don't forget.

With regard to the content of your web page titles, bear in mind that this is often the most prominent thing returned in search engine results pages. Keep titles clear, concise, and utterly to the point. Use too many words and the title will be clipped; use too few (or try to get "arty" with characters) and you may end up with something that stumps search engines and potential visitors, too.

Generally speaking, for the homepage at least, it's good to include the name of the site or organization, followed by an indication of the site's reason for existence (and location, if relevant). For instance, as shown in the following image, the Snub Communications title includes the organization's name, the primary services it offers, and its location.

Some designers use the same title throughout their site. This is a bad idea—web page titles are used as visual indicators by visitors trawling bookmarks or their browser's history. This is why I generally tend to use titles as a "breadcrumb" navigation of sorts, showing where a page sits within the website's hierarchy, like this:

```
<title>Company name - Services - Service name</title>
```

Meta tags

In the dim and distant past (the 1990s), the Web was awash with tips for tweaking meta tags. Although these tags are primarily there to provide information about the document, they were initially what most search engines used to categorize web pages and return results. It didn't take long for the shortfalls in the system to become apparent and for designers to abuse them. Thus, many meta tags are considered redundant these days, although some must still be taken into account when creating web pages, for the few search engines that still rely on them and for those tags that assist in other ways. Those tags of interest—for practical means or curiosity's sake—are explored in the sections that follow.

Keywords and descriptions

Unless you're a total newbie, you'll no doubt be aware of the keywords and description meta tags:

```
<meta name="keywords" content="keywords, separated, by, commas" />
<meta name="description" content="A short description about the Web site" />
```

> Because meta tags are empty tags, they must be closed using a space and trailing slash, as explained in Chapter 1.

The first of these tags, keywords, is supposed to contain a list of words that users might type into a search engine to find your site. Because of abuse (websites including thousands of words in the meta tag content, in order to try and create a catch-all in search engine results pages), such lists are rarely used these days. Instead, search engines tend to look at the entire content of a page to determine its relevance to someone's search. However, the tag is still worth adding. Generally, 30 or fewer words and short phrases are sufficient.

The contents of the description's content attribute are returned by some search engines in a results page along with the web page's title. As with the title, keep things succinct, otherwise the description will be cropped. Most search engines display a maximum of 200 characters, so 25 well-chosen words are just about all you can afford.

revisit-after, robots, and author

Other meta tags also use name and content attributes. These tags assist search engines. In the following example, the first tag provides an indication of how often they should return (useful for regularly updated sites) and the second tag states whether the page should be indexed or not.

```
<meta name="Revisit-After" content="30 Days" />
<meta name="robots" content="ALL,INDEX" />
```

The content attribute of the robots meta tag can instead include the values noindex and none, in order to block indexing, and follow or nofollow, depending on whether you want search engine robots to follow links from the current page or not.

Another method of controlling robots is to place a `robots.txt` file in your site root. See Chapter 12 for more information on creating such a file.

The author meta tag is of less use to search engines, and typically includes the page author's name and home URL. Designers sometimes use it as a means to declare the author's name and details, but it has little use beyond that.

```
<meta name="author" content="Craig Grannell for www.snubcommunications.com." />
```

Blocking smart tags and the image toolbar

The following tags block certain Microsoft "innovations." The first prevents "smart tags" from interfering with a web page (although at the time of this writing, this is not an issue), and the second stops Internet Explorer's image toolbar from appearing (which otherwise appears when you hover the cursor over an image, as shown in the image to the right).

```
<meta name="MSSmartTagsPreventParsing"
content="true" />
<meta http-equiv="imagetoolbar" content="false" />
```

Whether you should add a meta tag to turn off the image toolbar is debatable—doing so interferes with a browser's default behavior, and users can turn off this option if they wish. Ultimately, the decision is yours. Note also that the meta tag for controlling the image toolbar has an http-equiv attribute rather than a name attribute. Such tags usually control the action of browsers, although the distinction became muddied long ago. Just make sure you don't mix up name and http-equiv when using specific tags.

Stopping pages from being cached

A final meta tag worth mentioning is intended to prevent a web browser from caching a page locally, regardless of the settings within the browser's preferences. This is ideal for things like regularly updated news pages, but it should be used sparingly elsewhere.

```
<meta http-equiv="pragma" content="no-cache" />
```

There are other meta tags, but we're not going to cover them. Even those mentioned in this chapter aren't all supported to any great extent in all web browsers, and some are little more than curiosities. In the end, it's up to you how many you use. As a general rule, always use the tag that defines the character set, and usually include the keywords and description meta tags.

Attaching external documents

Although it's possible to work with JavaScript and CSS within an HTML document, this goes against the modular nature of web design. It's far easier to create, edit, and maintain a site if you work with separate files for each technology. (The exception is if your "site" is only a single page, therefore making it sensible to include everything in a single document.)

As already mentioned, XHTML documents are text files that are saved with the suffix .html (or .htm). CSS and JavaScript files are also text documents, and their file suffixes are .css and .js, respectively. When you start a project, having already set the relevant DOCTYPE and added meta tags, it's a good idea to create blank CSS and JavaScript files and to attach them to your web page, so you can then work on any element as you wish.

Attaching external CSS files: The link method

In the previous chapter, you were shown how to attach CSS to a web page (see the section "Adding styles to a web page" in Chapter 1), and we'll briefly recap the process here. There are two methods of attaching an external CSS file: the link method and the @import method.

The link tag specifies a relationship between the linked document and the document it's being linked to. In the context of attaching a CSS file, it looks something like this:

```
<link rel="StyleSheet" href="stylesheet.css" type="text/css" media="all" />
```

The attributes used are

- rel: Defines the relation from the parent document to the target
- href: The location of the target file
- type: The MIME type of the target document
- media: The target medium of the target document

In our example, we set the media attribute to all, specifying that this style sheet is intended for all devices. But it's feasible to attach multiple style sheets to a web page, and set the media attribute of each one to a different type. For instance, in the following example, two CSS files are attached, one for screen and the other for printed output:

```
<link rel="stylesheet" href="stylesheet.css" type="text/css" media="screen" />
<link rel="stylesheet" href="printcss.css" type="text/css" media="print" />
```

There are other media types, including aural, braille, projection, and tv, but few are supported well. However, toward the end of the book we'll look at style sheets for print, which is one of the alternatives to screen that is supported reasonably well in mainstream browsers.

Attaching CSS files: The @import method

The problem with the link method is that obsolete browsers see the style sheet but don't understand it. This results in garbled layouts—and often in unusable websites for those unfortunate enough to have to deal with such arcane web browsers. The solution is to hide the CSS from such browsers by using a command that they don't understand and so will ignore. This is often referred to as the @import method.

As shown in the following example, the style element is used to do this:

```
<style type="text/css" media="all">
@import url(stylesheet.css);
</style>
```

> The CSS specifications permit the use of the style sheet location as a quoted string instead of enclosing it in url(). The method shown here is more commonly supported, though.

The following image shows the result in obsolete browsers, such as Netscape 4. The CSS is hidden, so just the content is displayed.

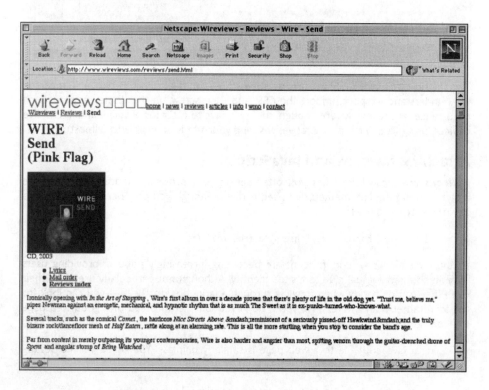

However, compliant browsers see the CSS and render the site accordingly:

This method isn't perfect. Some browsers think they can deal with CSS but can't, meaning they understand @import, import the CSS, and then screw up the display anyway. Such occurrences are relatively rare, though, so if you have to cater for obsolete and alternative devices, using @import is a wise move, ensuring your site is accessible to (almost) all.

Attaching favicons and JavaScript

Favicons are those little icons you often see in your browser's address bar. They are attached using the link method discussed earlier, although you only need to include two attributes, rel and href:

```
<link rel="shortcut icon" href="favicon.ico" />
```

At the time of this writing, favicons are becoming increasingly popular, providing users with an additional visual clue to a site's identity. Although not particularly useful on their own, they can be handy when trawling through a large bookmarks list—you can look for the icon rather than the text. However, don't rely on them instead of a good web page title, because favicons aren't supported by all browsers.

Attaching a JavaScript file to a web page is similarly painless. You do so via the script element, as follows:

```
<script type="text/javascript" src="javascriptfile.js"></script>
```

You may have used the language *attribute in the past, but this is now deprecated and will get you into trouble when validating if you're using XHTML Strict.*

Checking paths

When working with external files, ensure paths between files are complete and don't become broken as files are moved around, otherwise your web page may lose track of the CSS and JavaScript, affecting its display and functionality. If you're using document-relative links (i.e., links relative to the current document), remember to add paths accordingly. The majority of web designers will be aware of such things, but if this is new information for you, check out the guide in Chapter 5, at the beginning of the "Anchors (creating links)" section.

The body section

The body element is used to define the body of a web page, and it contains the document's content. **No document content should ever be placed outside of the body element**. Sorry for the bold type, but this is something I see on a regular basis, so I wanted to nip that one in the bud.

Although the body element has a number of possible attributes that can be included in its start tag, unless you're having a funny turn or want to go on a retro web adventure, these should be avoided, because they can all be dealt with using CSS (and therefore controlled sitewide, rather than in each individual page). Such attributes include the likes of alink, link, and vlink for defining link colors; text for defining the default text color; and background and bgcolor for defining a background pattern and color. There are also a number of proprietary attributes, which were intended to set padding around web page content:

> **For Netscape**: marginwidth and marginheight

> **For Internet Explorer**: leftmargin, topmargin, rightmargin, and bottommargin

> **For the web designer**: A big headache having to remember all these stupid attributes

> **For the web page**: A bulging body tag, full of junk

In this section, we'll look at a better way of setting content margins and padding, default font and color, and web page backgrounds.

Content margins and padding in CSS

Page margins and padding are better dealt with using CSS. You need to set the values only once, in an external file. To update your settings sitewide, you only have to upload the amended style sheet rather than every single page on your site that has an amended body tag.

Furthermore, in terms of page weight, CSS is more efficient. If using old methods, to cater for all browsers, you set the following body attributes:

```
<body marginwidth="0" marginheight="0" topmargin="0" leftmargin="0"
➥bottommargin="0" rightmargin="0">
```

The equivalent in CSS is

```
body {
margin: 0;
padding: 0;
}
```

> If a CSS setting is 0, there's no need to state a unit such as px or em.

The reason we set both margin and padding to 0 is because some browsers (notably Opera) have a default padding value. Therefore, even if you set all body margins to 0, there would still be a gap around your page content. Setting both the margin and padding to 0 in the body rule ensures that all browsers display your content with no gaps around it.

The previous CSS is used in pretty much every site I create. It's clean, it's efficient, and it's in shorthand, so I'd better explain how that works while I'm at it.

Working with CSS shorthand for boxes

Something worth getting to grips with is the ability to work in CSS shorthand. The previous example showed how to set page margins and padding to 0, and this was done in shorthand instead of writing out every single value. How CSS shorthand works for boxes is like this:

- **A single value (margin: 10px;)**: This is applied to all edges.
- **Two values (margin: 10px 20px;)**: The first setting (10px) is applied to the top and bottom edges. The second setting (20px) is applied to both the left and right edges (20px each, not in total).
- **Three values (margin: 10px 20px 30px;)**: The first setting (10px) is applied to the top edge. The second setting (20px) is applied to both the left and right edges. The third setting (30px) is applied to the bottom edge.
- **Four settings (margin: 10px 20px 30px 40px)**: Settings are applied clockwise from the top (i.e., top: 10px; right: 20px; bottom: 30px; left: 40px).

Shorthand's benefits become immediately obvious when comparing CSS shorthand with the equivalent properties and values written out in full. For instance, the following shorthand

```
body {
margin: 0;
padding: 0 100px;
}
```

looks like this when written out in full:

```
body {
margin-top: 0;
margin-right: 0;
margin-bottom: 0;
margin-left: 0;
padding-top: 0;
padding-right: 100px;
padding-bottom: 0;
padding-left: 100px;
}
```

Whether or not you use shorthand is up to you. Some designers swear by it and others because of it. Some web design applications have options to "force" shorthand or avoid it entirely. I reckon it's a good thing: CSS documents are usually more logical and shorter because of shorthand. But if you don't agree, feel free to keep on defining the margin and padding as relevant for every edge of every element.

Setting a default font and font color

Along with setting the spacing around body content, the body element attributes are used to deal with default text and background colors, link colors, and background images. In CSS, links are dealt with separately (see Chapter 5), and we'll look at how to use backgrounds later in this chapter.

At this point, it's worth noting that, when working with CSS, the body selector is often used to set a default font family and color for the website. We'll discuss working with text in more depth in the next chapter, but for now, check out the following CSS:

```
body {
font-family: Verdana, Arial, Helvetica, sans-serif;
color: #000000;
}
```

This is pretty straightforward. The font-family property sets a default font (in this case, Verdana) and fallback fonts in case the first choice isn't available on the user's system. The list must end with a generic family, such as sans-serif or serif, depending on your other choices. The fonts are separated by commas in the list, and if you're using multiple-word fonts, they must be quoted ("Courier New", not Courier New).

The color property's value defines the default color of text throughout the site. In the preceding example, its value is #000000, which is the hexadecimal (hex) value for black (when defining colors in CSS, it's most common to use hex values, although you can use comma-separated RGB values if you wish).

> Although it's possible to set a default size for text in the body declaration, we'll leave that for now, and instead explore how best to do so in the following chapter.

51

Web page backgrounds

Web page backgrounds used to be commonplace, but they became unpopular once designers figured out that visitors to web pages didn't want their eyes wrenched out by gaudy tiled background patterns. With text being as hard to read onscreen as it is, it's adding insult to injury to inflict some nasty paisley mosaic background (or worse) on the poor reader, too.

But, as affordable monitors continue to increase in size and resolution, designers face a conundrum. If they're creating a liquid design that stretches to fit the browser window, text can become unreadable, because the eye finds it hard to scan text in wide columns. And if they're creating a fixed-width design, large areas of the screen often end up blank. It's for the latter design style that backgrounds can be useful, both in drawing the eye to the content and providing some visual interest outside of the content area.

Like most things related to design, the use and style of backgrounds is subjective, but some rules are worth bearing in mind. The most obvious is that a background should not distract from your content. If you're using images, keep them simple, and when you're using color, keep contrast and saturation fairly low. Unless you're using a subtle watermark, it's bad form to put images underneath text—the low resolution of the Web means it will be harder to read than a print-based equivalent. Also, because backgrounds are not main site content, loading times should be kept as low as possible.

Web page backgrounds in CSS

Backgrounds are added to web page elements using a number of properties, as described in the sections that follow.

background-color

This property sets the background color of the element. In the following example, the page's body background color has been set to #ffffff (which is hex for white):

```
body {
background-color: #ffffff;
}
```

background-image

This property sets a background image for the relevant element:

```
body {
background-image: url(background_image.jpg);
}
```

By using this CSS, you end up with a tiled background, as shown in the following image.

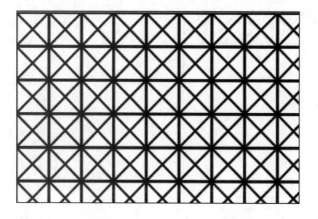

background-repeat

What we've done so far mimics deprecated HTML attributes, but CSS provides you with control over the background's tiling and positioning. The background-repeat property can take four values, the default of which is repeat, creating the tiled background just shown. If background-repeat is set to no-repeat, the image is shown just once:

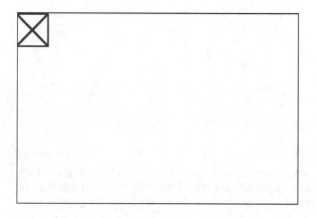

If this property is set to repeat-x, the image tiles horizontally only:

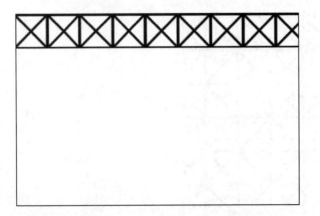

And if the property is set to repeat-y, the image tiles vertically only:

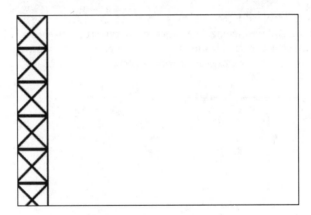

background-attachment

This property has two possible values: scroll and fixed. The default is scroll, in which the background works as normal, scrolling with the rest of the page. If you set the value to fixed, the background image remains stationary while the remainder of the page scrolls.

background-position

This property's values set the origin of the background by using two values that relate to the horizontal and vertical position. This is in relation to the content rather than the available browser window space (so if you set both horizontal and vertical values to center, the background will align itself dead center of your content, regardless of whether the content spans several screen heights; it won't align itself in the center of the browser window). The default background-position value is 0,0 (the top-left of the web page).

Along with keywords (center, left, and right for horizontal positioning; center, top, and bottom for vertical positioning), you can use percentages and pixel values. It's possible to use a combination of percentages and pixel sizes, but you cannot mix keywords with either. Therefore, it's typically recommended that designers stick with using percentages and pixel values—after all, keyword positioning can be emulated with numbers anyway (left top being the same as 0,0, for instance).

When using keywords, it's recommended to use the order horizontal-vertical, because both percentage- and pixel-based background positioning uses this order, and it's simpler to remember a single rule. In the following example, the background would be positioned on the left of the web page and positioned in the vertical center of the content:

```
body {
background-image: url(background_image.jpg);
background-repeat: no-repeat;
background-position: left center;
}
```

Again, when using percentages or pixel values, the first value relates to the horizontal position and the second to the vertical. So, to create the equivalent of our keyword example, we'd use the following CSS:

```
body {
background-image: url(background_image.jpg);
background-repeat: no-repeat;
background-position:  0 50%;
}
```

CSS shorthand for web backgrounds

As when defining margins and padding, you can use shorthand for web background values, bundling them into a single background property, although it's worth stating that the shorthand value overrides any previous settings in a CSS file for individual background properties. (For instance, if you use individual settings to define the background image, and then subsequently use the shorthand for setting the color, the background image will most likely not appear.)

When using shorthand, you can set the values in any order. Here's an example:

```
body {
background: #ffffff url(background_image.jpg) no-repeat fixed 50% 10px;
}
```

Generally speaking, it's best to use shorthand over separate background properties—it's quicker to type and easier to manage. You also don't have to explicitly define every one of the values; if you don't, the values revert to their defaults. Therefore, the following is acceptable:

```
body {
background: #ffffff url(background_image.gif) no-repeat;
}
```

Because the background-attachment value hasn't been specified, this background would scroll with the page, and because the background-position value hasn't been defined, it would be positioned at 0%, 0%—the top-left of the browser window.

Web page background ideas

Before finishing up this section on web page backgrounds, we'll run through some examples that show the CSS and the result, along with the background image used. For the HTML, which is the same in each case, we'll add several paragraphs within a div element with an id value of content, as follows:

```
<div id="content">
<p>...</p>
</div>
```

In CSS, we define the body, setting padding and margins to 0 and background to #ffffff (white):

```
body {
padding: 0;
margin: 0;
background: #ffffff;
}
```

Again in CSS, the top margin of paragraphs is set to 0, in order to ensure no extra padding is placed at the top of the content:

```
p {
margin-top: 0;
}
```

For the first few examples, we also define the content div by adding the following CSS rule:

```
#content {
background: #ffffff;
width: 500px;
margin: 0 auto;
padding: 10px;
}
```

We'll cover this sort of thing in more depth in the layout chapters (notably Chapter 8), but the preceding rule sets the div's width to 500px, sets the margins to 0 vertically and auto horizontally (thereby centering the page onscreen), and provides some internal padding. It also sets the background color to white, so the text will be readable.

> *Note that* margin: auto *doesn't work in Internet Explorer 5 and 5.5 for Windows. Later chapters explain workarounds for dealing with that browser's noncompliance.*

Striped backgrounds

The following CSS can be used to add a simple striped, tiled background to your web page:

```css
body {
padding: 0;
margin: 0;
background: #ffffff url(background_tile.gif);
}
```

The following screenshot shows a page with diagonal stripes, although you could use horizontal stripes, squares, or other simple shapes. Contrast has been kept fairly low, in order to not distract from the content. Also, the size of the background image (magnified to 300% in the screenshot) was set to 60 pixels square. This is because if you use tiles that are too small, some browsers end up running extremely slowly, or choke entirely.

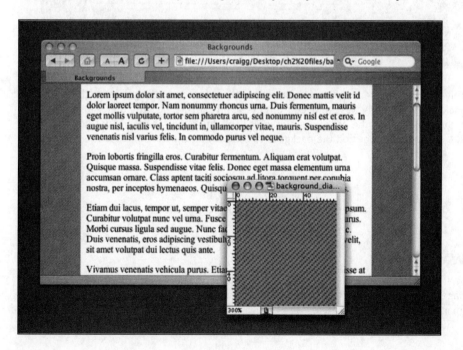

Drop shadows

The following image shows a page with a content area and drop shadow.

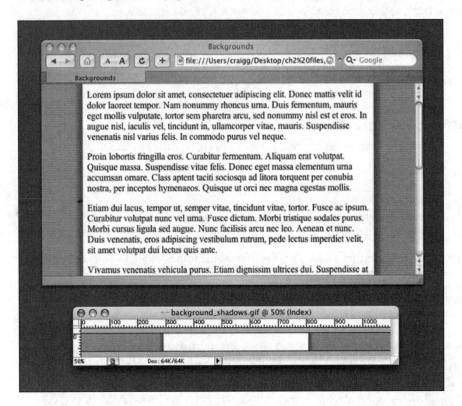

This effect was achieved by creating the depicted graphic and tiling it vertically. In CSS, the background property was removed from the #content rule, because the white background area is now part of the background graphic itself. In the body rule, the position was set to 50% 0 in order to position the background centrally on the horizontal axis.

```
body {
padding: 0;
margin: 0;
background: #ffffff url(background_shadows.gif) 50% 0;
}
```

Watermarks

The final example looks at utilizing a background image to assist in a left-aligned web page. In the following screenshot, we see the content area to the left, with a background image to the right of this area.

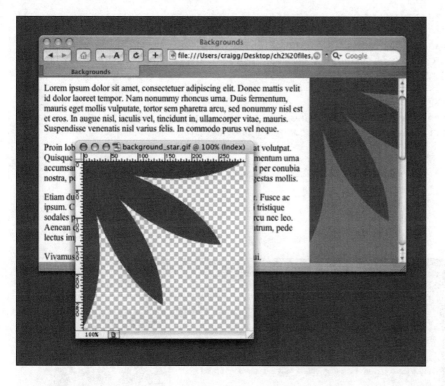

2

To achieve this effect, the margin setting in the #content rule was set to 0 (instead of 0 auto) to stop it from being centered. The body background value was then changed as follows:

```
background: #8b8b8b url(background_star.gif) no-repeat 520px 0;
```

The image used is a transparent GIF, so the background color setting was changed from white to a mid gray (#8b8b8b). The reasoning behind using a transparent GIF is explained in Chapter 4, but it relates to web browsers sometimes interpreting colors differently from graphics packages. Therefore, it's often easier to make the flat background color of a graphic transparent and then use the web page background color in place of it.

The repeat setting is set to no-repeat, because we don't want the image to tile. Finally, the background's position is set to 520px 0. The 0 setting means it hugs the top of the browser window, while the 520px setting means the image is placed at 520 pixels from the left. This is because we earlier defined the content area as 500 pixels wide with 10 pixels of padding, and 500 + 10 + 10 = 520. The full body rule is therefore as follows:

```
body {
padding: 0;
margin: 0;
background: #8b8b8b url(background_star.gif) no-repeat 520px 0;
}
```

> *Internet Explorer 5.5 for Windows places padding on the inside of elements rather than on the outside, so if you test a page such as this in that particular browser, it won't display correctly. I explain how to work around Internet Explorer 5.5 bugs in the layout chapters and in more depth in Chapter 12.*

As mentioned earlier, backgrounds can be added to any web page element. For instance, we can add a watermark to the content area by using the following CSS:

```
#content {
background: #ffffff url(background_watermark.gif) no-repeat 20px 20px;
width: 500px;
margin: 0;
padding: 10px;
}
```

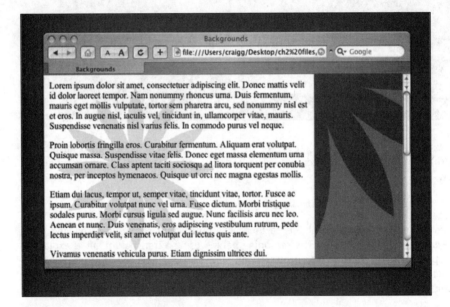

Body CSS styling summary

So far in this chapter, we've looked at setting margins and padding, the default font (and color), and web page backgrounds. We've not yet put everything together, though, so here's a handy summary of what a full body rule might look like:

```
body {
margin: 0;
padding: 0;
```

```
font-family: Verdana, Arial, Helvetica, sans-serif;
color: #000000;
background: #ffffff url(assets/image.jpg) no-repeat scroll 10px 20%;
}
```

Closing your document

Back at the start of the chapter, we examined basic HTML and XHTML documents. Regardless of the technology used, the end of the document should look like this:

```
</body>
</html>
```

There are no variations or alternatives. A body end tag terminates the document's content, and an html end tag terminates the document itself. No web page content should come after the body end tag, and no HTML content should come after the html end tag (white space is fine, and it's common practice with server-side technologies to put functions after the html end tag—just don't put any HTML there).

Also, you must only ever have **one** body and **one** head in an HTML document, as well as a single HTML start tag and a single HTML end tag.

This is important stuff to bear in mind, and even if you think it's obvious, there are millions of pages out there—particularly those that utilize server-side includes and server-side languages—that include multiple body tags and head tags, have content outside the body tag, and have HTML outside the html tag.

Don't do this in your own work.

Commenting your work

The rules for HTML, CSS, and JavaScript comments are simple, but the actual characters used are different in each case.

HTML comments begin with <!-- and end with -->, and can run over multiple lines, as follows:

```
<!-- this is a comment in HTML -->

<!--
Multiple-line
HTML
comment
-->
```

In XHTML, double dashes should not occur within the comment itself. Therefore, the following is not valid XHTML:

```
<!-- This is invalid -- as is the HTML below -->
<!----------------------------------------------------------->
```

The multiple-dash comment is commonly used by designers who favor hand-coding, to separate large chunks of code within a document. When working in XHTML, replace the dashes with a different character:

```
<!--ooooooooooooooooooooooooooooooooooooooo-->
<!--==================================-->
```

CSS comments are opened with /* and closed with */ and, like HTML comments, can run over multiple lines, as shown here:

```
/* This is a comment in CSS */

/*
Multiple-line
CSS
comment
*/
```

Multiple-line comments in JavaScript are the same as in CSS, but single-line comments are placed after double forward slashes:

```
// This is a JavaScript comment.
```

Don't use comments incorrectly. CSS comments in an HTML document won't be problematic—but they will be displayed. HTML comments in CSS can actually cause a CSS file to fail entirely.

> *Along with enabling you to comment your work, comments can be used to disable sections of code when testing web pages.*

Web page essentials checklist

Congratulations—you made it to the end of this chapter! I'm aware that some of this one was about as much fun as trying to work out complex quadratic equations in your head but, as mentioned at the start, you need to know this stuff. Imagine designing a site and it suddenly not working the way you thought it would. It looks fine in your web design package and also in some web browsers, but it starts falling apart in others. Just removing an XML declaration might be enough to fix the site.

If you take the elements of this chapter and form them into a simple checklist, you won't have to risk displaying those wonderful "Untitled Documents" to the entire world (or inadvertently advertising the package you used to create the page). To make your life easier, you can refer to this checklist:

1. Ensure the relevant DOCTYPE declaration and namespace is in place.

2. Remove the XML declaration if it's lurking.

3. Add a title tag and some content within it.

4. Add a meta tag to define your character set.

5. If required, add keywords and description meta tags.

6. Attach a CSS file (or files).

7. Attach a JavaScript file (or files).

8. If your web editor adds superfluous body attributes, delete them.

9. Ensure there are no characters prior to the DOCTYPE declaration and after the html end tag.

10. Ensure no web page content appears outside the body element.

CHAPTER 3
WORKING WITH TEXT

In this chapter

- Moving from old to new: from font tags to semantic markup and CSS
- Defining font colors, families, and other styles
- Understanding web-safe fonts
- Creating drop caps and pull quotes with ease
- Rapidly editing styled text
- Creating and styling lists

Styling text the old-fashioned way (or, Why we hate the font tag)

Styling text online used to be all about the font tag. When Netscape introduced this element—complete with size and color attributes—web designers jumped for joy. When Microsoft announced it would go further, adding a face attribute (enabling you to specify the font family), web designers were giddy with anticipation. But things didn't go according to plan. Page sizes bloated as designers created pages filled with fonts of myriad sizes and colors. Web users looked on aghast, wondering whether giant, orange body copy was really the way to go, and whether it was worth waiting twice as long for such abominations to download.

More important, it became apparent that font tags caused problems, including

- Inconsistent display across browsers and platforms
- The requirement for font tags to be applied to individual elements
- Difficulty ensuring fonts were consistent sitewide, because of having to style individual elements
- HTML geared toward presentation rather than logical structure
- Large HTML documents due to all the extra elements

In addition, working with font tags is a time-consuming, boring process, and yet some web designers remain blissfully ignorant of such problems. In my opinion, if font tags weren't an HTML element, I'd suggest they be taken out back and shot. Today, there is no reason whatsoever to stick with them. Text can be rapidly styled sitewide with CSS and, as we'll see later in this chapter, CSS provides you with a greater degree of control than font tags ever did. More crucially, font tags encourage badly formed documents, with designers relying on inline elements to style things like headings, when there are perfectly good HTML elements better suited to that purpose.

HTML should be reserved for content and structure, and CSS for design. Web pages should be composed of appropriate elements for each piece of content. This method of working, called **semantic markup**, is what we're going to discuss next.

A new beginning: Semantic markup

Some might argue that "semantic markup" is web designer fancy-talk for "using the appropriate tag at the relevant time," but there can be no denying the usefulness of well-formed, semantic markup. The following is an example of the *wrong* way of doing things, relying on font tags to create a heading and double line-breaks (

) for separating paragraphs:

```
<font size="7" color="red" face="Helvetica">Articleheading</font><br /><br />
```

```
Lorem ipsum dolor sit amet, consectetuer adipiscing elit. Sed aliquet elementum
➥erat. Integer diam mi, venenatis non, cursus a, hendrerit at, mi.<br /><br />
Quisque faucibus lorem eget sapien. In urna sem, vehicula ut, mattis et,
➥venenatis at, velit. Ut sodales lacus sed eros.
```

The likelihood of this displaying consistently across browsers and platforms is low. More important, the tags used don't relate to the content. Therefore, if the styling is removed, there's no indication regarding what role each element plays within the document structure and hierarchy—for instance, there would be no visual clues as to the importance of the heading. Also, the use of double line-breaks (

) instead of paragraph tags means the "paragraphs" cannot be styled in CSS.

Instead, the example should be marked up like this:

```
<h1>Article heading</h1>
<p>Lorem ipsum dolor sit amet, consectetuer adipiscing elit. Sed aliquet
➥elementum erat. Integer diam mi, venenatis non, cursus a, hendrerit at, mi.</p>
<p>Quisque faucibus lorem eget sapien. In urna sem, vehicula ut, mattis et,
➥venenatis at, velit. Ut sodales lacus sed eros.</p>
```

Here, the heading is marked up with the relevant tags, and double carriage-returns are replaced with paragraph tags. This means the page's structural integrity is ensured, and the markup is logical and semantic. If attached CSS styles are removed, the default HTML formatting still makes obvious to the end user the importance of the headings, and will visually display them as such.

In this section, we'll look at how to mark up paragraphs and headings, explore logical and physical styles, and discuss the importance of well-formed semantic markup.

Paragraphs and headings

With words making up the bulk of online content, the paragraph and heading HTML elements are of paramount importance. HTML provides six levels of headings, from h1 to h6, with h1 being the top-level heading. The adjacent image shows how these headings, along with a paragraph, typically appear by default in a browser.

```
<h1>Level one heading</h1>
<h2>Level two heading</h2>
<h3>Level three heading</h3>
<h4>Level four heading</h4>
<h5>Level five heading</h5>
<h6>Level six heading</h6>
<p>Default paragraph size.</p>
```

Level one heading

Level two heading

Level three heading

Level four heading

Level five heading

Level six heading

Default paragraph size.

By default, browsers put margins around paragraphs and headings, and this can vary from browser to browser, although it can be controlled by CSS. Therefore, there's no excuse for using double line-breaks to avoid default paragraph margins affecting web page layouts.

Despite the typical default sizes, level five and six headings are not intended as "tiny text," but as a way to enable you to structure your document, which is essential, as headings help with assistive technology, enabling the visually disabled to efficiently surf the Web.

Logical and physical styles

Once text is in place, it's common to add inline styles, which can be achieved by way of logical and physical styles. Many designers are confused by the difference between the two, especially because equivalents (such as the logical strong and physical b) tend to be displayed the same in browsers. The difference is that **logical styles** describe what the content *is*, whereas **physical styles** merely define what the content *looks like*. This subtle difference becomes more apparent when you take into account things like screen readers. In the markup I like to emphasize things, a screen reader emphasizes the text surrounded by the em tags. However, replace the em tags with i tags and the screen reader won't emphasize the word, although in a visual web browser the two pieces of markup will look identical.

Styles for emphasis (bold and italic)

Physical styles enable you to make text bold and <i>italic</i>, and these are the most commonly used inline physical styles. Of late, logical styles are becoming more widespread (the majority of web design applications now default to logical styles rather than physical ones). Typically, strong emphasis emboldens text in a visual web browser, and emphasis italicizes text.

Deprecated and nonstandard physical styles

Many physical elements are considered obsolete, including the infamous blink (a Netscape "innovation" used to flash text on and off, amusingly still supported in Firefox). Some physical styles are deprecated: u (underline) and s (strikethrough; also strike) have CSS equivalents using the text-decoration property (text-decoration: underline and text-decoration: line-through, respectively).

The big and small elements

The big and small elements cling on, and are sometimes used to increase and decrease the size of inline text (even text defined in pixels in CSS). However, because the actual change in size depends on individual web browsers, you're better off using span elements with a specific class relating to a font size defined in CSS (see the section "Creating alternatives with classes and spans" later in the chapter).

Teletype, subscript, and superscript

This leaves three useful physical styles. The first, tt, renders text in a monospace font (à la teletype text). The others, sub and sup, render text as subscript and superscript text, respectively. These are useful for scientific documents, although there is a drawback: characters are displayed at the same size, defined by the browser. You can get around this by using a CSS tag selector and defining a new font size for each element. The following code shows how to do this, and the screen shot below shows a default (top) and CSS styled (bottom) sup element in use.

```
sup {
font-size: 70%;
}
```

$e=mc^2$

$e=mc^2$

Logical styles for programming-oriented content

Several logical styles do similar jobs, are programming oriented, and are usually displayed in a monospace font:

```
<code>Denotes a code sample.</code>
<kbd>Indicates text entered by the user.</kbd>
<samp>Indicates a programming sample.</samp>
```

The var element also relates to programming, signifying a variable. However, it is usually displayed in italics.

Citations and definitions

The cite element indicates a citation (a reference to another document, such as an article) and is usually displayed in italics. To indicate the defining instance of a term, you use the dfn element. This is used to draw attention to the first use of such a term and is also as a rule displayed in italics.

Acronyms and abbreviations

Two logical styles assist with accessibility, enabling you to provide users with full forms of abbreviations and acronyms by way of the title attribute:

```
<abbr title="Cascading Style Sheets">CSS</abbr>
<acronym title="North Atlantic Treaty Organization">NATO</acronym>
```

This has two uses: users with disabilities (using screen readers) can access the full form of the words in question. But anyone using a visual web browser can access the information, too, because title attribute contents are usually displayed as a tooltip when you hover your mouse over elements they're used on.

To further draw attention to an abbreviation or acronym, style the tag in CSS (using a tag selector), thereby making all such tags consistent across an entire website. The following is an example of this, the results of which can be seen to the right (including the pop-up triggered by hovering over the abbr element, which has a title attribute).

```
abbr {
border-bottom: 1px dotted #000000;
background-color: yellow;
}
```

Simulating tracking features with logical styles

The del and ins elements simulate the look of tracking features of word processing packages, if not the functionality. The del element indicates deleted text and usually appears in strike-through format, whereas ins indicates inserted text and usually appears underlined. These tags cannot be nested inside each other, for obvious reasons.

```
<p>I <del>deleted this</del> and then <ins>inserted this</ins>.</p>
```

I ~~deleted this~~ and then <u>inserted this</u>.

The latter can be problematic online. Because links are often underlined, users may attempt to click text marked up as inserted text and wonder why nothing happens. It's a good idea to amend the tag's visual appearance by changing the underline color. This can be done by removing the default underline and replacing it with a bottom border:

```
ins {
text-decoration: none;
border-bottom: 1px solid red;
}
```

The bottom border resembles an underline, although it appears lower than the default underline, thereby further differentiating inserted text from hypertext links.

The importance of well-formed markup

Many logical styles are rarely used online, because they look no different from text marked up using the likes of the i element. However, as mentioned earlier, physical appearance alone misses the point of HTML. Always using the most appropriate relevant element means that you can later individually style each element in CSS, overriding the default appearance if you wish. If the likes of citations, defining instances, and variables are all marked up with i instead of cite, dfn, and var, there's no way of distinguishing each type of content and no way of manipulating their appearance on an individual basis. Well-formed markup is more than ensuring visual flexibility, though. Use of the cite tag, for instance, enables you to manipulate the Document Object Model (DOM) to extract a bibliography or list of quotations from a page or even a full website. The ability to style logical tags like this with CSS is likely to be of increasing rather than diminishing importance.

The importance of end tags

While we're on the subject of well-formed markup, we'll revisit the importance of end tags. As mentioned earlier, XHTML demands that all tags be closed. Most browsers let you get away with ignoring some end tags, though, such as on paragraphs. Many designers picked up this bad habit when such tags were optional in HTML. Omit many others at your peril. For instance, overlook a heading element end tag and a browser considers subsequent content to be part of the heading and displays it accordingly. As shown in the following image, two paragraphs are displayed as a heading, because the earlier heading element lacks an end tag.

A heading, not closed

Lorem ipsum dolor sit amet, consectetuer adipiscing elit. Morbi id tellus. Lorem ipsum dolor sit amet, consectetuer adipiscing elit. Mauris risus ante, dapibus vitae, venenatis id, rutrum at, purus.

Proin iaculis volutpat turpis. Cras bibendum hendrerit tortor. Mauris lorem lorem, suscipit sed, malesuada non, vehicula quis, lectus. Cras porta mattis pede. Class aptent taciti sociosqu ad litora torquent per conubia nostra, per inceptos hymenaeos.

A similar problem occurs when you accidentally omit end tags when using logical and physical elements. For instance, forget to close an emphasis element and the remainder of the web page may be displayed in italics.

> *Some designers create both start and end tags at the same time, and then populate them with content, so end tags are not forgotten.*

Styling text using CSS

HTML is intended as a structural markup language, but the Web's increasing popularity meant it got "polluted" with tags designed for presentation. This made HTML more complex than it needed to be, and such tags soon became a headache for web designers trying to style page elements, such as text. You'd often see source code like this:

```
<font face="Helvetica" size="3" color="#333333"> This markup is
➥<font size="+3"><small>really </small></font>bad, but it was sort of
➥the norm in the 1990s.</font>
```

WYSIWYG tools would insert tags to override others, adding to the page weight and making it tough to ensure visual consistency sitewide. By and large, CSS eradicates these problems and enables more control over text.

This is a boon for graphic designers who used to loathe HTML's lack of typographical control. However, the level of freedom evident in print design still isn't quite so on the Web. Restrictions imposed by browsers and the screen must be taken into account, such as it being harder to read type onscreen than in print. This is largely related to resolution. Even magazines with fairly low-quality print tend to be printed at around 250 dpi—several times the typical resolution of a monitor. This means very small text (favored by many designers, who think such small text looks neat) becomes tricky to read onscreen, because there aren't enough pixels to create a coherent image.

I'll note restrictions such as this at the appropriate times during this section on styling text with CSS, ensuring that you'll know how to strike a balance between the visual appearance and practicality of web-based text.

Defining font colors

In CSS, the color property value defines the foreground color of the relevant CSS element, which for text sets its color. This can be set using hex, keywords, or RGB. The following examples show each method in turn and all have the same result: setting paragraphs to black.

```
p {
color: #000000;
}

p {
color: black;
}

p {
color: rgb(0,0,0);
}
```

Declaring colors using RGB is rare in web design—hex is most popular, especially because CSS supports so few keywords (see the section "Working with hex" in Chapter 4).

Remember to test your choices on both Windows and Mac, because there are differences in the default color space for each platform. In general terms, the Mac default display settings are brighter (or Windows is darker, depending on your outlook on life); if you use subtle dark tones on the Mac, or very light tones on Windows, the result might be tricky to view on the other platform. This should cause few problems with text, but some designers insist on rendering text with very little contrast to the background color, and this ends up being even harder to read on a different platform from the one on which it was created.

The main tip to keep in mind for color with regard to web-based text is simple: always provide plenty of contrast so that your text remains readable.

Defining font families

The font-family property enables you to specify a list of font face values, starting with your first choice, continuing with alternates (in case your choice isn't installed on the user's machine), and terminating in a generic font family, which causes the browser to substitute a similar font (think of it as a last resort). Generic font family names in general use are serif and sans-serif, although when you're using monospace fonts (such as Courier New), you should end your list with monospace.

Multiple-word font family names must be quoted (such as "Trebuchet MS" and "Times New Roman"). You can use single or double quotes—just be consistent. Single-word font family names should never be quoted. Examples of font-family in use are as follows:

```
h1 {
font-family: Arial, Helvetica, sans-serif;
}

p {
font-family: Georgia, "Times New Roman", serif;
}

pre {
font-family: Courier, "Courier New", Monaco, monospace;
}
```

> pre *is the element for preformatted text, used to display monospace text in an identical fashion to how it's formatted in the original HTML document. It's commonly used for online FAQs, film scripts, and the like.*

Web-safe fonts

Print designers have a world of fonts at their disposal, but the same isn't true online. Rather than being limited by installed fonts, you're restricted by common fonts across various platforms. If end users don't have installed the same fonts as you, they won't see your design like you do, rendering your choices pointless.

Sans-serif fonts for the Web

Arial is a common font choice, largely because of its dominance on Windows. Its poor design makes it unreadable at small sizes and a poor choice for body copy, although it can be of use for headings. Mac users should be wary of choosing Helvetica—it's an excellent font, but it's not generally shipped with Windows. Although you can specify fallback fonts in CSS, again, there's little point in making your first choice something that the majority of people won't see.

> *Despite its lack of penetration on Windows, Helvetica is often used as a fallback sans-serif font, due to its prevalence on Linux.*

Better choices for body copy are Trebuchet MS or Verdana. The latter is especially good, because its spacious nature makes it readable at any size. Its bubbly design renders it less useful for headings, though. See the following images for a comparison of these fonts on Windows (left) and Mac (right).

Arial (bold, 24px)
Arial (24px)
Arial (12px)
Arial (9px)

Arial (bold, 24px)
Arial (24px)
Arial (12px)
Arial (9px)

Trebuchet MS (bold, 24px)
Trebuchet MS (24px)
Trebuchet MS (12px)
Trebuchet MS (9px)

Trebuchet MS (bold, 24px)
Trebuchet MS (24px)
Trebuchet MS (12px)
Trebuchet MS (9px)

Verdana (bold, 24px)
Verdana (24px)
Verdana (12px)
Verdana (9px)

Verdana (bold, 24px)
Verdana (24px)
Verdana (12px)
Verdana (9px)

Serif fonts for the Web

Although popular in print, serif fonts fare less well online. If using serifs, ensure you render them large enough so that they don't break down into an illegible mess. Georgia is the best available web-safe serif, especially when used at sizes of 12px and above (or the equivalent), and it's more suitable than a sans-serif if you're working with traditional subject matter, or if you're attempting to emulate print articles (such as in the following screenshot of the online column Revert to Saved, www.reverttosaved.com).

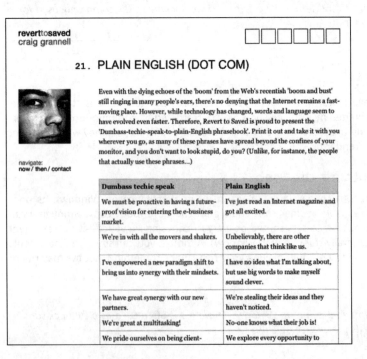

The other commonly available serif font, Times New Roman, is inferior to Georgia at every size. Like Arial, its popularity is the result of its prevalence as a system font. See below for a comparison of Georgia and Times New Roman on Windows (left) and Mac (right).

Georgia (bold, 24px) Georgia (24px) Georgia (12px) Georgia (9px)	**Georgia (bold, 24px)** Georgia (24px) Georgia (12px) Georgia (9px)
Times New Roman (bold, 24px) Times New Roman (24px) Times New Roman (12px) Times New Roman (9px)	**Times New Roman (bold, 24px)** Times New Roman (24px) Times New Roman (12px) Times New Roman (9px)

Display fonts for the Web

The remaining fonts are generally only useful as display fonts—or, in some cases, for pointing and laughing at, and then making a solemn vow never to use. One example is Comic Sans MS, which is inexplicably popular with novice web designers. To give the font its due, it is readable, but its quirky and unprofessional nature makes it unsuitable for most purposes (even comic artists eschew it in favor of personalized fonts).

Courier New is more useful and a good choice when you need a monospace font, such as for displaying code and other technical information (or for when you want to pretend you're in *The Matrix*, prior to coming to your senses and using a different font instead). Arial Black and Impact are reasonable choices for headings, although they must be handled with care. The bold version of Impact looks terrible (and isn't displayed at all in some browsers), and some browsers by default render headings in bold, so this must be overridden in CSS. The following image shows this collection of fonts, again with Windows versions on the left and Mac versions on the right.

Arial Black (24px) **Arial Black (12px)** **Arial Black (9px)**	**Arial Black (24px)** **Arial Black (12px)** **Arial Black (9px)**
Comic Sans MS (bold, 24px) Comic Sans MS (24px) Comic Sans MS (12px) Comic Sans MS (9px)	**Comic Sans MS (bold, 24px)** Comic Sans MS (24px) Comic Sans MS (12px) Comic Sans MS (9px)
Courier New (bold, 24px) Courier New (24px) Courier New (12px) Courier New (9px)	**Courier New (bold, 24px)** Courier New (24px) Courier New (12px) Courier New (9px)
Impact (24px) **Impact (12px)** **Impact (9px)**	**Impact (24px)** **Impact (12px)** **Impact (9px)**

Using images for text

Limitations imposed by web-safe fonts lead some designers to seek out alternative methods of creating online type. It's common to use graphics (mostly GIFs, but sometimes Flash, due to its vector-based, scalable nature) for text. If you have to follow a corporate design style under pain of death, the ability to use graphics can be a lifesaver—after all, most browsers happily render images, and they can be marked up within heading elements, so you can control things like margins via CSS and also retain the structural integrity of your document.

However, graphical text has its share of problems:

- Unless you're using Opera, you cannot resize graphical text in a browser.
- Because the Web is low resolution, when a page is printed out, graphical text looks pixelated and poor quality.
- Although GIF-based text tends to be small in terms of file size, it's still larger than HTML-based text.
- People using alternate browsers cannot "see" graphical text (although you can use the alt attribute to compensate).
- Graphical text cannot be copied and pasted.
- Graphical text cannot be read by search engines.
- Graphical text is a pain to update. To change a word, you must rework the original image, export and upload it and, if the image size has changed, you must edit the appropriate HTML documents and upload those, too.

In my opinion, graphics should be used as a last resort. A company's style can be made apparent by the use of a corporate logo and other imagery rather than by the use of a font. Also, **never, ever render body copy as an image**. There are many sites out there with body copy rendered as an image and, quite frankly, every one of them makes me want to scream. Such sites are often full of typos (perhaps because amending them requires the entire graphic to be reworked, re-exported, and uploaded again), cannot be printed at quality, and cannot be copied to a text editor. Some suggest this means the site's text is "secure." But this goes against one of the fundamental benefits of the Web: that people can share information, and that it can be easily copied and sent on to others. Sure, this presents copyright implications, but everything online is subject to copyright anyway. Also, plenty of sites commit the cardinal sin of rendering things like contact details as a graphic—I'm sure their customers really appreciate having to type such things out by hand rather than just being able to copy them into their digital address books.

In conclusion, avoid graphical text. If you have to, use it for headings, but take care when doing so. And on no occasion use graphics for body copy—you'll just end up annoying people, and there are already quite enough annoyed people in the world.

Defining font size and line height

In theory, defining font sizes should be easy enough. You use the font-size property, and then you can set the value to an absolute size, a relative size, a length, or a percentage. For instance, you might set the following:

```
h1 {
font-size: 20px;
}

p {
font-size: 12px;
}
```

Setting text in pixels

In fact, many designers specify font sizes in pixels, because pixels are the only measurement that enables you to know, with a large degree of certainly, that your text will look pretty much identical wherever it's viewed. Unfortunately, unlike every other major browser, Internet Explorer for Windows cannot resize pixel-based text (although a user can chose to ignore font sizes via little-known Accessibility controls), and this creates an accessibility problem.

Therefore, if you decide to size text in pixels, ensure your text is *very* readable. Test it on various people and listen to feedback. If complaints come your way regarding the fact that someone "had trouble reading the words," or that another rooted around for a microscope before giving up and playing Solitaire, you need to increase your pixel size settings. Sure, the resulting page might not look quite as "designery," but at least people will be able to read it.

A better alternative for sizing text in CSS

Some designers use point values, but they're better off left for print; others battle with ems and percentages, and end up bashing their head against nearby objects when cascading values multiply in unruly browsers, creating either massive or tiny text.

Keywords are a better alternative for setting the default text size in CSS. The available values are xx-small, x-small, small, medium, large, x-large, and xx-large—pretty straightforward, unless you can only think in numbers these days. Keyword values don't compound, and most modern browsers set a lower limit, even on xx-small, so text never enters the realms of the illegible.

Despite the flexibility of keywords and the fact that, unlike text set in pixels, Internet Explorer for Windows can resize text set with keywords, most designers avoid them. Perhaps this is because browsers have historically dealt with keywords badly. Early releases of Netscape 4 ignored keywords entirely, and later releases followed the original specification to the letter, which was updated accordingly when it was discovered that anything smaller than medium looked like an ink-footed ant had taken a stroll across your monitor.

Internet Explorer 4 and 5 got things totally wrong, welding CSS keywords to Netscape font size tags. In times gone by, `<font size=3>` was the default, and it should have logically mapped to the medium CSS keyword (as called for in the CSS1 specification). But because the CSS small keyword was third from the bottom of the list, Internet Explorer ended up mapping it to that instead, resulting in keyword-based text being displayed too small in that browser.

Things have moved on since then, largely due to the excellent work of Todd Fahrner and Tantek Çelik. Çelik's box model hack exploits a bug in Internet Explorer before version 6, enabling you to "hack" your CSS to set one set of values to cater solely for it and let well-behaved browsers get on with displaying the correct values. Although the hack is mostly used to get unruly browsers to correctly layout CSS-based designs, Fahrner noted how it could be used to get earlier versions of Internet Explorer to correctly deal with CSS font keywords. An example rule using this method looks like this:

```
body, body div, body p, body th, body td, body li, body dd {
font-size: x-small;
voice-family: "\"}\"";
voice-family: inherit;
font-size: small;
}
```

If you've just had a panic attack, calm down—it's not as complex as it looks. The comma-separated selectors just group a bunch of common HTML elements that text might sit within. (Unless overriding a linked CSS, you can ditch these and just replace them with a body tag selector.) The next line defines a default text size for Internet Explorer 4 and 5. The next two lines "trick" Internet Explorer 4 and 5 into terminating the rule, but enable compliant browsers to continue. The final line sets a value for well-behaved browsers, which is one size bigger than the one set for Internet Explorer 4 and 5 (because what Internet Explorer 4 and 5 think is x-small is actually small).

In a nutshell, early versions of Internet Explorer see x-small as the value and stop reading, whereas compliant browsers continue to the second font-size value, which overrides the first.

In an even smaller nutshell, the same size text is shown in all browsers, even those that normally get keywords wrong.

Actually, that's not entirely true. Older versions of Opera are stumped by the box model hack, and therefore actually display text one size too small when using the previous rule. This can be dealt with by using Çelik's "be nice to Opera" rule, which is placed in your CSS after the previous rule.

```
html>body, html>body div, html>body p,html>body th, html>body td, html>body li,
➥html>body dd {
font-size: small;
}
```

The other browser to throw a fit over this method is Netscape 4, but if the preceding CSS is imported (see the section "Attaching CSS files: The @import method" in Chapter 2), that browser doesn't see the CSS anyway. Should you want to style fonts in Netscape 4, it is recommended that you do so in pixels via a linked style sheet (see the section "Attaching external CSS files: The link method" in the previous chapter). You can do so with a rule like this:

```
body, div, p, th, td, li, dd {
font-family: Verdana, Arial, Helvetica, sans-serif;
font-size: 11px;
}
```

Problems with keyword-sized CSS text

Although I recommend using keywords to define the default font size, there are some problems with this method. If users of Internet Explorer set their fonts to Small using View ➤ Text Size, keyword-set CSS text can become hard to read, but that depends on user choice, and users can increase the text size by using a more sensible setting. Also, some Mac users still attempt to set their browsers back to the old 72 ppi Mac standard, instead of the generally accepted 96 ppi. But again, that's a user preference and not the default. In my opinion, having a tiny minority of users screwing up their own settings and potentially ending up with unreadable text is better than the vast majority not being able to resize the text because it's set in pixels. Ultimately, though, the final decision is up to you.

Setting line-height

Graphic designers will be familiar with **leading**, and the CSS line-height property enables you to set this. Available values are a number, length, or percentage:

```
p {
font-size: 100%;
line-height: 1.5em;
}

h1 {
font-size: 14px;
line-height: 20px;
}
```

The difference between the font-size and line-height measurements is the leading value. Half the value is applied above the text and half below. Should you use a number, rather than a length or percentage, that value is multiplied by the font-size setting to define the line-height. (For instance, if font-size is set to 10px and line-height is set to 1.5, the line-height value is effectively 15px.)

Many web designers who have no graphic design experience ignore the line-height property, but it can be useful. Setting it higher than you might in print results in increased white space between lines of text, which is easier to read online, as shown in the following screenshots. To the left is the default spacing, and to the right is increased line-height, which results in increased legibility.

Line-height set to 1

Lorem ipsum dolor sit amet, consectetuer adipiscing elit. Sed ante pede, scelerisque sit amet, gravida sed, vehicula vel, eros. Nullam vitae mi. Fusce consectetuer mattis ipsum. Sed scelerisque blandit augue. Sed tincidunt lectus sit amet est. Donec quam. Vivamus suscipit enim in wisi. Etiam ac pede vitae erat elementum egestas. Aliquam aliquet, tellus volutpat molestie sagittis, purus lacus lobortis pede, eget ornare nibh diam vitae sapien. Morbi tempor felis eu dui. Pellentesque habitant morbi tristique senectus et netus et malesuada fames ac turpis egestas. In porta, elit et dapibus placerat, mi ante tristique quam, et lacinia augue tellus eget mi.

Phasellus tempus neque id justo. Nullam scelerisque, lacus ac viverra volutpat, est ligula iaculis ante, quis vehicula justo pede nec arcu. Aliquam dignissim lacus. In hac habitasse platea dictumst. Phasellus facilisis pede et nulla. Nunc porta. Donec non magna vel enim aliquet faucibus. Sed placerat purus non ipsum luctus vehicula. Nullam a magna. Donec ullamcorper magna quis libero. Aenean ultricies ullamcorper risus. Vivamus commodo enim rutrum pede. Donec pharetra justo id purus. Praesent commodo lacus at urna. Pellentesque vel orci. In hac habitasse platea dictumst. Integer tincidunt, neque et gravida porta, augue lectus rhoncus nibh, sed gravida tortor arcu et nunc. Duis sem. Suspendisse iaculis, lorem a dictum dignissim, urna metus feugiat lectus, in luctus metus wisi tempor felis. Nulla at est in ante accumsan dignissim.

Maecenas rutrum porttitor massa. Donec posuere purus non quam. Vestibulum at eros. Cras volutpat. Morbi ut nunc vel neque euismod suscipit. Fusce congue ligula ac neque. Cras odio libero, posuere sit amet, iaculis vehicula, sollicitudin vel, mauris. Integer wisi. Nunc ac quam eget est imperdiet vestibulum. Proin rutrum tortor non arcu. Nullam urna tortor, mollis et, convallis sed, mattis eu, nulla.

Line-height set to 1.4

Lorem ipsum dolor sit amet, consectetuer adipiscing elit. Sed ante pede, scelerisque sit amet, gravida sed, vehicula vel, eros. Nullam vitae mi. Fusce consectetuer mattis ipsum. Sed scelerisque blandit augue. Sed tincidunt lectus sit amet est. Donec quam. Vivamus suscipit enim in wisi. Etiam ac pede vitae erat elementum egestas. Aliquam aliquet, tellus volutpat molestie sagittis, purus lacus lobortis pede, eget ornare nibh diam vitae sapien. Morbi tempor felis eu dui. Pellentesque habitant morbi tristique senectus et netus et malesuada fames ac turpis egestas. In porta, elit et dapibus placerat, mi ante tristique quam, et lacinia augue tellus eget mi.

Phasellus tempus neque id justo. Nullam scelerisque, lacus ac viverra volutpat, est ligula iaculis ante, quis vehicula justo pede nec arcu. Aliquam dignissim lacus. In hac habitasse platea dictumst. Phasellus facilisis pede et nulla. Nunc porta. Donec non magna vel enim aliquet faucibus. Sed placerat purus non ipsum luctus vehicula. Nullam a magna. Donec ullamcorper magna quis libero. Aenean ultricies ullamcorper risus. Vivamus commodo enim rutrum pede. Donec pharetra justo id purus. Praesent commodo lacus at urna. Pellentesque vel orci. In hac habitasse platea dictumst. Integer tincidunt, neque et gravida porta, augue lectus rhoncus nibh, sed gravida tortor arcu et nunc. Duis sem. Suspendisse iaculis, lorem a dictum dignissim, urna metus feugiat lectus, in luctus metus wisi tempor felis. Nulla at est in ante accumsan dignissim.

Mac vs. Windows: Leading and anti-aliasing

While we're on the subject of sizing fonts in CSS, it's a suitable time to note two aspects of fonts that differ on Mac and Windows. The first is leading/line-height, which tends to be slightly larger in Windows-based browsers than in Mac-based browsers, unless the value is set in pixels. This isn't generally a problem, unless you're designing a pixel-perfect layout, in which case you're most likely using pixels to set text sizes anyway.

More noticeable is the Mac's tendency (as of Mac OS X) to anti-alias onscreen text, which can affect spacing (in fact, various anti-aliasing algorithms mean text can look slightly different in each browser on the Mac). On Windows, aliased text makes for jagged edges. This isn't a major problem for body copy (in fact, many people prefer aliased text when reading onscreen); however, set a heading to 40px and you'll discover the results are less than visually pleasing.

The difference is hard to get across in print, so I've enlarged some text. In the following image, you can see Windows text on the left and Mac text on the right.

Windows displays a simpler version of the original font, reduced to a black and white bitmap, whereas the Mac attempts to emulate the soft curves of the original by introducing gray pixels at the edges.

Although arguments rage regarding which is the best method of displaying fonts onscreen, this is a moot point for web designers, because you don't control the end user's setup and therefore must be aware of every possibility. For instance, Mac-based designers must take care not to use large text that looks great on their system, without checking how it looks on Windows, too.

Even what I've mentioned so far is simplifying matters. Windows-based laptops often have font-smoothing technology that approximates the Mac's anti-aliasing. Also, Windows XP has a technology called ClearType that more or less does the same but, for a reason I've never managed to fathom, it's turned off by default.

In conclusion, you can't be as precious about web-based text as you can with print-based copy. (The same, in fact, goes for the majority of web design—try to get into the habit of a "good enough" aesthetic, rather than trying to get everything exact on all platforms and in all browsers—for that way lies madness.)

Defining font-style, font-weight, and font-variant

These three properties are straightforward. The first, font-style, enables you to set italic or oblique text. The former is often a defined face within the font itself, whereas the latter is usually computed. Typically, web browsers treat both the same, and only the italic value is in general use (except for the occasional use of normal—the default—in order to override something set elsewhere).

An element's font-style is set like this:

```
h2 {
font-style: italic;
}
```

The font-weight property is intended to make a font heavier or lighter, and despite the various available values (detailed in full in the reference section of this book), only bold and normal are in general use.

```
.introParagraph {
font-weight: bold;
}
```

The font-variant property has two available values: the default (normal) and small-caps. Small caps are often used to de-emphasize uppercase letters in abbreviations and acronyms, and are a similar size to a typeface's lowercase characters. Display of small caps varies across browsers and platforms, and older versions of Internet Explorer simply render such text entirely in normal caps (i.e., in standard uppercase letters).

CSS shorthand for font properties

The CSS properties discussed so far can be written in shorthand, enabling you to cut down on space and manage your CSS font settings with greater ease. Like some other shorthand properties, some rules apply:

- Some browsers are more forgiving than others regarding required and optional values, but you should always specify the font-size and font-family values, in that order.

- Omitted values revert to default settings.

- The font-style, font-weight, and font-variant values, if included, should be placed at the start of the rule, in any order, prior to the font-size value.
- The font-size and line-height values can be combined using the syntax font-size/line-height (for example, 12px/16px for 12px font-size and 16px line-height).

A complete font declaration might look like this:

```
p {
font: italic small-caps bold 100%/1.3em Arial, Helvetica, sans-serif;
}
```

An invalid font declaration is as follows. The font-weight value (bold) is incorrectly placed after the font-family value, and the font-size value is missing.

```
p.invalid {
font: Arial, Helvetica, sans-serif bold;
}
```

Controlling text element margins

By default, browsers place margins around block-level text-based elements (such as headings and paragraphs), which can be overridden by CSS. However, many designers get confused when dealing with margins, so a good rule of thumb is to set the top margin of elements to 0 and control spacing via the bottom margins:

```
h1, p {
margin-top: 0;
}

h1 {
margin-bottom: 10px;
}

p {
margin-bottom: 1em;
}
```

In this case, the margins below headings are small, enabling the eye to rapidly travel from the heading to the related body copy. The margin at the bottom of each paragraph is one character high, as is seemingly traditional these days.

Using text-indent for printlike paragraphs

Because of people's familiarity with nonintended paragraphs on the Web, the W3C recommends staying away from indented ones. However, there are times when designers yearn for a more print-based design. In theory, the following CSS should create printlike web page paragraphs:

```
p {
margin-top: 0;
margin-bottom: 0.3em;
}

p+p {
text-indent: 1.5em;
}
```

The first rule sets the top margin of paragraphs to 0 and makes the bottom one very slight—much smaller than usual. The second rule (which uses an adjacent sibling selector) states that if a paragraph follows another paragraph, text-indent should be set to 1.5em, which indents the first line of the affected paragraph(s). (Hanging indents can also be achieved by setting this to a negative value.)

Most browsers support this, but Internet Explorer for Windows doesn't support adjacent sibling selectors. You therefore have two choices. The first is to just have Internet Explorer indent every paragraph (by setting text-indent: 1.5em in the paragraph tag selector). After all, the convention of not indenting the leading paragraph is just that—a convention. Alternatively, do this and then also create a class called firstParagraph, set text-indent to 0, and apply the class to the first paragraph on each page.

In CSS:

```
p.firstParagraph {
text-indent: 0;
}
```

In HTML:

```
<p class="firstParagraph">This is the start of the first paragraph...
```

Although this is extra markup, and technically superfluous, it's not a major imposition if it provides you with the effect you require.

Setting letter-spacing and word-spacing

Both of these properties work in the same way, taking length values or a default of normal. For letter-spacing, the value increases white space between characters, and for word-spacing, the defined value increases white space between words. Negative values are permitted, which cause characters or words to bunch together (or **kern**, if you're a graphic designer). A certain amount of experimentation is recommended if you decide to use these properties. Because the Web's resolution is low, subtle kerning changes are hard to achieve online, and the results often end up looking clunky. Also, spacing varies from platform to platform.

The following CSS increases the letter spacing in the h1 element and decreases the word spacing in the h2 element. The results are compared with default spacing in the subsequent screenshot.

```
h1 {
letter-spacing: 3px;
}

h2 {
word-spacing: -0.5em;
}
```

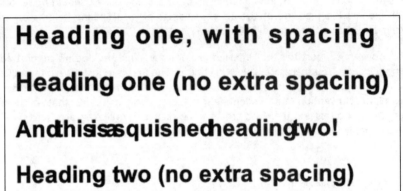

Controlling case with text-transform

This useful property enables you to change the case of letters within an element. Available values are capitalize, uppercase, lowercase, and none (the default). uppercase and lowercase force the text of the applied element into the relevant case regardless of the original content, whereas capitalize sets the first letter of each word in uppercase.

In the following example, we'll style the first heading as uppercase, the second as lowercase, and the paragraph as capitalize. This will make the typographers out there cry into their soup (if they're currently eating soup—if not, they may just cry), but this is, after all, just an example, and not a display of magical typography.

```
<h1>A heading</h1>
<h2>Another heading</h2>
<p>A small, but perfectly formed, paragraph of text.</p>
```

The CSS, then, is as follows:

```
h1 {
text-transform: uppercase;
}

h2 {
text-transform: lowercase;
}

p {
text-transform: capitalize;
}
```

A HEADING

another heading

A Small, But Perfectly Formed,
Paragraph Of Text.

The resulting web page is shown in the image above. See how the `text-transform` settings override the case of the original content? This can be useful in ensuring headings are consistent to style guides sitewide.

Creating alternatives with classes and spans

There will be many cases when a web page requires alternatives to the rules set for tag selectors (h1, h2, p, and so on). In such cases, you can define a class in the CSS and then use a `class` attribute to apply it to an element. Should you only want a portion of some text to take on the style, you can surround the selection with a span element and apply the class to that instead.

For example, if we want to create some "warning" text, we can use the following CSS:

```
.warningText {
color: #ff0000;
font-size: 120%;
}
```

This can then be applied as follows:

```
<p class="warningText">This paragraph takes on the styles defined in the
➥warningText class</p>
<p>Only <span class="warningText">this portion</span> of this paragraph takes
➥on the warningText class styles.</p>
```

Avoid overusing spans, though. Text works best when it's consistent across the page.

> Note that the preceding CSS style has a capital letter halfway through it (also known as **lowerCamelCase**). This is one way of dealing with multiple-word style names, because underscores and spaces must be avoided in CSS. Take care if you do this, because styles are case sensitive. If you set a `class` attribute value to `warningtext` instead of `warningText`, many browsers fail to display the style, reverting to the default style for the relevant element.

Exercise: Styling semantic markup

Taking into consideration what you've seen in the chapter so far, you're now going to style some semantic markup, showing how rapidly you can create great-looking text when working with CSS. The markup that you'll use is as follows, and the default web page, prior to any work being carried out, can be seen to the right. All exercise steps are carried out in CSS.

Article heading

Lorem ipsum dolor sit amet, consectetuer adipiscing elit. Sed aliquet elementum erat. Integer diam mi, venenatis non, cursus a, hendrerit at, mi. Morbi risus mi, tincidunt ornare, tempus ut, eleifend nec, risus.

Curabitur sit amet risus

Quisque faucibus lorem eget sapien. In urna sem, vehicula ut, mattis et, venenatis at, velit. Ut sodales lacus sed eros. Pellentesque tristique senectus et netus et malesuada fames ac turpis egestas.

Praesent rutrum

Nam scelerisque dignissim quam. Ut bibendum enim in orci. Vivamus ligula nunc, dictum a, tincidunt in, dignissim ac, odio.

Habitant morbid

Phasellus tempor felis vel molestie vehicula nibh est...

```
<h1>Article heading</h1>
<p>Lorem ipsum dolor sit amet, consectetuer adipiscing elit. Sed aliquet
➥elementum erat. Integer diam mi, venenatis non, cursus a, hendrerit at, mi.
➥Morbi risus mi, tincidunt ornare, tempus ut, eleifend nec, risus.</p>
<h2>Curabitur sit amet risus</h2>
<p>Quisque faucibus lorem eget sapien. In urna sem, vehicula ut, mattis et,
➥venenatis at, velit. Ut sodales lacus sed eros. Pellentesque tristique senectus
➥et netus et malesuada fames ac turpis egestas.</p>
<h3>Praesent rutrum</h3>
<p>Nam scelerisque dignissim quam. Ut bibendum enim in orci. Vivamus ligula
➥nunc, dictum a, tincidunt in, dignissim ac, odio.</p>
<h3>Habitant morbid</h3>
<p>Phasellus tempor felis vel molestie vehicula nibh est...</p>
```

1. **Define page defaults**. Using a body selector, background and foreground colors are defined, along with padding, so content doesn't hug the browser window edges. In this example, body copy will be set as a serif font, Georgia, falling back to Times New Roman and the generic serif setting.

Article heading

Lorem ipsum dolor sit amet, consectetuer adipiscing elit. Sed aliquet elementum erat. Integer diam mi, venenatis non, cursus a, hendrerit at, mi. Morbi risus mi, tincidunt ornare, tempus ut, eleifend nec, risus.

Curabitur sit amet risus

Quisque faucibus lorem eget sapien. In urna sem, vehicula ut, mattis et, venenatis at, velit. Ut sodales lacus sed eros. Pellentesque tristique senectus et netus et malesuada fames ac turpis egestas.

Praesent rutrum

Nam scelerisque dignissim quam. Ut bibendum enim in orci. Vivamus ligula nunc, dictum a, tincidunt in, dignissim ac, odio.

Habitant morbid

Phasellus tempor felis vel molestie vehicula nibh est...

```
body {
background-color: #ffffff;
color: #333333;
padding: 10px;
font-family: Georgia, "Times New Roman", serif;
}
```

2. **Set font sizes**. Using the Fahrner method discussed earlier in this chapter, set the default body copy size by using a second body rule—it *doesn't* replace the body rule created in step 1. You want nice, readable text, so set it to medium. (Prior to the box model hack, the value is set to small for Internet Explorer 4 and 5, which looks the same as medium in that browser. See earlier in the chapter for a full explanation of the box model hack.)

```
body {
font-size: small;
voice-family: "\"}\"";
voice-family: inherit;
font-size: medium;
}


html>body {
font-size: medium;
}
```

> *You can combine the body rules, but I prefer to separate them, to have one rule for the page essentials and another for font sizes.*

3. **Style paragraphs**. Using the p tag selector, style the web page's paragraphs. To make them more readable, set line-height to 1.4em, providing white space between the lines. The medium-set text is slightly too big, so set font-size to 90% (because you've used the Fahrner method, end users on any browser can resize this). The padding-left property is set to 1.4em, offsetting the paragraphs and making them easier to differentiate from headings. Finally, remove the top margin and set the bottom margin to 1em.

Article heading

Lorem ipsum dolor sit amet, consectetuer adipiscing elit. Sed aliquet elementum erat. Integer diam mi, venenatis non, cursus a, hendrerit at, mi. Morbi risus mi, tincidunt ornare, tempus ut, eleifend nec, risus.

Curabitur sit amet risus

Quisque faucibus lorem eget sapien. In urna sem, vehicula ut, mattis et, venenatis at, velit. Ut sodales lacus sed eros. Pellentesque tristique senectus et netus et malesuada fames ac turpis egestas.

Praesent rutrum

Nam scelerisque dignissim quam. Ut bibendum enim in orci. Vivamus ligula nunc, dictum a, tincidunt in, dignissim ac, odio.

Habitant morbid

Phasellus tempor felis vel molestie vehicula nibh est...

```
p {
font-size: 90%;
line-height: 1.4em;
padding-left: 1.4em;
margin-top: 0;
margin-bottom: 1em;
}
```

4. **Style main headings**. You want the main head-ings (h1 and h2) to have a common style, so use a grouped selector (h1, h2). These headings are set in lowercase, gray (#555555), Arial font (falling back to Helvetica and sans-serif). The sans-serif font contrasts nicely with the serif body copy, further helping to differentiate between headings and body copy and enabling users to rapidly scan the text. The font-weight property is set to normal; usually you needn't set default states on properties, but it's useful here, because some browsers default headings to bold, and you don't want to use the bold form of Arial for the headings. Set the margins to 0, except the bottom one, which you set to 10px.

```
h1, h2 {
text-transform: lowercase;
color: #555555;
font-weight: normal;
font-family: Arial, Helvetica, sans-serif;
margin: 0 0 10px 0;
}
```

You might think it odd to use pixel values for margins when the fonts are styled in rela-tive units, but it makes sense from a layout perspective. The margin setting never inter-feres with the resizing of fonts, but ensures that the body copy sits a uniform distance under the headings.

5. **Refine main headings**. The headings are too large, and you should set explicit values for each to differentiate them. You'll therefore add a rule for each one. (Remember, you can style the same element as many times as you like in the same CSS, although if you set the same *property* more than once, the setting closest to the element on the web page is the one that's used.) For h1, the font size is set to 150% (making it one and a half times the default font size set earlier), and for h2, it is set to 120%.

```
h1 {
font-size: 150%;
}
```

```
h2 {
font-size: 120%;
}
```

6. **Style subheadings**. The level-three headings on this page are used as subhead-ings and don't need to be as prominent as the other headings. The bottom margin setting is reduced, making the eye flow more rapidly from heading to copy. The

font-size value is set to the same as the body copy. To differentiate the headings, the color setting is varied from the paragraph one, and a bold version of Arial is chosen for the font. Finally, to align the headings with the offset paragraphs, set padding-left to 1.35em. This is a slightly smaller value than the padding-left set for paragraphs, and the reason for this is because it looks better to the eye. This sort of tweaking is simple when using CSS.

```
h3 {
margin: 0 0 5px 0;
font-size: 90%;
color: #444444;
font-family: Arial, Helvetica, sans-serif;
font-weight: bold;
padding-left: 1.35em;
}
```

7. **Add a border to headings**. Now add a subtle border to the bottom of the main headings, to further enhance the page layout. This is done by editing the h1, h2 rule. The padding value ensures the border doesn't hug any descenders (the part of the letters that "hang").

```
h1, h2 {
text-transform: lowercase;
color: #555555;
font-weight: normal;
font-family: Arial, Helvetica, sans-serif;
margin: 0 0 10px 0;
border-bottom: 1px dotted #555555;
padding: 0 0 2px 0;
}
```

> *Remember always to test in various browsers. Here, the "dotted" value more resembles a dashed line in Internet Explorer for Windows.*

Exercise: Rapidly editing text styles

You know how it is: you're working on a website, and you're just about to hit the deadline, when the client phones and asks for all manner of changes. In many cases, working with CSS enables you to rapidly change things, as you'll see in this exercise. In two minutes, the text created in the previous exercise will be reformatted and made suitable for a quite different site.

1. **Change the default font**. You're going for a contemporary look here, so amend the body rule's font-family to Verdana, falling back to Arial, Helvetica, and the default sans-serif. The color setting is also lightened.

```
body {
background-color: #ffffff;
color: #444444;
padding: 10px;
font-family: Verdana, Arial, Helvetica, sans-serif;
}
```

2. **Change the paragraph settings**. Because Verdana is a bubbly font, reduce the paragraph font size from 90% to 80% and increase the offset.

```
p {
font-size: 80%;
line-height: 1.4em;
padding-left: 2.5em;
margin-top: 0;
margin-bottom: 1em;
}
```

3. **Edit the headings**. For this design, you want the main headings in uppercase, which is achieved by editing the text-transform value. The headings are emboldened by setting font-weight to bold, and you also lighten the color. By using CSS borders, you create square, boxlike markers to the left of the headings, making them stand out. This is achieved by setting the border-left width value to a figure slightly larger than 1em (use 1.2em), in order to get a square, and the style value to solid. The padding setting ensures the heading content (the text) doesn't hug the border. Finally, although you want to be able to differentiate between level one and two headings in the code (to retain structural integrity for the document, and to enable you to differentiate between them later, should you want to), you want both to look the same onscreen (for design/layout reasons), hence you amend the font-size value in the h1 rule.

```
h1, h2 {
text-transform: uppercase;
color: #666666;
font-weight: bold;
font-family: Arial, Helvetica, sans-serif;
margin: 0 0 10px 0;
border-left: 1.2em solid #cccccc;
padding: 0 0 0 10px;
}

h1 {
font-size: 120%;
}
```

4. **Amend the subheadings**. Amend the sub-headings by changing the padding-left and color values within the h3 rule to suit (primarily to match the changes made to the p rule).

```
h3 {
margin: 0 0 5px 0;
font-size: 90%;
color: #555555;
font-family: Arial, Helvetica, sans-serif;
font-weight: bold;
padding-left: 2.25em;
}
```

3

Exercise: Creating drop caps with CSS

For this exercise, you're going to use CSS to create a **drop cap**—one of those large letters that magazines love using at the start of an article. They can look pretty good online, too (depending on your design), and pre-CSS you'd have had to embed the relevant character in a table. Not anymore.

This exercise introduces one of the most important CSS properties: float. Any element can be floated left or right in CSS, and this causes subsequent content to wrap around it, saving messing around creating tables for the same purpose.

1. **Write some text**. Here's the text that you'll use for this exercise:

```
<p>This paragraph of text begins with a drop cap! Lorem ipsum dolor sit amet,
➥consectetuer adipiscing elit. Sed aliquet elementum erat. Integer diam mi,
➥venenatis non, cursus a, hendrerit at, mi. Morbi risus mi, tincidunt ornare,
➥tempus ut, eleifend nec, risus.</p>
```

2. **Wrap the drop cap in a span**. Wrap the relevant letter in a span element, and then add a class attribute with the value dropCap.

```
<p><span class="dropCap">T</span>his paragraph begins with a drop cap!</p>
```

Remember the span end tag, otherwise subsequent content will take on styles intended only for the drop cap.

3. **Set the basics**. In CSS, rules are added to provide padding around the web page content (so it doesn't hug browser window edges) via the body rule. The p tag rule sets the top margin of paragraphs to 0 and line height to 1.3em.

```
body {
padding: 10px;
}


p {
margin-top: 0;
line-height: 1.3em;
}
```

4. **Create a new class**. Next, you need to add a CSS class rule for the drop cap.

```
.dropCap {


}
```

5. **Set the basics**. In the declaration, set the affected part of the web page (the drop cap letter) to float left, and define the background and foreground colors.

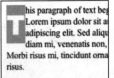

```
.dropCap {
float: left;
background: #aaaaaa;
color: #ffffff;
}
```

All subsequent CSS property/value pairs should be placed within the declaration above (i.e., inside the curly brackets).

6. **Define the font**. Using CSS font shorthand (explained earlier), set the drop cap font to something nice and chunky: Arial Black, at three times the size of the body text.

```
font: 300% "Arial Black", Arial, sans-serif;
```

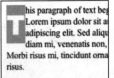

7. **Set the line height**. Setting line-height to 100% reduces the height of the drop-cap box to something more suitable and not so ungainly.

```
line-height: 100%;
```

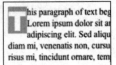

8. Define margins. Setting margins enables you to set white space around the drop cap, as you would in print typography, making the design less cluttered.

```
margin: 0 0.2em 0 0;
```

You may have to add a small bottom margin, otherwise subsequent page content may hug the underneath of the drop cap.

9. Set padding. The drop cap no longer hugs the web page content, but it's rather close to its containing borders. Therefore, add some padding. To keep it centered, apply equal values to the top and bottom padding (0.1em), and to the left and right padding (0.2em).

```
padding: 0.1em 0.2em;
```

If a skewed approach is required, pushing the letter to one side of the box, the padding values can be amended accordingly.

```
padding: 0.1em 0.1em 0.1em 0.6em;
```

10. Add a border. Borders help web page elements stand out, especially when the contrast between a background and the web page isn't strong enough. Using CSS shorthand, the following rule adds a thin border around the drop cap:

```
border: 1px solid #444444;
```

11. Change the background. Should the flat-colored background prove boring, it can be spiced up by the addition of a background image. Use a grayscale GIF that gradually lightens from top to bottom. Add it by replacing the background property/value pair added in step 5 with the following:

```
background: url(dropcap_gradient.gif) top left;
```

Should the image not be big enough, or the text on the page be considerably increased in size, the image starts to tile. In such scenarios, the best course of action is to stop the background tiling vertically (by setting the repeat value to repeat-x) and set the background color of the drop cap to the same as the lightest color of the gradient.

```
background: #b4b4b4 url(dropcap_gradient.gif) repeat-x top left;
```

Compare the drop cap before (left) and after (right) this fix was applied.

his paragraph of text begins with a drop cap! Lorem ipsum dolor sit amet, consectetuer adipiscing elit. Sed aliquet elementum erat. Integer diam

his paragraph of text begins with a drop cap! Lorem ipsum dolor sit amet, consectetuer adipiscing elit. Sed aliquet elementum erat. Integer diam

You can now control all elements of the drop cap's design from an external document, which wouldn't have been possible using obsolete methods. For one page alone, this is a bonus, but if this style were to be used throughout an entire website, the time savings for a later design tweak could be massive.

Exercise: Creating CSS pull quotes

Drop caps are primarily decorative, so this next exercise looks at creating something that adds function to your web pages: pull quotes. These are often used to draw someone's attention to a quote or highlight of an article. Historically, web designers used tables for pull quotes, but all we now need is the addition of a class attribute to the relevant paragraph of text and some deft use of CSS to style it.

1. **Add a class attribute**. Mark up the web page as normal and ensure the pull quote content is within a standard paragraph. Add a class attribute with a value of pullQuote to the start tag.

```
<p class="pullQuote">"Morbi adipiscing. Pellentesque habitant morbi tristique
➥senectus et netus et malesuada fames ac turpis egestas. Nunc gravida elementum
➥diam. Praesent quis mauris et quam vehicula volutpat"</p>
```

2. **Set defaults**. Next, set padding around the content. Set a font for paragraphs and remove their top margin.

```
body {
padding: 10px;
}

p {
font: Georgia, "Times New Roman", serif;
margin-top: 0;
}
```

3. Use the all-important float property. Create a CSS rule for the pull quote, and then use the `float` property to float the pull quote to the right. The width setting is required, otherwise the pull quote spans the entire page.

```
.pullQuote {
float: right;
width: 180px;
}
```

Sed fermentum. Praesent mattis, velit vel hendrerit egestas, turpis risus cursus velit, nec luctus turpis sem ac sapien.

Vivamus rutrum risus in lorem. Mauris blandit varius sem. Cras dignissim sem elementum sapien. Phasellus felis arcu, fringilla vitae, fringilla ut, egestas malesuada, augue. Donec mauris erat, semper nec, aliquam congue, fringilla non, nisl. Integer libero. Nullam urna.

"Morbi adipiscing. Pellentesque habitant morbi tristique senectus et netus et malesuada fames ac turpis egestas. Nunc gravida elementum diam. Praesent quis mauris et quam vehicula volutpat"

Duis aliquet, sapien sit amet rutrum volutpat, eros odio cursus quam, id laoreet lectus eros vel dolor. Fusce commodo lectus non mauris. Aenean in justo. Donec quis felis. Lorem ipsum dolor sit amet, consectetuer adipiscing elit. Sed augue risus, ornare id, mollis condimentum, egestas vitae, turpis.

4. Add margins. Like the drop cap, you don't want the pull quote hugging other page content, so set some margins:

```
margin: 0 10px 5px 10px;
```

5. Use a different font. The pull quote still doesn't stand out, so amend the font. Using the CSS font shorthand property, set the text to italic, bold, 110% of the body copy size, and Arial, so it's easy to distinguish from the other page copy.

```
font: italic bold 110% Arial,
➥Helvetica, sans-serif;
```

turpis risus cursus velit, nec luctus turpis sem ac sapien.

Vivamus rutrum risus in lorem. Mauris blandit varius sem. Cras dignissim sem elementum sapien. Phasellus felis arcu, fringilla vitae, fringilla ut, egestas malesuada, augue. Donec mauris erat, semper nec, aliquam congue, fringilla non, nisl. Integer libero. Nullam urna.

"Morbi adipiscing. Pellentesque habitant morbi tristique senectus et netus et malesuada fames ac turpis egestas. Nunc gravida elementum diam. Praesent quis mauris et quam vehicula volutpat"

Duis aliquet, sapien sit amet rutrum volutpat, eros odio cursus quam, id laoreet lectus eros vel dolor. Fusce commodo lectus non mauris. Aenean in justo. Donec quis felis. Lorem ipsum dolor sit amet,

6. Add borders. Add borders, at the top and bottom, to draw the eye inside the quote—10px is quite enough. Add padding to provide some space around the quote and ensure the content doesn't hug the borders.

```
padding: 10px;
border-top: 10px solid #666666;
border-bottom: 10px solid #666666;
```

turpis risus cursus velit, nec luctus turpis sem ac sapien.

Vivamus rutrum risus in lorem. Mauris blandit varius sem. Cras dignissim sem elementum sapien. Phasellus felis arcu, fringilla vitae, fringilla ut, egestas malesuada, augue. Donec mauris erat, semper nec, aliquam congue, fringilla non, nisl. Integer libero. Nullam urna.

"Morbi adipiscing. Pellentesque habitant morbi tristique senectus et netus et malesuada fames ac turpis egestas. Nunc gravida elementum diam. Praesent quis mauris et quam vehicula volutpat"

Duis aliquet, sapien sit amet rutrum volutpat, eros odio cursus quam, id laoreet lectus eros vel dolor. Fusce commodo lectus non mauris. Aenean in justo. Donec quis felis. Lorem ipsum dolor sit amet, consectetuer adipiscing elit. Sed augue risus, ornare id, mollis condimentum, egestas vitae, turpis.

Exercise: Creating CSS pull quotes, take two

The previous example works well, but to be more creative with the page, let's try again, starting with the original unstyled HTML paragraphs.

1. **Change the colors**. This time, the page is almost reversed, setting white text on a dark gray background.

```
body {
padding: 10px;
background: #666666;
color: #ffffff;
}
```

2. **Use the same paragraph settings**.

```
p {
font-family: Georgia, "Times New Roman", serif;
margin-top: 0;
}
```

3. **Set the float, width, margin, and font**. After adding the pullQuote class to the CSS, use property values to float it right, and then set a width, the margins, and the font weight, size, and family. This time, the font is smaller than the surrounding copy and set to bold and a sans-serif font, to differentiate it from other page copy.

ultricies. Integer est. Cras eu lorem quis augue scelerisque cursus. Sed fermentum. Praesent mattis, velit vel hendrerit egestas, turpis risus cursus velit, nec luctus turpis sem ac sapien.

Vivamus rutrum risus in lorem. Mauris blandit varius sem. Cras dignissim sem elementum sapien. Phasellus felis arcu, fringilla vitae, fringilla ut, egestas malesuada, augue. Donec mauris erat, semper nec, aliquam congue, fringilla non, nisl. Integer libero. Nullam urna.

"Morbi adipiscing. Pellentesque habitant morbi tristique senectus et netus et malesuada fames ac turpis egestas. Nunc gravida elementum diam. Praesent quis mauris et quam vehicula volutpat"

Duis aliquet, sapien sit amet rutrum volutpat, eros odio cursus quam, id laoreet lectus eros vel dolor. Fusce commodo lectus non mauris. Aenean in justo. Donec quis felis. Lorem ipsum dolor sit amet, consectetuer adipiscing elit. Sed augue risus, ornare id,

```
.pullQuote {
float: right;
width: 180px;
margin: 0 10px 5px 10px;
font: bold 80% Verdana, Helvetica, sans-serif;
}
```

4. **Add a background image**. Overlay the pull quote on a photograph. The background image used here is a landscape with plenty of sky, over which the text will be displayed. (Always ensure backgrounds aren't too busy when using a method such as this, otherwise the text will be difficult to read.) Because the background

ultricies. Integer est. Cras eu lorem quis augue scelerisque cursus. Sed fermentum. Praesent mattis, velit vel hendrerit egestas, turpis risus cursus velit, nec luctus turpis sem ac sapien.

Vivamus rutrum risus in lorem. Mauris blandit varius sem. Cras dignissim sem elementum sapien. Phasellus felis arcu, fringilla vitae, fringilla ut, egestas malesuada, augue. Donec mauris erat, semper nec, aliquam congue, fringilla non, nisl. Integer libero. Nullam urna.

"Morbi adipiscing. Pellentesque habitant morbi tristique senectus et netus et malesuada fames ac turpis egestas. Nunc gravida elementum diam. Praesent quis mauris et quam vehicula volutpat"

Duis aliquet, sapien sit amet rutrum volutpat, eros odio cursus quam, id laoreet lectus eros vel dolor. Fusce commodo lectus non mauris. Aenean in justo. Donec quis felis. Lorem ipsum dolor sit amet, consectetuer adipiscing elit. Sed augue risus, ornare id,

image is a set size and pinned to the bottom of the pull quote (using the values no-repeat left bottom) the background color is set to #b6c7df. The image itself is then edited and a gradient overlaid from transparent to #b6c7df at the top, which means there will be a seamless transition from image to background color.

```
background: #b6c7df url(pullquote_background.jpg) no-repeat left bottom;
```

5. **Use padding for positioning.** Here, set 10px on each side, so the text doesn't hug the edges of the background image. The exception is at the bottom, where the setting is 80px, ensuring the text is largely over the sky area of the image, where it's easiest to read.

```
padding: 10px 10px 80px 10px;
```

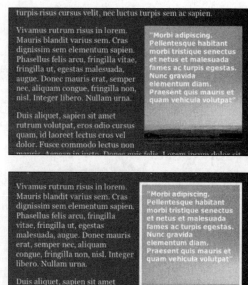

6. **Use borders to emulate a photo.** Solid white borders are set around the image. The larger bottom border brings to mind old Polaroid shots, making for a rather different pull quote from the relatively plain one created earlier.

```
border-style: solid;
border-color: #ffffff;
border-width: 5px 5px 15px 5px;
```

Working with lists

This chapter concludes with the last of the major type elements: the list. We'll first look at the different types of lists—unordered, ordered, definition—and also see how to nest them. Then we'll move on to cover how to style lists in CSS, list margins and padding, and inline lists.

Unordered lists

The **unordered list**, commonly referred to as a **bullet point list**, is the most frequently seen type of list online. The list is composed of an unordered list element (<ul></ul>) and any number of list items within <li></li>. An example of an unordered list follows, and the resulting browser display is shown to the right. As you can see, browsers typically render an unordered list with solid black bullet points.

```
<ul>
    <li>List item one</li>
    <li>List item two</li>
    <li>List item 'n'</li>
</ul>
```

- List item one
- List item two
- List item 'n'

> Unlike HTML, XHTML lists require end tags on all list elements. In HTML, the </li> end tag was optional.

Ordered lists

On occasion, list items must be stated in order, whereupon an **ordered list** is used. It works in the same way as the unordered list, the only difference being the containing element, which is <ol></ol>.

```
<ol>
    <li>List item one</li>
    <li>List item two</li>
    <li>List item 'n'</li>
</ol>
```

1. List item one
2. List item two
3. List item 'n'

Web browsers automatically insert the item numbers when you use ordered lists. However, it's sometimes useful to control the numbering directly, which you can do via the start attribute, the value of which dictates the first number of the ordered list. Although this attribute is deprecated, the CSS equivalent is pretty much unsupported across the board, so the HTML attribute has to do for now.

```
<ol start="5">
    <li>List item one</li>
    <li>List item two</li>
    <li>List item 'n'</li>
</ol>
```

5. List item one
6. List item two
7. List item 'n'

Definition lists

A **definition list** isn't a straightforward list of items. Instead, it's a list of terms and explanations. This type of list isn't common online, but it has its uses, at least in a structural sense. The list itself is enclosed in the definition list element (<dl></dl>), and within the element are placed terms and definitions, marked up with <dt></dt> and <dd></dd>, respectively. Generally speaking, browsers display the definition with an indented left-hand margin.

```
<dl>
  <dt>Cat</dt>
  <dd>Four-legged, hairy animal, with an inflated
➥sense of self-importance</dd>
  <dt>Dog</dt>
  <dd>Four-legged, hairy animal, often with an
➥inferiority complex</dd>
</dl>
```

Cat	
	Four-legged, hairy animal, with an inflated sense of self-importance
Dog	
	Four-legged, hairy animal, often with an inferiority complex

Nesting lists

Lists can be nested, but designers often do so incorrectly, screwing up their layouts and rendering web pages invalid. The most common mistake is placing the nested list outside any list items, as shown in the following *incorrect* example:

```
<ul>
  <li>List item one</li>
    <ul>
      <li>Nested list item one</li>
      <li>Nested list item two</li>
    </ul>
  <li>List item two</li>
  <li>List item 'n'</li>
</ul>
```

Nested lists must be placed inside a list item, after the relevant item that leads into the nested list. Here's an example:

```
<ul>
  <li>List item one
    <ul>
      <li>Nested list item one</li>
      <li>Nested list item two</li>
    </ul>
  </li>
  <li>List item two</li>
  <li>List item 'n'</li>
</ul>
```

- List item one
  - Nested list item one
  - Nested list item two
- List item two
- List item 'n'

Always ensure that the list element that contains the nested list is closed with an end tag. Not doing so is another common mistake, and although it's not likely to cause as many problems as the incorrect positioning of the list, it can still throw your layout.

Styling lists with CSS

Lists can be styled with CSS, making it easy to amend item spacing or create custom bullet points. I tend to think bullet points work well for lists. They're simple and—pardon the pun—to the point. However, I know plenty of people would rather have something funkier, which is where the list-style-image property comes in.

list-style-image property

The list-style-image property replaces the standard bullet or number from an unordered or ordered list with whatever image you choose. If we set the following in our CSS, the resulting list looks like that shown to the right. (Note that this is the nested list created earlier in this chapter.)

```
ul {
list-style-image: url(bullet.gif);
}
```

☒ List item one
    ☒ Nested list item one
    ☒ Nested list item two
☒ List item two
☒ List item 'n'

In Chapter 1, I mentioned **contextual selectors** (see the section "Types of CSS selectors"). These enable you to style things in context, and this is appropriate when working with lists. We can style list items with one type of bullet and nested list items with another. The original rule stays in place but is joined by a second rule:

```
ul {
list-style-image: url(bullet.gif);
}

li ul {
list-style-image: url(bullet_level_two.gif);
}
```

☒ List item one
    Σ Nested list item one
    Σ Nested list item two
☒ List item two
☒ List item 'n'

This second rule's selector is li ul, which means the declaration is applied only to lists within a list item (i.e., nested lists). The upshot is that the top-level list items remain with the original custom bullet, but the nested list items now have a different bullet graphic.

With this CSS, each subsequent level would have the nested list bullet point, but it would be feasible to keep changing the bullet graphic for a third or fourth (and so on) level, by using increasingly complex contextual selectors.

> *When using custom bullet images, be wary of making them too large. Some browsers, such as Safari, clip the left of the bullet image, and most place the list contents at the foot of the image. In all cases, the results look terrible.*

list-style-position property

This property has two values: inside and outside. The latter is how list items are usually displayed: the bullet is placed in the list margin and the left margin of the text is always indented. However, if you use inside, the affected list items have the bullet placed where the first character would usually go, meaning that the text wraps underneath the bullet.

list-style-type property

The list-style-type property is used to amend the bullets in an unordered or ordered list, enabling you to change the default bullets to something else (other than a custom image). In an unordered list, this defaults to disc (a black bullet), and in an ordered list, this defaults to decimal (resulting in a numbered list), but it has other values, some of which are depicted in the following image on the right. (On the left are alternatives for unordered lists: circle, square, and none, which results in no bullet points; on the right are alternatives for ordered lists: decimal, lower-roman, and upper-alpha.) A full list of supported values is in the reference section.

o Circle	1. Decimal
o List item	2. List item
o List item	3. List item
▪ Square	i. Lower-roman
▪ List item	ii. List item
▪ List item	iii. List item
None	A. Upper-alpha
List item	B. List item
List item	C. List item

Generally speaking, the values depicted are the best supported, along with the upper and lower versions of roman and alpha for ordered lists. If a browser doesn't understand the numbering system used for an ordered list, it usually defaults to decimal. The W3C recommends using decimal (the default ordered list) whenever possible, because it makes web pages easier to navigate. I agree: things like alpha and roman are too esoteric for general use, plus there's nothing in the CSS specifications to tell a browser what to do in an alphabetic system after z is reached.

List style shorthand

As elsewhere in CSS, there is a shorthand property for list styles, the aptly named list-style. Therefore, in the following example, this piece of CSS

```
ul {
list-style-type: square;
list-style-position: inside;
list-style-image: url(bullet.gif);
}
```

could be rewritten as

```
ul {
list-style: square inside url(bullet.gif);
}
```

List margins and padding

Browsers don't seem to be able to agree on how much padding and margin to place around lists by default, and also how margin and padding settings affect lists in general. This can be frustrating when developing websites that rely on lists *and* pixel-perfect element placement. By creating a list and using CSS to apply a background color to the list, and a different color to list items, then removing the page's padding and margins, you can observe how each browser creates lists and indents the bullet points and content.

In Gecko browsers (Mozilla, Firefox, etc.) and Safari, the list background color is displayed behind the bullet points, suggesting those browsers place bullet points within padding (because backgrounds extend into an element's padding). Internet Explorer and Opera show no background color, suggesting they place bullet points within margins (by default, Opera also places a margin under each list item—it's the only browser to do so).

This is confirmed if you set the margin property to 0 for a ul selector in CSS. The Gecko and Safari list is unaffected, but the bullet points in the Opera and Internet Explorer list disappear, and the list butts up to the edge of the web browser window. Conversely, setting the padding to 0 makes the bullet points vanish in Gecko browsers and Safari, but not in Internet Explorer or Opera.

To get all browsers on a level playing field, you must therefore set margin and padding to 0 in a ul selector, and also cater for Opera's default padding on list elements by setting margin to 0 in an li selector.

```
ul {
margin: 0;
padding: 0;
}

li {
margin: 0;
}
```

This is a good starting point when styling lists in CSS, because all browsers render them the same with these settings. Of course, with these settings, your lists have no bullet points. To bring those back, you either set the margin-left value to 1em (i.e., set margin: 0 0 0 1em) and leave padding set to 0, or you set the padding-left value to 1em (i.e. set padding: 0 0 0 1em) and leave margin set to 0. The difference is that if you set padding-left to 1em, any background applied to the list will appear behind the bullet points, but if you set margin-left to 1em, it won't. Note that 1em is a big enough value to enable the bullet points to display; setting a higher value places more space to the left of the bullet points.

Safari exhibits slightly different behavior, with the bullet points slightly further to the left. Bear this in mind if you're working on pixel-perfect layouts.

Inline lists

Although most people think of lists as being vertically aligned, you can also display list items inline. This is particularly useful when creating navigation bars, as we'll see in Chapter 5. To set a list to display inline, you simply add display: inline; to the ul selector. Adding list-style-type: none; as well ensures the list sits snug to the left of its container (omitting this tends to indent the list).

If your list items consist of images or have background colors, you may find gaps appearing between them. This happens when browsers interpret white space in the HTML document as a gap (which, strictly speaking, they shouldn't). The workaround is inconvenient, but simple: remove the white space between the list item elements.

```
<ul>
<li>List item</li><li>List item</li><li>List item</li>
</ul>
```

Just another example of how knowing a bit of hand-coding can stop you from tearing your hair out in the wonderful world of web design.

Well, that just about wraps things up for online type. After all that text, it's time to change track. The next chapter looks at working with images on the Web, before you combine what you've learned so far and add anchors into the mix to cover web navigation in Chapter 5.

3

CHAPTER 4

WORKING WITH IMAGES

In this chapter

- Introducing graphics editors
- Introducing color theory and web-safe colors
- Choosing the best image format
- Avoiding common mistakes
- Working with images in XHTML
- Using alt text to improve accessibility
- Using CSS when working with images
- Displaying random images using JavaScript

Introduction

Although text makes up the bulk of the Web's content, it's inevitable that you'll end up working with images at some point—that is, unless you favor terribly basic websites akin to those last seen in 1995 (in which case you may as well stop reading now and get back to perfecting your time machine or watching John Hughes movies).

Unsurprisingly, images are now rife online, comprising the bulk of interfaces, the navigation of millions of sites, and a considerable amount of actual content, too. As the Web continues to barge its way into every facet of life, this trend can only continue; visitors to sites now expect a certain amount of visual interest, just as readers of a magazine expect illustrations or photographs.

Like anything else, use or misuse of images can make or break a website—so, like elsewhere in this book, this chapter covers more than just the relevant HTML and CSS when working with images. Along with providing an overview of graphics editors and color theory, I've compiled a brief list of the most common mistakes that people make when working with images for the Web—after all, even the most dedicated web designers pick up bad habits without even realizing. Finally, at the end of the chapter, I'll introduce your first piece of JavaScript, providing you with a handy cut-out-and-keep script to randomize images on a web page.

Graphics editors

Earlier we discussed the myriad applications available for web design—the choice of graphics editors is similarly large. However, when it comes down to it, the vast majority of web designers are fans of either Adobe or Macromedia (perhaps due to those companies becoming the industry "standards" for desktop publishing software and web software, respectively)—and some designers get quite irritable when forced to use the other company's software.

Adobe's main powerhouse is Photoshop (www.adobe.com/products/photoshop), which comes bundled with ImageReady, an application that provides further scope for creating web graphics. The reason for ImageReady's inclusion (and indeed its entire existence) is that although Photoshop is the bitmap editor of choice in design circles, its web support used to be weak. A rather awkward workflow "innovation" enables you to switch between the two applications while working on graphics. However, unless you're creating animations, you can do everything in Photoshop these days.

Photoshop's main rival in the web space is Macromedia's Fireworks (www.macromedia.com/software/fireworks). Fireworks and Photoshop seem to be on a collision course: if you've watched them both evolve over recent years, you might surmise that the applications will eventually be exactly the same. Anyone who's exported web graphics from both applications will know what I mean—the interfaces are virtually identical. Fireworks has some benefits over Photoshop, including a slightly more intuitive workflow with regard to shapes and vectors, marginally more mature web tools, and a simpler means of working with animations (in that everything can be done within Fireworks itself). On the flip side, not everyone's convinced by Macromedia's text anti-aliasing technology. Ultimately, it's up to you which application to use, but in my experience, the final choice often comes down to which interface someone prefers.

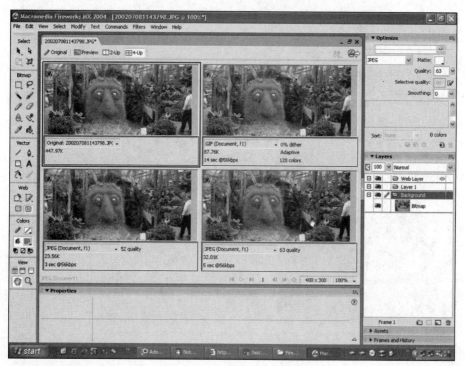

Vector applications

Although the Web is primarily a bitmap-based medium, that doesn't mean you can't use vector-based graphics tools such as Adobe Illustrator (www.adobe.com/products/illustrator) and Macromedia Freehand (www.macromedia.com/software/freehand) in your workflow process. In fact, designers are increasingly using Adobe Illustrator to create mock-ups, because vector tools often feel more suited to creating CSS-based website layouts. The main advantage of using such tools is that they enable you to edit each individual element without affecting something else (something that's rarely true in bitmap applications, even when using dozens of layers). Of course, the companies creating the bitmap applications are well aware of this trend, and many recent updates to the applications have involved adding tools suitable for web design.

Budget applications

If you're just starting out, the price of software can be quite daunting. For web designers, web design software takes priority, and sometimes there's little left in the kitty for working with graphics. Luckily, there are low-cost alternatives available, meaning you don't have to spend many hundreds of dollars to get a decent graphics application.

Jasc Paint Shop Pro (www.jasc.com/products/paintshoppro) is a favorite of many Windows users, some of whom swear that it's just as good as Photoshop. Although I wouldn't go that far, there's no denying that it's powerful and includes many features found in much more expensive applications.

Mac users are out of luck with Paint Shop Pro, though, because Jasc's software is Windows only. For them, Photoshop Elements is the best bet, although this application is also available for Windows (see www.adobe.com/products/photoshopelmac/main.html and www.adobe.com/products/photoshopelwin/main.html for information on the Mac and Windows versions, respectively). In many ways, this application is a cut-down Photoshop. It lacks CMYK support (CMYK is the format required for print work), although it can convert CMYK images to RGB when opening them. It also lacks some of Photoshop's other niceties, but it does have support layers and many Photoshop effects and filters.

In any case, the particular application you use is actually not all that important, as long as you can export to the relevant formats and you understand the best way to work—which is what we'll deal with next.

Avoiding dated export methods

One of the main thrusts of this book is to present modern work methods that will enable you to create cutting-edge websites. Many designers are used to working with applications that make their lives easier (at least in theory), but by letting applications do all the work, the results suffer as a consequence. For instance, most graphics applications enable you to carve up web layouts into slices. You click a button, and the application spews out dozens of oddly named image files and HTML so complicated that even FrontPage would be offended if you suggested it might have originated in that application. Instead of having graphics applications dictate how your layout should work, it's better to plan things, work out the actual structure of your web page, and then manually export the relevant parts of the layout document. For some layouts, you may actually be able to use CSS for most things (anything with flat color and borders, for instance); in other cases, you may need many more graphics, but you could still use CSS to position them or tile repeating sections, rather than exporting a much larger area.

In essence, I'm suggesting that you should stop and think before letting a graphics application dictate how your website works. We'll be exploring the details of website layout later in this book, in Chapters 6 through 9.

Color theory

Color plays a massively important role in any field of design, and web design is no exception. However, web designers come from varied backgrounds, many of which are technically oriented, so some of the people reading this book may not have a grounding in color theory. With this in mind, I've decided to provide a brief primer on color theory and working with colors on the Web.

Color wheels

Even if you have a great eye for color and can instinctively create great schemes for websites, it still pays to have a color wheel handy. These days, you don't have to rely on dodgy reproductions in books or hastily created painted paper wheels pinned to your wall.

Instead, there are numerous digital color wheels that enable you to experiment rapidly and easily, my favorite of which is Color Consultant Pro for the Mac (www.code-line.com/software/colorconsultantpro.html), shown in the following screenshot. Similar applications for Windows include Color Wheel Pro (www.color-wheel-pro.com) and ColorImpact (www.tigercolor.com/Default.htm).

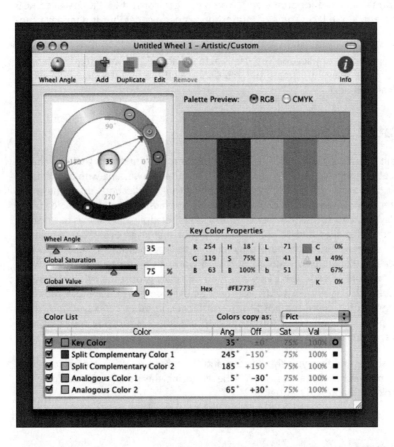

The most common type of color wheel has the primary colors—red, yellow, and blue—evenly spaced around the wheel, with the secondary colors—orange, green, and purple—positioned between the primary colors.

Colors adjacent to each other on the wheel are said to work harmoniously, creating a gentle color scheme. Complementary colors—those opposite to each other on the wheel—contrast with each other, grabbing the viewer's attention. Such combinations (red/green, orange/blue, yellow/purple) should be used in moderation, though, since overusing them can result in a garish display.

Artists often favor the triadic scheme, using three colors that are spaced equally around the wheel. This provides visual contrast, but is more subtle than the complementary scheme.

How colors "feel" also plays a part in how someone reacts to them—colors can feel warm or cool, depending on cultural ideas or what they're juxtaposed against. For instance, yellow on white appears warm, but mild. On black, yellow has an aggressive brilliance.

Working with hex

The CSS specifications support just 17 color names: aqua, black, blue, fuchsia, gray, green, lime, maroon, navy, olive, orange, purple, red, silver, teal, white, and yellow. All other colors should be written in hexadecimal format. Colors written in hex comprise a hash sign followed by six digits. The six digits are comprised of pairs, representing the red, green, and blue color values, respectively.

- #XXxxxx: Red color value
- #xxXXxx: Green color value
- #xxxxXX: Blue color value

Because the hexadecimal system is used, the digits can range in value from 0 to F, with 0 being the null value and F being the highest. Therefore, if we set the first two digits to full (ff) and the others to null, we get #ff0000, which is the hex color value for red. Likewise, #00ff00 is green and #0000ff is blue.

Of course, there are plenty of potential combinations—16.7 million of them, in fact. Luckily, any half-decent graphics application will do the calculations for you, so you won't have to work out for yourself that black is #000000, white is #ffffff, and—to take an HTML color name at random—LightGoldenRodYellow is #fafad2.

> HTML color names are another method of stating colors on the Web, and they refer to colors within the web-safe palette (see the following section). As I stated, though, these names should not be used in CSS, apart from the 17 listed earlier.

Web-safe colors

Because even the most basic PCs and Macs tend to come with fairly powerful graphics cards these days, it's often hard to remember that this hasn't always been the case. In fact, many computers that are still in common use cannot display millions of colors. Back in the 1990s, palette restrictions were even more ferocious, with many computers limited to a paltry 256 colors (8 bit). Cleverly, Microsoft and Apple couldn't agree on which colors to use—hence the creation of the web-safe palette, which comprises a mere 216 colors that are supposed to work accurately on both platforms without dithering. (For more information about dithering, see the GIF section later in this chapter.) Applications such as Photoshop have built-in web-safe palettes, including one from VisiBone (see the accompanying illustration) that acts rather like a color wheel. (For other useful web-safe tools, visit the VisiBone website: www.visibone.com.) The color pickers in most graphics applications also enable you to snap to web-safe colors.

Colors in the web-safe palette are made up of combinations of RGB in 20% increments, and as you might expect, the palette is pretty limited. Even more discouragingly, David Lehn and Hadley Stern reported on Webmonkey (http://hotwired.lycos.com/webmonkey/00/37/index2a.html) that all but 22 of these colors were incorrectly shifted in some way when tested on a variety of platforms and color displays—in other words, only 22 of the web-safe colors are actually totally web-safe.

Although the rise of PDAs means the web-safe palette may make a comeback in specialist circles, most designers these days tend to ignore it. The majority of people using the Web have displays capable of millions of colors, and most everyone else can view at least thousands of colors. Unless you're designing for an audience with restricted hardware, stick with sRGB (the default color space of the Web—see www.w3.org/Graphics/Color/sRGB) and design in millions of colors. And consider yourself lucky that it's not 1995.

Choosing formats for images

In order to present images online in the best possible way, it's essential to choose the best file format when exporting and saving them. Although the save dialogs in most graphics editors present a bewildering list of possible formats, the Web typically uses just two: JPEG and GIF. In addition to these, we'll also cover the GIF89 and PNG formats in this section.

JPEG

The JPEG (Joint Photographic Experts Group) format is used primarily for images that require smooth color transitions and continuous tones, such as photographs. JPEG supports millions of colors, and very little image detail is lost even when compression settings are fairly high. This is because the format uses **lossy compression**, which removes information that the eye doesn't need. As the compression level increases, this becomes increasingly obvious, as shown in the following images. As you can see from the image on the right, which is more compressed than the one on the left, nasty artifacts become increasingly dominant as the compression level increases. At extreme levels of compression, the image will appear to be composed of linked blocks.

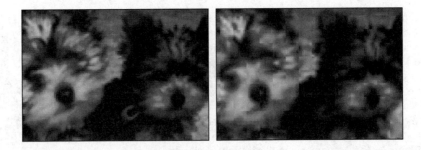

In general, 50% compression is the highest level you should use—less if the image in question is particularly important (for instance, if you're a graphic designer presenting a portfolio, it makes sense to compress your images less). If the download time for an image is unacceptably high, try reducing the dimensions rather than the quality—a small, detailed image usually looks better than a large, heavily compressed image.

Be aware that applications have different means of referring to compression ratios. Some, such as Adobe applications, use a quality scale, in which 100 is uncompressed and 0 is completely compressed. Others, such as Paint Shop Pro, use compression values, in which higher numbers indicate increased compression. Always be sure you know which scale you're using.

Some applications have the option to save **progressive JPEGs**. Typically, this format results in larger file sizes, but it's useful because it enables your image to download in multiple passes. This means that a low-resolution version will display rapidly and gradually progress to the quality you saved it at, allowing viewers to get a look at a simplified version of the image without having to wait for it to load completely.

4

GIF

The Graphics Interchange Format is in many ways the polar opposite of JPEG. The GIF format is **lossless**, meaning that there's no color degradation when images are compressed. However, the format is restricted to a maximum of 256 colors, thereby rendering it ineffective for color photographic images. Using GIF for such images tends to produce banding, in which colors are reduced to the nearest equivalent. A fairly extreme example of this is shown in the following illustration.

GIF is useful for displaying images with large areas of flat color, such as logos, line art, and type. As I mentioned in the previous chapter, you should generally avoid using graphics for text on your web pages, but if you do, GIF is the best choice of format.

Although GIF is restricted to 256 colors, it's worth noting that you don't have to use the *same* 256 colors every time. Most graphics applications provide a number of palette options, such as **perceptual**, **selective**, and **Web**. The first of those, perceptual, tends to prioritize colors that the human eye is most sensitive to, thereby providing the best color integrity. Selective works in a similar fashion, but balances its color choices with web-safe colors, thereby creating results more likely to be safe across platforms. Web refers to the 216 color web-safe palette discussed earlier. Additionally, you often have the option to lock colors, which forces your graphics application to use only the colors within the palette you choose.

Images can also be dithered, which prevents continuous tones from becoming bands of color. Dithering simulates continuous tones, using the available (restricted) palette. Most graphics editors allow for three different types of dithering: **diffusion**, **pattern**, and **noise**—all of which have markedly different effects on an image. Diffusion applies a random pattern across adjacent pixels, whereas pattern applies a half-tone pattern rather like that seen in low-quality print publications. Noise works rather like diffusion, but without diffusing the pattern across adjacent pixels. In the following example, you can see four examples of how dithering affects an image that began life as a smooth gradient. The first image (1) has no dither, and the gradient has been turned into a series of solid, vertical stripes. The second image (2) shows the effects of diffusion dithering; the third (3), pattern; and the fourth (4), noise.

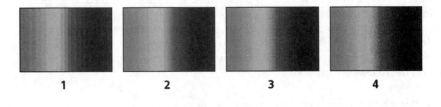

1   2   3   4

GIF89

The GIF89 file format is identical to GIF, with one important exception: you can remove colors, which provides a very basic means of transparency and enables the background to show through. Because this is not alpha transparency (a type of transparency that enables a smooth transition from solid to transparent, allowing for many levels of opacity), it doesn't work in the way many graphic designers expect. You cannot, for instance, fade an image's background from color to transparent and expect the web page's background to show through—instead, GIF89's transparency is akin to cutting a hole with a pair of scissors: the background shows through the removed colors only. This is fine when the "hole" has flat horizontal or vertical edges. But if you try this with irregular shapes—such as in the adjacent image of the cloud with drop shadow— you'll end up with ragged edges. In the example, the idea was to have the cloud casting a shadow onto the gray background. However, because GIFs can't deal with alpha transparency, we instead end up with an unwanted white outline. (One way around this is to export the image with

114

the same background color as that of the web page, but this is only possible if the web page's background is a plain, flat color.)

Because of these restrictions, GIF89s are not used all that much these days. They do cling on in one area of web design, though: as spacers for stretching table cells, in order to lay out a page. I'll cover this briefly later in the book, but this type of technique is generally to be avoided in these enlightened times—you can lay out precisely spaced pages much more easily by using CSS.

PNG

"A ha!" you might say, "I thought you said there were just two formats available, and yet you've already mentioned three, and now a fourth!" Well, GIF89 is effectively a subset of GIF—and that, along with JPEG, is what the vast majority of web designers tend to use. So, why bother mentioning PNG, then? Because it's great—at least potentially.

The **PNG** (Portable Network Graphics) format comes in two flavors, and can be used as a replacement for both GIF and JPEG. Interestingly, PNG enables full alpha transparency, thereby enabling all manner of fancy graphical effects. Unfortunately, Internet Explorer for Windows doesn't support this feature. (Boo!) There are workarounds, but they're all extremely ugly and inflexible hacks, so I won't be covering them in this book.

For more information about this format, check out the PNG website at www.libpng.org/pub/png.

What about other formats?

What about them, indeed? You may have worked on pages in the past and added the odd BMP or TIFF file, or seen another site do the same. These are not standard formats for the Web, though, and while they may work fine in some cases, they require additional software in order to render in some browsers (in many cases, they won't render at all, or they'll render inconsistently across browsers). Furthermore, JPEG, GIF, and PNG are well-suited to web design because they enable you to present a lot of visual information in a fairly small file. Presenting the same in a TIFF or BMP won't massively increase the image's quality (when taking into account the low resolution of the Web), but it will almost certainly increase download times. Therefore, quite simply, don't use any formats other than JPEG, GIF, or PNG for your web images (and if you decide to use PNG transparency, be sure that your target audience will be able to see the images).

Common web image gaffes

As mentioned earlier, the same mistakes tend to crop up again and again when designers start working with images. In order to avoid making them, read on to find out about ten common mistakes (and how to avoid them).

Incorrect resolution

The rule for resolution with regard to web images is simple: they should be exported at 72 dpi—no more, no less. However, you shouldn't scan in images you want to include on your site at 72 dpi. Instead, scan things in at 300 dpi so you've got more pixels to play with. Only once satisfied with your edit should you resample the image to 72 dpi. This enables you to get more detail in the initial scan, and you're therefore more likely to get a pleasing result when you export and optimize your image for the Web.

Using graphics for body copy

This is one of my greatest bugbears with regard to web design. As I said in Chapter 3, using graphics for body copy will cause your text to print poorly—much worse than HTML-based text). Additionally, it means your text can't be read by search engines, it can't be copied and pasted, and it can't be enlarged (unless using Opera—and even then it will be pixelated). If you need to update graphical text, that means reworking the original image (which could include messing with line wraps, if you need to add or remove words), re-exporting it, and re-uploading it. To some extent, the same is true for any graphical copy on websites—so wherever possible, use HTML-based text for headings, too.

Not working from original images

This perhaps warrants some explaining. Say you start with a brand-spanking new, top-quality TIFF (a format that ensures images don't degrade when resaved) and then turn it into a compressed JPEG for your web page. If you then decide that this image needs to be changed in any major way, you should start again from the original source material. Continually saving a compressed image reduces its quality each time. And, under no circumstances whatsoever should you increase the size of a compressed JPEG. Doing so leads to abysmal results every time.

Overwriting original documents

The previous problem gets worse if you've deleted your originals. Therefore, be sure that you never overwrite the original files you're using. If resampling JPEGs from a digital camera for the Web, work with copies so you don't accidentally overwrite your only copy of that great photo you've taken with a much smaller, heavily compressed version. More important, if you're using Photoshop for creating Web layouts, save copies of the layered documents prior to flattening them for export—otherwise you'll regret it when having to make that all-important change and having to start from scratch.

Lack of contrast

Many designers have a tendency to use pale text on an only slightly darker background, and sometimes this lack of contrast finds its way into other things, such as imagery comprising interface elements. In some cases, this isn't a problem: such designs can look stylish if a subtle scheme is used with care. You should, however, ensure that usability isn't affected—it's all very well to have a subtle color scheme, but it's not so great if it stops visitors from being able to easily find things like navigation elements, or from being able to read the text (see the adjacent example).

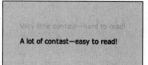

Using the wrong image format

Exporting photographs as GIFs, using BMPs or TIFFs online, rendering soft and blotchy line art and text as a result of using the JPEG format, using PNG transparency in the face of browsers that can't handle it—these are all things to avoid in the merry world of creating images for websites. See the section "Choosing formats for images," earlier in this chapter, for an in-depth discussion of formats.

Resizing in HTML

This is a very common occurrence that largely came about when WYSIWYG design tools became prevalent, leading many designers to forget about or ignore the underlying code of a web page. You should never resize an image by stretching it in the visual view of a web design application, nor should you amend the width and height attributes of any image tags. Doing so is likely to distort your image, as shown in the rather extreme example that follows.

There are exceptions to this rule, however, although they are rare. For instance, if you work with pixel art saved as a GIF, you can proportionately enlarge an image, making it large on the screen. Despite the image being large, the file size will be tiny.

Not balancing quality and file size

Bandwidth can be a problem in image-heavy sites—both in terms of the host getting hammered when visitor numbers increase, and in terms of the visitors—many of whom may be stuck with dial-up modems—having to download the images. Therefore, you should always be sure that your images are highly optimized, in order to save on hosting costs and ensure that your website's visitors don't have to suffer massive downloads. (In fact, they probably won't—they'll more than likely go elsewhere.)

But this doesn't mean that you should compress every image on your website into a slushy mess (and I've seen a *lot* of sites where the creator has exported JPEGs at what looks like 90% compression—"just in case").

Err on the side of caution, but remember: Common interface elements are cached, so you can afford to save them at a slightly higher quality. Any image that someone requests (such as via a thumbnail on a portfolio site) is something they *want* to see, so these too can be saved at a higher quality because the person is likely to wait. Also, there is no such thing as an "optimum" size for web images. If you've read in the past that no web image should ever be larger than 50KB, it's hogwash. The size of your images depends entirely on context, the type of site you're creating, and the audience you're creating it for.

Text overlays

I've lost count of the number of occasions on which I've seen a perfectly good image (often a product shot or part of a portfolio) totally ruined by some garish text overlay, proudly exclaiming who holds the copyright to the image—see right for a good example of how to ruin an image. OK, so anyone can download images from your website to their hard drive—big deal. If someone else uses your images, they're breaking the law, and you can deal with them accordingly (and, if they link directly to images on your server, just try

This image is © Craig Grannell.

changing the affected images to something text-based, stating "the scumbag whose site you're visiting stole images from me"). If you're worried about someone downloading your images and using them offline, that's not going to happen—a 72 dpi compressed JPEG isn't going to set the world on fire when appropriated for a brochure.

While on the subject of text overlays, I should mention some other irritating habits of some web designers: splitting images into several separate files or placing invisible GIFs over images to try to stop people from downloading them. Don't do this—there are simple workarounds in either case, and you just end up making things harder for yourself when updating your site. Sometimes you even risk compromising the structural integrity of your site when using such methods.

Stealing images and designs

I'm sure that you've never contemplated doing such a thing, but just in case, always remember that copyright exists on the web just like everywhere else. Unless you have permission to reuse an image you've found online, you shouldn't do so. If discovered, you may get the digital equivalent of a slap on the wrist, but you could also be sued for copyright infringement.

Although it's all right to be influenced by someone else's design, you should also ensure you don't simply rip off a creation found on the Web—otherwise you could end up in legal trouble, or the subject of ridicule as a feature on Tim Murtaugh's excellent website, www.pirated-sites.com.

Working with images in XHTML

The img element is used to add images to a web page. It's an empty tag, so it takes the combined start and end tag form with a trailing slash, as outlined in Chapter 1. The following code block shows an example of an image element, complete with relevant attributes:

```
<img src="sunset.jpg" height="200" width="400" alt="A photo of a sunset" />
```

Perhaps surprisingly, the height and width attributes are actually optional, although I recommend including them because they assist the browser in determining the size of the image before it downloads (thereby speeding up the process of laying out the page). The only two image element attributes required in XHTML are src and alt. The first, src, is the path to the image file to be displayed; and the second, alt, provides some alternative text for when the image is not displayed.

Using alt text for accessibility benefits

Alt text is often ignored or used poorly by designers, but it's essential for improving the accessibility of your web pages. Visitors using screen readers rely on the alt attribute's value to determine what an image is. Therefore, always include a succinct description of the image's content and avoid using the image's file name, because that's often of little help. Ignoring the alt attribute not only renders your page invalid according to the W3C recommendations, but it also means that screen readers (and browsers that cannot display images) end up with something like this for output: [IMAGE][IMAGE][IMAGE]—not very helpful, to say the least.

Images often take on dual roles, being used for navigation purposes as well as additional visual impact. In such cases, the fact that the image is a navigation aid is likely to be of more significance than its visual appearance. For instance, many companies use logos as links to a homepage—in such cases, using "Company X homepage" for alt text would be far more useful than "Company X logo." An example of this can be seen in the screenshot that follows: the highlighted link (Snub Communications homepage) is actually a graphical logo that links back to the homepage, but the alt text enables someone using a screen reader to access the image's function.

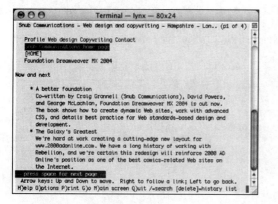

> *The previous image shows the web page in Lynx, a text-based browser. Using a text browser is a good way of finding out whether your site is usable when stripped of all images and layout. If you don't fancy installing Lynx, Opera's User mode can emulate a text browser.*

Null alt attributes for interface images

In some cases, images have no meaning at all (for instance, if they're a part of an interface), and there is some debate regarding the best course of action to take with regard to such images' alt values. Definitely never type something like spacer or interface element, otherwise screen readers and text browsers will drive their users crazy, relaying these values back to them. Instead, it's recommended that you use a **null alt attribute**, which takes the form alt="".

Null alt attributes are unfortunately not interpreted correctly by all screen readers; some, upon discovering a null alt attribute, go on to read the image's src value. A common workaround is to use empty alt attributes, which just have blank space for the value (alt=" "). However, the null alt attribute has valid semantics, so it should be used despite some screen readers not being able to deal with it correctly.

Using alt text for tooltips

I'm guessing that a couple of veteran web designers just spat out their coffee. Don't worry, though, because I'm not actually recommending using alt text for tooltips—in fact, quite the opposite. As I've already said, alt text is intended for displaying alternative text when an image isn't available, for whatever reason. Although the W3C specifically states that alt text shouldn't be visible if the image can been seen, several browsers totally ignore this and display alt text as a tooltip when the mouse cursor hovers over an image, as shown in the adjacent example.

Windows-based users of Internet Explorer are most likely accustomed to this by now, and, indeed, you may have used alt text to create tooltips in your own work. If so, it's time to stop. This behavior is not recommended by the W3C and it's also not common across all browsers and platforms.

> *If an image requires a tooltip, most browsers display the value of a title attribute as one. In spite of this, if the text you're intending for a pop-up is important, you should instead place it within the standard text of your web page, rather than hiding it where most users won't see it.*

Using the object element to embed images

Often a source of confusion for designers the world over, the object element was the W3C's reaction to the ever-increasing functionality of the Web. When some bright spark had the idea of enabling designers to include images in web pages, the img element was born, and there was much joy—except at the W3C where there was much wailing and gnashing of teeth. The W3C advised that the object element should be used instead (and also for embedding other objects, such as media files). Designers ignored this advice, and now—several years and many millions of websites later—the img tag rules, while the object element remains relatively unused.

When you look at what the object element can do, this may seem surprising. For instance, you can use it to specify fallbacks for any one object, for which browsers are supposed to render the first object they can. If a browser can't handle any of the defined formats, you can set plain text as the final fallback. This works rather like alt text, except that this text can be fully styled HTML. For instance, the following example shows an img element and the equivalent object element:

```
<img src="sunset.jpg" height="200" width="400" alt="A photo of a sunset" />

<object data="sunset.jpg" height="200" width="400" type="image/jpeg">
  <p>A photo of a sunset</p>
</object>
```

In theory, the object element is superior, enabling styling of the fallback text and explicitly defining the image's MIME type. The only snag is that it doesn't work. Support for this element over the years has been flaky at best, and sadly, things aren't much better today. By and large, Opera, the various Mozilla browsers, and Safari deal with the object element fairly well, although there are quirks (for instance, Opera 7 treats objects like inline frames, causing them to vanish if support for inline frames has been disabled).

Internet Explorer for Windows, on the other hand, messes up in dramatic fashion. Because Microsoft's browser treats object elements as ActiveX controls, it whacks a border and scroll bars around them. And, for good measure, if you set Internet Explorer's security settings to high, thereby disabling ActiveX controls, you won't even be able to see object elements that have nothing to do with ActiveX (such as the innocent sunset image from the previous example code). There are workarounds, but they are complex and more effort than they're worth. For now, stick with the img element for adding images to web pages.

> *There was a lot of panic when it was announced that XHTML 2 will most likely unceremoniously dump the* img *element in favor of* object. *It's worth noting, though, that XHTML 2 is not a replacement for XHTML 1, so you can continue using* img *for the foreseeable future, and perhaps begin using* object *when mainstream browser support is more reliable.*

4

Useful CSS when working with images

In the following section, we're going to look at relevant CSS for web page images. You'll see how best to apply borders to images and how to wrap text around them, along with defining spacing between images and other page elements.

Applying CSS borders to images

You may have noticed earlier that I didn't mention the border attribute when working through the img element. This is because the border attribute has been deprecated; adding borders to images is best achieved and controlled by using CSS. (Also, because of the flexibility of CSS, this means that if you only want a simple surrounding border composed of flat color, you no longer have to add borders directly to your image files.) Should you want to add a border to every image on your website, you could do so with the following CSS:

```
img {
border: 1px solid #000000;
}
```

In this case, a 1-pixel solid border, colored black (#000000 in hex), would surround every image on the site. Using contextual selectors, this can be further refined. For instance, should you only want the images within a content area (marked up as a div with an id value of content) to be displayed with a border, you could write the following CSS:

```
div#content img {
border: 1px solid #000000;
}
```

Borders can be set on a per-side basis, as demonstrated when working on the second pull quote example in the previous chapter. If you wanted to style a specific image to resemble a Polaroid, you could set equal borders on the top, left, and right, and a larger one on the bottom. In HTML, you would add a class attribute to the relevant image:

```
<img class="photo" src="sunset.jpg" height="300" width="300"
➥alt="Sunset photo" />
```

In CSS, you would write the following:

```
.photo {
border-width: 8px 8px 20px 8px;
border-style: solid;
border-color: #ffffff;
}
```

The results of this can be seen in the image to the right. (Obviously, the white border only shows if you have a contrasting background—you wouldn't see a white border on a white background!)

Using CSS to wrap text around images

You can use the `float` and `margin` properties to enable body copy to wrap around an image. The method is similar to the pull quote example in the previous chapter, so we won't dwell too much on this. Suffice to say that images can be floated left or right, and margins can be set around edges facing body copy in order to provide some white space. For example, expanding on the previous example, you could add the following rules, to ensure that the surrounding body copy doesn't hug the image:

```
.photo {
border-width: 8px 8px 20px 8px;
border-style: solid;
border-color: #ffffff;
float: right;
margin-left: 20px;
margin-bottom: 20px;
}
```

This results in the following effect:

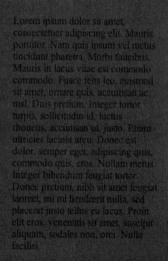

Displaying random images using JavaScript

The final thing we're going to look at in this chapter is how to create a simple system for displaying a random image from a selection. This has several potential uses, such as randomizing banners (yes, we know that a banner is often a horrible thing, but it can be very useful if you run a commercial site). It also creates the impression that the site is updated more often than it is by showing visitors some new content each time they arrive. (And for things like portfolios, it's always useful to present a random piece of work from a selection.)

Prior to starting work, you need to prepare your images. Unless you're prepared for subsequent layout elements to shift upon each visit to the page, aim to export all your images with equal dimensions. Should this not be an option, try to keep the same height setting. Note, however, that you can use different file formats for the various images. It's good housekeeping to keep these images in their own folder, too; for this exercise, the images are going to be within assets/random_images, and we'll assume the JavaScript and HTML documents are both in the site root.

Exercise: Creating a JavaScript-based image randomizer

1. **Create a function**. First, start writing the function, which has been dubbed randomContent. Most of you will most likely be somewhat familiar with JavaScript—if not, you should know that content from subsequent steps must be inserted into the space between the curly brackets.

```
function randomContent()
{

}
```

2. **Add an array for image file names**. Next, add an array to house the file names of your images.

```
var chosenImage=new Array();

// filenames of images in this array
chosenImage[1]="stream.jpg";
chosenImage[2]="river.jpg";
chosenImage[3]="road.jpg";
```

> If you require another image in your array, copy the last line and increase the bracketed number by one—for example, **chosenImage[4]="something_else.jpg";**

3. **Add an array for alt text**. Because the alt text may differ for each image, you need to set up a second array to house it. Note that you must take care with the order of items in the array; the alt text of the first item in this array relates to the first item of the array created in the previous step.

```
var chosenAltCopy=new Array();

// title and alt copy for images goes here
chosenAltCopy[1]="A photo of a stream";
chosenAltCopy[2]="A photo of a river";
chosenAltCopy[3]="A photo of a road";
```

4. **Create a random value**. The following JavaScript provides you with a random value.

```
var getRan=Math.ceil(Math.random()*chosenImage.length);
```

5. **Create JavaScript to write HTML to the web page**. The final line of JavaScript prints HTML back to the web page when the script is called. Note that the src value includes the path to the images, and width and height have been defined. Should your images be of varied sizes, leave out the height and width attributes—otherwise your images will be distorted. This code should all be on one line without any line breaks.

```
document.write('<img src=\"assets/random_images/'+chosenImage[getRan]+'"
➡alt=\"'+chosenAltCopy[getRan]+'\" width=\"300\" height=\"300\"
➡class=\"imageBorder\" />');
```

6. **Define borders in CSS**. In CSS, you need to define a border style, as outlined earlier in the chapter in the section entitled "Applying CSS borders to images."

```
.imageBorder {
border: solid 1px #000000;
}
```

7. **Add a script element to the web page**. Finally, on the web page, you need to add a script element to wherever you want the image to be displayed.

```
<script type="text/javascript">
randomContent();
</script>
```

> You may be familiar with using the language attribute within the script element, but this was deprecated in HTML 4.01 and is not supported in the XHTML 1.0 Strict DTD, although it is still supported under the XHTML 1.0 Transitional DTD. In any case, there's no real need to use it, so we're not going to.

4

Upon testing the completed files in a browser, each refresh should show a random image from the selection, as shown below.

Finally, here's the entire script, should you wish to use it in your own work:

```
function randomContent()
{
var chosenImage=new Array();

// filenames of images in this array
chosenImage[1]="stream.jpg";
chosenImage[2]="river.jpg";
chosenImage[3]="road.jpg";

var chosenAltCopy=new Array();

// title and alt copy for images goes here
chosenAltCopy[1]="A photo of a stream";
chosenAltCopy[2]="A photo of a river";
chosenAltCopy[3]="A photo of a road";
```

```
var getRan=Math.ceil(Math.random()*chosenImage.length)

document.write('<imgsrc=\"assets/random_images/'+chosenImage[getRan]+'"
➥alt=\"'+chosenAltCopy[getRan]+'\" width=\"300\" height=\"300\"
➥class=\"imageBorder\" />')
}
```

Hopefully you've found this chapter of interest and now feel you have a good grounding in working with images on the Web. It's amazing to think how devoid of visual interest the Web used to be in contrast to today, now that images are essential to the vast majority of sites. As I mentioned before, the importance of images on the Web lies not only in content, but in interface elements as well, such as navigation—a topic we're covering in the very next chapter.

4

CHAPTER 5
CREATING NAVIGATION

In this chapter

- Introducing web navigation
- Creating links
- Controlling CSS link states
- Mastering the cascade
- Looking at links and accessibility
- Examining a JavaScript alternative to pop-ups
- Creating CSS-based rollovers

Introduction to web navigation

The primary concern of most websites is the provision of information. The ability to enable nonlinear navigation via the use of links is one of the main things that sets the Web apart from other media. But without organized, coherent, and usable navigation, even a site with the most amazing content will fail.

During this chapter, we'll work through how to create various types of navigation. Instead of relying on large numbers of graphics and clunky JavaScript, we'll create rollovers that are composed of nothing more than simple HTML lists and a little CSS. And rather than using pop-up windows to display large graphics when a thumbnail image is clicked, we'll cover how to do everything on a single page.

Navigation types

There are essentially three types of navigation online:

- **Inline navigation**: General links within web page content areas
- **Site navigation**: The primary navigation area of a website, commonly referred to as a **navigation bar**
- **Search-based navigation**: A search box that enables you to search a site via terms you input yourself

Although I've separated navigation into these three distinct categories, lines blur, and not every site includes all the different types of navigation. Also, various designers call each navigation type something different, and there's no official name in each case, so in the following sections, we'll expand a little on each type.

Inline navigation

Inline navigation used to be the primary way of navigating the Web, which, many moons ago, largely consisted of technical documentation. Oddly, inline navigation—links within a web page's body copy—has become increasingly rare. Perhaps this is due to the increasing popularity of visually oriented web design tools, leading designers to concentrate more on visuals than usability. Maybe it's because designers have collectively forgotten that links can be made anywhere and not just in navigation bars. In any case, links—inline links in particular—are the main thing that differentiates the Web from other media, making it unique. For instance, you can make specific words within a document link directly to related content. A great example of this is Wikipedia (www.wikipedia.org), the free encyclopedia.

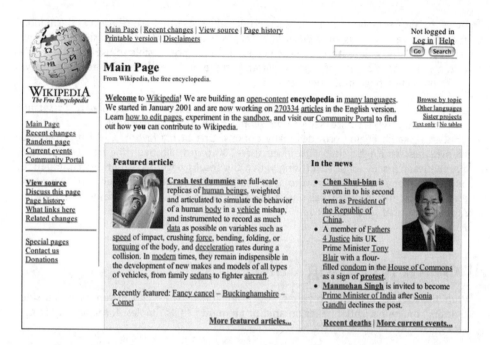

Site navigation

Wikipedia showcases navigation types other than inline. To the left, underneath the logo, is a navigation bar that is present on every page of the site, allowing users to quickly access each section. This kind of thing is essential for most websites—long gone are the days when users were happy to keep returning to a homepage to navigate to new content. (Actually, to be fair, they weren't ever too happy about it, but there you go.)

As Wikipedia proves, just because you have a global navigation bar, that doesn't mean you should skimp on inline navigation. In recent times, I've seen a rash of sites that say things like Thank you for visiting our website. If you have any questions, you can contact us by clicking the contact details link on our navigation bar. Quite frankly, this is bizarre. A better solution is to say Thank you for visiting our website. If you have any questions, please contact us, and to turn contact us into a link to the contact details page. This might seem like common sense, but not every web designer thinks in this way.

Search-based navigation

Wikipedia has a search box at the top-right corner of each page. It's said there are two types of web users: those who eschew search boxes and those who head straight for them. The thing is, search boxes are not always needed, despite the claims of middle managers the world over. Indeed, most sites get by with well-structured and coherent navigation.

However, sites sometimes grow very large (typically those that are heavy on information and that have hundreds or thousands of pages, such as technical repositories, review archives, or large online stores). In such cases, it's often not feasible to use standard navigation elements to access information. Attempting to do so leads to users getting lost trying to navigate a huge navigation "tree."

Unlike other types of navigation, search boxes aren't entirely straightforward to set up yourself, and they require server-side scripting for their functionality. A quick trawl through a search engine provides many options. One of my favorites, which provides a simple, free service for sites with fewer than 500 pages (although the free version also automatically places some advertising within the results page), is Atomz Search. If you're one of the many web designers who aren't particularly technically minded, you'll be interested to hear that Atomz takes only a few minutes to set up. For more details, visit the Atomz website at www.atomz.com.

Anchors (creating links)

With the exception of search boxes, which are forms based and driven by server-side scripting, online navigation relies on **anchor elements**. In its simplest form, an anchor tag looks like this:

```
<a href="http://www.friendsofed.com/">A link to the friends of ED website</a>
```

> By placing a trailing slash in this type of URL, you make only one call to the server instead of two. Also, some incorrectly configured Apache servers generate a "File not found" error if the trailing slash is omitted.

The href attribute value is the URL of the destination document, which is often another HTML file, but can in fact be any file type (MP3, PDF, JPEG, and so on). If the browser can display the document type (either directly or via a plug-in), it does so; otherwise, it downloads the file (or brings up some kind of download prompt).

> Never omit end tags when working with links. Omitting </a> is not only shoddy and invalid XHTML, but most browsers then make all subsequent content on the page into a link!

There are three ways of linking to a file: absolute links, relative links, and root-relative links. We'll cover these in the sections that follow, and you'll see how to create internal page links, style link states in CSS, and work with links and images. We'll also discuss enhanced link accessibility and usability, and link targeting.

Absolute links

The preceding example shows an **absolute link**, sometimes called a **full URL**, which is typically used when linking to external files (i.e., other websites). This type of link provides the entire path to a destination file, including the file transfer protocol, domain name, any directory names, and the file name itself. A longer example is

```
<a href="http://www.wireviews.com/lyrics/instar.html">Instar lyrics</a>
```

In this case, the file transfer protocol is http://, the domain is wireviews.com, the directory is lyrics, and the file name is instar.html.

> *Depending on how the target site's web server has been set up, you may or may not have to include www prior to the domain name when creating this kind of link. Usually it's best to include it, to be on the safe side.*

If you're linking to a website's homepage, you can usually leave off the file name, as in the earlier link to the friends of ED site, and the server will automatically pick up the default document (assuming one exists), which can be index.html, default.htm, index.php, index.asp, or some other name, depending on the server type. However, adding a trailing slash after the domain is beneficial (such as http://www.wireviews.com/).

Relative links

A relative link is one that locates a file in relation to the current document. Taking the Wireviews example, if we were on the instar.html page, located inside the lyrics directory, and we wanted to link back to the homepage via a relative link, we would write

```
<a href="../index.html">Wireviews homepage</a>
```

The index.html file name is preceded by ../, which tells the web browser to move up one directory prior to looking for index.html. Moving in the other direction is done in the same way as with absolute links: by preceding the file name with the path. Therefore, to get from the homepage back to the instar.html page we write

```
<a href="lyrics/instar.html">Instar lyrics</a>
```

In some cases, you need to combine both methods. For instance, this website has HTML documents in both the lyrics and reviews folders. To get from the instar.html lyrics page to a review, you have to go up one level, and then down into the relevant directory to locate the file:

```
<a href="../reviews/alloy.html">Alloy review</a>
```

Root-relative links

Root-relative links work in a similar way to absolute links, but from the root of the website. They ensure you point to the relevant document without your having to type an absolute link or mess around with relative links. For instance, regardless of how many directories deep you are in the Wireviews website, a root-relative link to the homepage always looks like this:

```
<a href="/index.html">Homepage</a>
```

And a link to the `instar.html` page within the `lyrics` directory always looks like this:

```
<a href="/lyrics/instar.html">Instar lyrics</a>
```

The initial forward slash tells the browser to start the path to the file from the root of the current website.

> All paths in href attributes must contain forward slashes only. Some software—notably some by Microsoft—both creates and permits backward slashes (i.e., `lyrics\ wire\154.html`), but this is nonstandard and does not work in non-Microsoft web browsers.

Internal page links

Along with linking to other documents, it's possible to link to another point in the same web page. This is handy for things like a FAQ (frequently asked questions) list, enabling the visitor to jump directly to an answer and then back to the list of questions.

Creating such a system is simple. For a list of questions, we can have something like this:

```
<ul id="questions">
  <li><a href="#answer1">Question one</a></li>
  <li><a href="#answer2">Question two</a></li>
  <li><a href="#answer3">Question three</a></li>
</ul>
```

Later on in the document, the first two answers might look like this:

```
<p id="answer1">The answer to question 1!</p>
<p><a href="#questions">Back to questions</a></p>

<p id="answer2">The answer to question 2!</p>
<p><a href="#questions">Back to questions</a></p>
```

In each case, the link href value is prefixed by a hash sign (#). When the link is clicked, the web page jumps to the element with the relevant id value. Therefore, clicking the Question one link, which has an href value of #answer1, jumps to the paragraph with the id value of answer1. Clicking the Back to questions link, which has an id value of #questions, jumps back to the list, because the unordered list element has an id of questions.

> *It's worth bearing in mind that the page only jumps directly to the linked element if there's enough room underneath it. If the target element is at the bottom of the web page, you'll see it plus a browser window height of content above.*

Backward compatibility/fragment identifiers

Note that obsolete browsers such as Netscape 4 often don't understand this system when working solely with the id attribute. Instead, you have to use a **fragment identifier**, which is an anchor tag with a name attribute, but no href attribute. For instance, a fragment identifier for the first answer is

```
<p><a id="answer1" name="answer1">Answer 1!</a></p>
```

The reason for "doubling up," using both the name and id attributes, is because the former is on borrowed time in web specifications, and it should therefore only be used for backward compatibility.

Top of page links

Internal page links are sometimes used to create a Back to top link, which is useful for navigating lengthy pages and returning to the top of the document, which usually houses the navigation. The problem here is that the most common internal linking method actually fails in the majority of web browsers.

```
<a href="#top">Back to top</a>
```

You've likely seen the previous sort of link countless times, but unless you're using Internet Explorer for Windows, it's as dead as a dodo. There are various workarounds, though, one of which is to include a fragment identifier at the top of the document. At the foot of the web page we have the Back to top link shown previously, and at the top of the web page we place the fragment identifier:

```
<a id="top" name="top"></a>
```

This technique isn't without its problems, though. Some browsers totally ignore empty elements such as this (some web designers therefore populate the element with a single space); it's tricky to get the element right at the top of the page and not to interfere with subsequent content; and, if you're working with XHTML Strict, it's not valid to have an inline element on its own, outside of a block element, such as p or div. A potential solution is to nest the fragment identifier within a block element, and then style the block element to sit at the top-left of the web page.

HTML:

```
<div id="topOfPageAnchor">
<a id="top" name="top"> </a></div>
```

CSS:

```
div#topOfPageAnchor {
position: absolute;
top: 0;
left: 0;
height: 0;
}
```

Setting the div's height to 0 means it takes up no space and is therefore not displayed; setting its positioning to absolute means it's outside the normal flow of the document, so it doesn't affect subsequent page content. You can test this by setting the background color of a following element to something vivid—it should sit tight to the edge of the browser window edges.

Another common solution to the Top of page link problem is to use JavaScript. You should be wary of using JavaScript for essential web page elements, though, because not everyone surfs the Web with JavaScript on (according to estimates, between one in ten and one in twenty turn it off). However, by combining two methods, we can create a catchall (well, "catch nearly all") solution:

```
<a href="#top" onclick="javascript: scrollTo(0,0);">Top of page</a>
```

Included is the standard link to #top, which works fine in Internet Explorer for Windows. Also included is some very simple JavaScript:

```
onclick="javascript: scrollTo(0,0);"
```

This is pretty self-explanatory: upon an onclick event (i.e., when you click the link), the page scrolls to location 0,0, which is the top-left corner.

> JavaScript is case sensitive, so ensure that you are careful when writing it. And when working in XHTML, JavaScript event handlers must be all lowercase (so onclick, not onClick).

As a slight extension to this, it's possible to add some JavaScript that upon a mouseover event (the cursor hovering over the link) updates the status text, and upon the mouseout event (the cursor moving off the link) returns the status to a blank state.

```
<a href="#top" onclick="javascript: scrollTo(0,0);"
↪onmouseover="window.status='Return to the top of the page'; return true;"
↪onmouseout="window.status='';">Top</a>
```

Again, the JavaScript is pretty obvious and can be repurposed for any link. Note that you need to be consistent with regard to quote marks:

```
onmouseover="window.status='Return to the top of the page'; return true;"
```

Here, the onmouseover value is enclosed in double quotes and the nested value in single quotes. Using double quotes on both breaks the script, terminating it early. (It's possible to swap the use of double and single quotes. As mentioned, just be consistent.) Likewise, the onmouseout window.status value is simply nothing within two single quotes. It is *not* a single double quote!

Link states

By default, links are displayed underlined and in blue when viewed in a web browser. However, links have four states, and their visual appearance varies depending on the current state of the link. The four states are

- link: The link's standard state, before any action has taken place
- visited: The link's state after having been clicked
- hover: The link's state while the mouse cursor is over it
- active: The link's state while being clicked

visited and active also have a default appearance. The former is displayed in purple and the latter in red. Both are underlined.

If every site adhered to this default scheme, it would be easier to find where you've been and where you haven't on the Web. However, most designers prefer to dictate their own color schemes rather than having blue and purple links peppering their designs. In my view, this is fine. Despite what some usability gurus claim, most web users these days probably don't even know what the default link colors are, and so hardly miss them.

In HTML, you can set custom colors for the link, active, and visited states via the link, alink, and vlink attributes of the body element. These attributes are deprecated, though, and should be avoided. This is a good thing, because you need to define them in the body element of every page of your site, which is a tiresome process—even more so if they later need changing—and, as you might have guessed, it's easier to define link states in CSS.

Defining link states with CSS

CSS has advantages over the obsolete HTML method of defining link states. You gain control over the hover state and can do far more than just edit the state colors—although that's what we're going to do first.

The default link state is defined by using a tag selector:

```
a {
color: #3366cc;
}
```

In this example, all links are turned to a medium blue. Individual states can be defined by using **pseudo-class selectors** (so called because they have the same effect as applying a class, even though no class is applied to the element):

```
a:link {
color: #3366cc;
}
a:visited {
color: #666699;
}
a:hover {
color: #0066ff;
}
a:active {
color: #cc00ff;
}
```

The difference between "a" and "a:link"

Many designers don't realize the subtle difference between the selectors a and a:link in CSS. Essentially, the a selector styles all anchors, but a:link styles only those that are clickable links (i.e., those that include an href attribute) that have not yet been visited. This means that, should you have a site with a number of fragment identifiers, you can use the a:link selector to style clickable links only, avoiding styling fragment identifiers, too. (This avoids the problem of fragment identifiers taking on underlines.) However, if you define a:link and not a, you then need to define the visited, hover, and active states, too, otherwise they will appear in their default appearances.

Correctly ordering link states

The various states have been defined in a very specific order in previous examples: link, visited, hover, active. This is because certain states override others, and those "closest" to the link on the web page take precedence.

It makes sense for the link to be a certain color when you hover over it, and then a different color on the active state (when clicked). However, if you put the hover and active states in the other order (active, hover), you may not see the active one when the link is clicked. This is because you're still hovering over the link even when you click it.

> A simple way of remembering the state order is to think of the words "**love**, **hate**": **l**ink, **v**isited, **h**over, **a**ctive.

Editing link styles using CSS

Along with changing link colors, CSS enables you to style links just like any other piece of text. You can define specific fonts; edit padding, margins, and borders; change the font weight and style; and also amend the standard link underline, removing it entirely if you wish (by setting the text-decoration property to none).

```
a:link {
color: #3366cc;
font-weight: bold;
text-decoration: none;
}
```

Removing the standard underline is still controversial, even in these enlightened times, and causes endless (and rather tedious) arguments among web designers. My view is that it can be okay to do so, but with some caveats.

If you remove the standard underline, ensure your links stand out from the surrounding copy in some other way. Having your links in the same style and color as other words *and* not underlined is, quite frankly, stupid (that is, unless you don't want people to find the links and click them, or you want them to guess—perhaps for a children's game or educational site).

Just using a different color may not be enough—after all, a significant proportion of the population has some form of color blindness. A commonly quoted figure for color blindness in Western countries is 8%, with the largest affected group being white males (the worldwide figure is lower, at approximately 4%). Therefore, a change of color (to something fairly obvious) *and* a change of font weight to bold often does the trick.

Whatever your choice, be consistent—don't have links change style on different pages of the site. Also, it's useful to reinforce the fact that links are links by bringing back the underline on the hover state.

The example shown to the right is from the Snub Communications website, and it works in the way outlined previously. Links are bold and orange, making them stand out from surrounding text. On the hover state, the link darkens to gray and the standard underline returns. This is achieved by setting text-decoration to underline in the a:hover declaration. Note that even when presented in grayscale, such as in this book, these two states can be distinguished from surrounding text.

Multiple link states: The cascade

A common problem web designers come up against is multiple link styles within a document. I know, I know—I just told you to be consistent. But there are very specific occasions when it's okay to have different link styles. One of these times is for site navigation. Web users are quite happy with navigation bar links differing from standard inline links. Other occasions that spring to mind are for a web page's footer, where links are often displayed in a smaller font than that of the other web page copy, and for areas where background colors are different and the standard link color wouldn't stand out (although in such situations it would perhaps be best to amend either the background or your default link colors).

Some designers apply a class to every link they want to have a style that's not the default, but that method is little better than mucking around with font tags—you end up with loads of inline junk that can't be easily amended at a later date. Instead, by the careful use of divs (with unique ids) on the web page and contextual selectors in CSS, we can rapidly style links for each section of the web page.

For instance, the following is a basic page content structure. There are three divs: navigation, content, and footer. The first houses an unordered list that forms the basis of the navigation bar. The second is the content area, which has an inline link within a paragraph. The third is the footer, which is commonly used to repeat the navigation bar, albeit in a simpler manner.

```
<div id="navigation">
  <ul>
    <li><a href="index.html">Homepage</a></li>
    <li><a href="products.html">Products</a></li>
    <li><a href="contact_details.html">Contact details</a></li>
  </ul>
</div>

<div id="content">
  <p>Hello there. Our new product is a <a href="banjo.html">fantastic
➥banjo</a>!</p>
</div>

<div id="footer">
  <a href="index.html">Homepage</a> | <a href="products.html">Products</a> |
➥<a href="contact_details.html">Contact details</a>
</div>
```

This isn't the most feature-packed web page in the world, but it's perfect for this example. Using contextual selectors, we style the link and hover states for links within the navigation area. As mentioned earlier, the hover state returns the default underline that's turned off in the link state:

```
#navigation a:link {
font-weight: bold;
font-size: 200%;
text-decoration: none;
color: #666666;
}

#navigation a:hover {
text-decoration: underline;
}
```

We then set the default link style:

```
a:link {
font-weight: bold;
color: #aaaaaa;
}
```

And finally, we use a contextual selector to style the footer links (which are commonly the same as those within the general page body, but smaller, hence only defining the font-size property):

```
#footer a {
font-size: 80%;
}
```

And there we have it: three different link styles on the same page, without messing around with classes.

However, as you can see from the screenshot, if we don't explicitly state a value for a property, the ones from the standard link styles (a:link, a:visited, a:hover, and a:active) are used. This explains the color and font weight of the footer links (gray and bold, respectively), despite us not explicitly defining them in the rules created earlier.

This sort of thing trips up a lot of designers, so take care when working with numerous link styles. For a second example, if you set the active link state background color to red (as in the following CSS), all links on the page—including those in the navigation and footer divs—have a red background when clicked.

```
a:active {
background-color: red;
}
```

This can be overridden by explicitly setting the background color in the relevant CSS rule(s), such as

```
#navigation a:active {
background-color: transparent;
}
```

Also remember that if you define a:link, but not a (as just shown), there is no default for undefined states. Clicking one of the navigation links invokes the visited state, which we haven't defined. This means the links appear in their default state: purple, underlined, and in the default size and font. This is most obvious in the visited navigation link, which is now significantly smaller than the other navigation links (see right).

Therefore, in addition to what we've done so far, we must define all states in each context or the a selector for each style of link we intend to have on the page (i.e., #navigation a, a, and so on).

Links and images

Although links are primarily text-based, it's possible to wrap anchor tags around an image, thereby turning it into a link:

```
<a href="a_link.html"><img src="linked_image.gif" width="40" height="40" /></a>
```

Most Windows-based browsers border linked images with whatever link colors have been stated in CSS (or the default colors, if no custom ones have been defined), which looks nasty and can displace other layout elements. There are two ways around this. The most common is to include the border attribute in your images and set it to 0, something that many web design applications tend to do by default.

```
<a href="a_link.html"><img src="linked_image.gif"width="40" height="40"
➥border="0" /></a>
```

However, this is deprecated, so it's best to use a CSS contextual selector to define images within links as having no border:

```
a img {
border: 0;
}
```

Additionally, you can set a border in CSS for the preceding rule and then use a pseudo-class selector to set a hover state that changes the border color (as we did earlier for links). This can be used (when appropriate) to help users to differentiate those images that are links from those that are not.

In any case, you must always have usability and accessibility at the back of your mind when working with image-based links. With regard to usability, is the image's function obvious? Plenty of websites use icons instead of straightforward text-based navigation, resulting in frustrated users if the function of each image isn't obvious. People don't want to learn what each icon is for, and they'll soon move on to competing sites. With regard to accessibility, remember that images cannot be increased in size (unless you're using Opera), so if an image-based link has text within it, ensure it's big enough to read easily. Wherever possible, offer a text-based alternative to image-based links, and never omit alt attributes. Therefore, the example from earlier becomes

```
<a href="a_link.html"><img src="linked_image.gif"width="40" height="40"
➥alt="purpose of link" /></a>
```

Here, I've placed a subtle hint for you regarding alt text content: when linking images, alt text should provide an idea of the image's *function*, and not merely what the image actually depicts. For instance, if using a logo to link to your homepage, don't set the alt text as logo; instead, set it as Back to homepage.

Image maps

Image maps enable you to define multiple links within a single image. There are both server-side and client-side versions of image maps. Server-side image maps are obsolete, and even client-side ones should generally be avoided, because they can cause accessibility problems. However, they occasionally prove useful. For instance, the Met Office website at www.met-office.gov.uk uses image maps to enable users to click a map of the UK and find the weather forecast for their region (see right).

Crown Copyright Met Office

5

Regardless of the complexity of the image and the defined regions, the method of creating an image map remains the same. Here's the image we're going to turn into an image map:

The image is added to the web page in the usual way, but with the addition of a usemap attribute, whose value must be preceded by a hash sign (#).

```
<img src="shapes.gif" alt="Shapes" width="398" height="398" border="0"
➥usemap="#shapes" />
```

The value of the usemap attribute must correlate with the name and id values of the associated map element. Note that the name attribute is only required for backward compatibility, whereas the id attribute is mandatory.

```
<map id="shapes" name="shapes">
</map>
```

Because the map element isn't displayed, it can be placed anywhere in the HTML document. On the rare occasions I use image maps, I place the map element under the relevant image (or its containing block element), but other designers group map elements at the end of the document, after all other content.

The map element acts as a container for specifications regarding the map's active areas, which are added as area elements.

```
<map name="shapes">
  <area shape="rect" coords="29,27,173,171" href="square.html"
➥alt="Squares page" />
  <area shape="circle" coords="295,175,81" href="circle.html"
➥alt="Circles page" />
  <area shape="poly" coords="177,231,269,369,84,369" href="triangle.html"
➥alt="Triangles page" />
</map>
```

Each of the preceding area elements has a shape attribute that corresponds to the intended active link area. The first, rect, defines a rectangular area, and the coords (coordinates) attribute contains two pairs that define the top-left and bottom-right corners in terms of pixel values (which you either take from your original image or guess, should you have amazing pixel-perfect vision). The circle value is used to define a circular area. Of the three values within the coords attribute, the first two define the horizontal and vertical position of the circle's center, and the third defines the radius. Finally, the poly value enables you to define as many coordinate pairs as you wish, enabling you to define active areas for complex and irregular shapes. In this example, three pairs define each corner of the triangle. In the Met Office's map of the UK, the county shapes are complex, thereby necessitating many pairs of values.

> Creating image maps is a notoriously tedious process, and it's one of the few occasions when I strongly advise using a visual web design tool, if you have one handy. However, take care not to overlap defined regions—this is easy to do, and it can cause problems with regard to each link's active area.

Enhanced link accessibility and usability

We've already looked at accessibility and usability concerns during this chapter, so we'll now briefly run through a few attributes that can be used with anchors (and some with area elements) to enhance your web page links.

The title attribute

Regular users of Internet Explorer for Windows may be familiar with its annoying (or helpful, depending on your opinion) habit of popping up alt text as a tooltip. This has encouraged web designers to wrongly fill alt text with explanatory copy for those links that require an explanation, rather than using the alt text for a succinct overview of the image's content or functional purpose. Should you require a pop-up, add a title attribute to your anchor ele-

ment. The majority of web browsers display its value when the link is hovered over for a couple of seconds (see right), although some older browsers, such as Netscape 4, don't provide this functionality.

```
<area title="This is a square. No, really." shape="rect"
➥coords="29,27,173,171" href="square.html" alt="Squares page" />
```

Behavior varies slightly between browsers. Although Firefox and Opera display the title attribute value when it's added to area elements, Internet Explorer for Windows doesn't (although the Mac version does). Opera goes further, displaying the link location.

Of course, this is kind of a moot point, anyway—if you really need to explain a link (or an area within an image map), you're not doing your job as a designer properly. For reinforcement or clarification, title attribute text can be of use, but it should never be the sole means of relaying information.

Using accesskey and tabindex

I've bundled these two attributes because they have similar functions—that is, enabling keyboard access to various areas of the web page. Most browsers enable you to use the Tab key to cycle through links, although if you end up on a web page with dozens of links, this can be a soul-destroying experience. (And before you say "So what?", throw your mouse out of the window and then try using the Web. Many web users cannot use a mouse. You don't have to be severely disabled or elderly to be in such a position either—something as common as repetitive strain injury affects plenty of people, both young and old.)

The accesskey attribute can be added to anchor and area elements. It assigns an access key to the link. In tandem with your platform's assigned modifier key (ALT for Windows and CTRL for Mac), you press the key to highlight or activate the link, depending on how the browser you're using works.

```
<a href="contact_details.html" accesskey="c">Contact us [c]</a>
```

The attribute's value must be a single character, and it's best to stick to standard key characters. Generally, providing at least the main navigation of the site with an access key per link is a good idea. If possible, ensure things remain intuitive by making the access key the first letter of the link's name and, should you use anything more complex, place a full list of access keys used on an accessibility page.

The tabindex attribute works in a similar way. Simply define the attribute's value as anything from 0 (which excludes the element from the tabbing order, which can be useful) to 32767 and its place in the tab order is defined, although if you have 32,767 tabbable elements on your web page, you really do need to go back and reread the earlier advice on information architecture (see Chapter 3). Note that tab orders needn't be consecutive, so it's wise to use tabindex in steps of ten, so you can later insert extra ones without renumbering everything.

Not all browsers enable tabbing to links, and others require that you amend some preferences to activate this function. It's also worth noting that tabindex comes in handy when working with forms, as we'll see in Chapter 10.

Link targeting

From accessibility enhancements to something of an accessibility snafu. **Link targeting** is extremely popular, but I don't recommend it. The target attribute can be added to anchor and area elements. Its value specifies the name of the window (or frame; see Chapter 9) that the link should be displayed in. A popular value is _blank, which opens the target document in a new, blank web browser window.

If you're scratching your head and thinking "So what?" I am well aware that this is common practice. Some argue that opening external links in a new window is beneficial, because it enables users to look at external content and then return to your site. However, what it actually does is take control of the browser *away* from users (after all, if they want to open content in a new window, they can do so using keyboard commands and/or contextual menus). More important, opening documents in new windows breaks

5

the history path. For many, this might not be a huge issue, but for those navigating the Web via a screen reader, pop-ups are a menace. New content opens up, is deemed to not be of interest, and the Back function is invoked. But this is a new window, with its own *blank* history. Gnashing of teeth ensues.

There are exceptions to this rule—notably when using frames, as you'll see in Chapter 9—but in general it's best to avoid target. The W3C agrees: although the target attribute is valid when working with XHTML Transitional, it's not when using XHTML Strict.

Links and JavaScript

Although we've used a little JavaScript during this chapter, we're going to work through some slightly more advanced scripts in this section, to show some methods of integrating JavaScript and links to provide web pages with enhanced interactivity and functionality. As mentioned earlier, though, always provide a non-JavaScript backup to essential content for those who choose to surf the Web with JavaScript disabled. In all cases, JavaScript can be added either to external JavaScript files attached to your HTML documents (which is the preferred method; see the section "Attaching favicons and JavaScript" in Chapter 2) or in a script element within the head of the HTML page:

```
<script type="text/javascript">
// <![CDATA[

(script goes here)

// ]]>
</script>
```

Specifically, we'll look at pop-up windows, swapping images using JavaScript, and toggling div visibility with JavaScript.

Pop-up windows

I imagine at least one person just threw this book out of the window upon seeing pop-up windows as a heading, but they really should have read on a bit. I'm not going to sit here advocating pop-up windows. They're mostly a serious pain in the backside, especially when automated, and they have the same problems as with the new, blank browser windows that I was moaning about earlier (except many JavaScript pop-ups also remove things like browser controls).

However, there are some occasions when pop-up windows can be useful. For instance, if you want to provide a user with brief access to terms and conditions without interrupting the checkout process, you might open the terms in a new window. Many portfolio sites also use pop-up windows to display larger versions of images (although we'll later see a much better method of creating an online gallery).

Should you require a pop-up window of your very own, the JavaScript is simple:

```
function newWindow()
{
window.open("location.html");
}
```

And this HTML calls the script using the onclick attribute:

```
<a href="#" onclick="newWindow()">Open a new window!</a>
```

Creating a system to open windows with varied URLs requires only slight changes to both script and HTML. The script changes to this:

```
function newWindow(webURL)
{
window.open(webURL);
}
```

and the HTML changes to this:

```
<a href="#" onclick="newWindow('location_one.html');">Open location one in a new
➥window!</a>
<a href="#" onclick="newWindow('location_two.html');">Open location two in a new
➥window!</a>
```

Note how the target location is now within the single quotes of the onclick value. This could be any file name, and the link type can be absolute, relative, or root-relative.

Controlling pop-up windows

By using the script so far, the pop-up windows open in whatever state the browser currently has set (usually that of the most recently closed window), but you may want to control the settings of a pop-up window, along with its name, so it can be targeted. To do so, the script needs to be amended, as follows:

```
function newWindow(webURL)
{
var newWin = window.open(webURL,"new_window","toolbar,location,directories,
➥status,menubar,scrollbars,resizable,copyhistory,width=300,height=300");
newWin.focus();
}
```

The values within the set of quotes that begin "toolbar, location..." enable you to set the pop-up window's dimensions and appearance. There must be no white space in the features list, and it must all be on one line. Most of the items are self-explanatory, but

5

some that may not be are location, which defines whether the browser's address bar is visible, and directories, which defines whether secondary toolbars such as the links bar are visible. Note that if you specify one or more of these, any you don't specify will be turned off—therefore, you must specify *all* the features you want in the pop-up window.

Now, a word of warning: as alluded to earlier, having control of the web browser wrenched away from them makes some users want to kick a puppy. Therefore, don't use JavaScript to pop up windows without the user knowing that's going to happen. Don't create a site that automatically pops up a window and removes the window controls. And don't start any spurious arguments regarding aesthetics, because there are no real reasons for using pop-up windows in the aforementioned manner, but there are plenty of counterarguments, such as taking control from the user, the general annoyance factor, and so on. Finally, there are methods for forcing pop-up windows to full screen, but that also makes users want to pull teeth. Not only does this take control away from users, but it means the new pop-up window covers up everything else that's onscreen—irritating for the many people who don't surf the Web at full screen, and who work with several browser windows visible at once.

Swapping images using JavaScript

I mentioned earlier that we would explore a better way of creating an online gallery. Instead of using pop-up windows when thumbnails are clicked, we're going to use JavaScript to swap out an image that's on the web page, replacing it with another. Before we begin, we require three full-size images (which have the same dimensions, because it makes things a whole lot easier and the page looks better) and three thumbnail versions.

Exercise: Creating an online gallery

1. **Add the script**. The JavaScript that drives the swappable images is straightforward:

```
function swapPhoto(photoSRC) {
document.images.imgPhoto.src = "assets/" + photoSRC;
}
```

As stated earlier, JavaScript should be added to an external JavaScript document linked to your HTML (see the section in Chapter 2 titled "Attaching favicons and JavaScript") or to a script element within the head of your HTML. Be aware of the case-sensitive nature of JavaScript and also the path to the images, which is set here as assets/.

2. **Add the main image**. This requires an id attribute (and a name attribute, if you're maintaining backward compatibility) that correlates with the one provided in step 1 (imgPhoto). Leave off the height and/or width attributes if your images have varied dimensions.

```
<img src="assets/dogs_1.jpg" width="400" height="300" id="imgPhoto"
➥name="imgPhoto" alt="Main photo" />
```

3. Add thumbnails. In each case, the swapPhoto value is the file name of the image to be loaded. Remember that the path to the images was defined in step 1, so it's not needed here.

```
<a href="javascript:swapPhoto('dogs_1.jpg')"><img src="assets/thumbnail_1.jpg"
➥alt="thumbnail" width="100" height="75" /></a>

<a href="javascript:swapPhoto('dogs_2.jpg')"><img src="assets/thumbnail_2.jpg"
➥alt="thumbnail" width="100" height="75" /></a>

<a href="javascript:swapPhoto('dogs_3.jpg')"><img src="assets/thumbnail_3.jpg"
➥alt="thumbnail" width="100" height="75" /></a>
```

And that's all there is to it. The solution is elegant and doesn't require pop-up windows. Instead, users can see thumbnails on the same page as the main image, making navigation through the portfolio that much easier. Of course, users must have JavaScript turned on for this functionality, so if the images are essential, you should provide an alternate means of accessing them, too. This can be done by using an ordinary file as the value of the href attribute, and then by using return false to prevent the page from being called in JavaScript-enabled browsers. For example, the first link in step 3 can therefore be amended to the following:

```
<a href="dogs_1.html" onclick="swapPhoto('dogs_1.jpg'); return false">
```

149

Toggling div visibility with JavaScript

The DOM enables you to access and dynamically control various aspects of a web page, and this allows you to use a nifty little trick to toggle the visibility of divs. This trick has numerous uses, from providing a method of hiding "spoiler" content unless someone wants to see it, to various navigation-oriented uses.

Exercise: Setting up a div toggler

1. **Add the script**. The script in this case can be copied verbatim and requires no editing. Again, if you want to use the script on multiple pages, it's best to add it to your external JavaScript document rather than the head of any web pages. Unlike previous JavaScript examples in this book, this method is not backward compatible; therefore, it doesn't work in obsolete web browsers.

```
function swap(targetId){

   if (document.getElementById)
        {
        target = document.getElementById(targetId);

            if (target.style.display == "none")
                {
                target.style.display = "block";
                }

            else
                {
                target.style.display = "none";
                }

        }
}
```

2. **Add a link**. A toggle link looks like this:

```
<div><a href="#" title="Toggle section" onclick="swap('hiddenDiv');return
➥false;">Toggle div!</a>
</div>
```

The value within single quotes—hiddenDiv—is the id value of the div that this link toggles.

3. **Add the div to be toggled**. Here is the div mentioned in step 2—note the id value. You can also see that an inline style attribute is included. This is required if the div is initially to be hidden. Don't put this style elsewhere (an external style sheet or the head of the document), otherwise the div toggler won't work.

```
<div id="hiddenDiv" style="display: none;"><p>Hello!</p>
</div>
```

In the screenshots (see right), CSS has been used to color the div's background, to make more obvious what's going on when the link is clicked.

A combination of the previous two exercises can be seen in action at the Images from Iceland website: www.snubcommunications.com/iceland. This site expands on the div toggler by also toggling the arrow images when a section is toggled, and it shows what you can do with some fairly straightforward JavaScript, some decent photographs, and a bit of imagination. With a little lateral thinking, you can apply this knowledge to the list-based navigation discussed in the next part of the chapter, which will enable you to toggle various parts of a navigation bar.

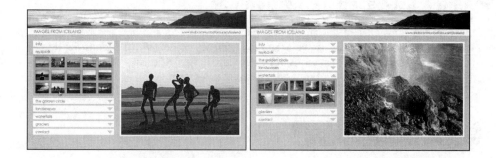

Creating navigation bars

The chapter has so far concentrated on inline navigation, so we'll now turn our attention to navigation bars. Before getting immersed in the technology, you need to decide what names you're going to use. When designing the basic structure of the site, content should have been grouped into categories, and this is often defined by what the user can do with it. It therefore follows that navigation bar links tend to one of the following:

- Action based (buy now, contact us, read our history)
- Site audience (end users, resellers, employees)
- Topic based (news, services, contact details)

Wherever possible, keep to one of the preceding categories rather than mixing topics and actions. This sits easier with readers. Navigation links should also be succinct, to the point, and appropriate to the brand and tone of the website.

In this section, we'll cover using lists for navigation, styling list-based navigation bars, working with inline lists, and creating graphical navigation bars with rollover graphics.

Lists for navigation

Think back to what we've covered to this point about semantic markup. Of the HTML elements that exist, which is the most appropriate for a navigation bar? If you said "A table," go to the back of the class. Using tables for navigation bars might be a rapid way of getting them up and running, but it's not structurally sound. Instead, we see navigation bars as a list of links to various pages on the website. It therefore follows that HTML lists are a logical choice to mark up navigation bars.

When creating the initial pass of the website, just create the list as it is, along with all the associated pages, and let people play around with the bare-bones site. This enables users to get a feel for its structure, without getting distracted by content, colors, and design. However, sooner or later, you're going to want to make that list look a little fancier.

Styling a list-based navigation bar

Much of the remainder of this chapter is concerned with CSS and how it can be used to style lists. From a plain HTML list, you can rapidly create exciting visual designs—and ones that are easy to update, both in terms of content and design. After all, adding another navigation link is usually just a matter of adding another list item.

Exercise: Using CSS to style a list

1. **Create a list**. By using nested lists, you can provide the navigation bar with a hierarchical structure (and you can style each level in CSS). In this example, the list has two levels. (Refer to Chapter 3 for an overview of correctly formatting lists.) This list is nested within a div with an id value of navigation, which we'll later take advantage of by using contextual selectors.

```
<div id="navigation">
<ul>
  <li><a href="#">Section one</a>
    <ul>
      <li><a href="#">A link to a page</a></li>
      <li><a href="#">A link to a page</a></li>
      <li><a href="#">A link to a page</a></li>
      <li><a href="#">A link to a page</a></li>
    </ul>
  </li>
  <li><a href="#">Section two</a>
    <ul>
      <li><a href="#">A link to a page</a></li>
      <li><a href="#">A link to a page</a></li>
```

- Section one
  - A link to a page
  - A link to a page
  - A link to a page
  - A link to a page
- Section two
  - A link to a page
  - A link to a page
  - A link to a page
  - A link to a page
- Section three
  - A link to a page
  - A link to a page
  - A link to a page
  - A link to a page

```
        <li><a href="#">A link to a page</a></li>
        <li><a href="#">A link to a page</a></li>
      </ul>
    </li>
    <li><a href="#">Section three</a>
      <ul>
        <li><a href="#">A link to a page</a></li>
        <li><a href="#">A link to a page</a></li>
        <li><a href="#">A link to a page</a></li>
        <li><a href="#">A link to a page</a></li>
      </ul>
    </li>
  </ul>
</div>
```

> In this example, all href attributes have a value of #. This is a quick way of creating a "dummy" link, and it doesn't distract from what you're working on by using a load of fake web page file names.

2. **Style the page body**. You now set the background color to gray, add some padding, and set the font size to small:

```
body {
background-color: #aaaaaa;
padding: 20px;
margin: 0;
font-size: small;
}
```

3. **Style the list**. The unordered list itself needs to be styled, so you'll remove default items like bullet points, margins, and padding. This is done via the following rule, which also defines a set width, font, and font size:

```
#navigation ul {
list-style-type: none;
padding: 0;
margin: 0;
width: 140px;
font-family: Arial, Helvetica, sans-serif;
font-size: 100%;
}
```

4. **Style list items**. For the benefit of Opera, you also set the list item margins to 0:

```
#navigation li {
margin: 0;
}
```

5. **Style buttons**. You'll use a contextual selector to style links within the navigation div (i.e., the links within this list). These styles initially affect the entire list, but you'll later override them for level two links. Therefore, the styles you're working on now are intended only for level one links (which are for sections or categories).

This first set of property/value pairs turns off the default link underline, sets the list items to uppercase, and defines the font weight as bold.

```
#navigation a {
text-decoration: none;
text-transform: uppercase;
font-weight: bold;
}
```

6. **Set button display and padding**. Still within the same rule, set the buttons to display as block, thereby making the entire container an active link (rather than just a link text). Add some padding so the links don't hug the edge of the container.

```
display: block;
padding: 3px 12px 3px 8px;
```

7. **Define colors**. Define the button background and foreground colors, setting the former to gray and the latter to white.

```
background-color: #666666;
color: #ffffff;
```

8. **Use borders for a 3D effect**. Borders can be styled individually. By setting the left and top borders to a lighter shade than the background, and the right and bottom borders to a darker shade, a 3D effect is achieved. (Don't use black and white, because they are too harsh.)

```
border-top: 1px solid #dddddd;
border-right: 1px solid #333333;
border-bottom: 1px solid #333333;
border-left: 1px solid #dddddd;
```

This completes the #navigation a rule.

9. **Define other states**. The hover state is defined by just changing the background color, making it slightly lighter.

```
#navigation a:hover {
background-color: #777777;
}
```

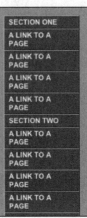

The active state enables you to build on the 3D effect: the padding settings are changed to move the text up and left by 1 pixel, the background and foreground colors are made slightly darker, and the border colors are reversed.

```
#navigation a:active {
padding: 2px 13px 4px 7px;
background-color: #444444;
```

```
color: #eeeeee;
border-top: 1px solid #333333;
border-right: 1px solid #dddddd;
border-bottom: 1px solid #dddddd;
border-left: 1px solid #333333;
}
```

10. **Style page buttons**. The selector `#navigation li li a` enables you to style links within a list item that are themselves within a list item (which happen to be in the navigation div). In other words, you can create a declaration for level two links.

These need to be differentiated from the section links, so you'll set them to lowercase and normal font weight (instead of bold). The padding settings indent these links more than the section links, and the background and foreground colors are different, being black on light gray rather than white on a darker gray.

```
#navigation li li a {
text-decoration: none;
text-transform: lowercase;
font-weight: normal;
padding: 3px 3px 3px 17px;
background-color: #999999;
color: #111111;
}
```

11. **Style page button hover and active states**. This is done in the same way as per the section links, changing colors as appropriate and again reversing the border colors on the active state.

```
#navigation li li a:hover {
background-color: #aaaaaa;
}
```

```
#navigation li li a:active {
padding: 2px 4px 4px 16px;
background-color: #888888;
color: #000000;
border-top: 1px solid #333333;
border-right: 1px solid #dddddd;
border-bottom: 1px solid #dddddd;
border-left: 1px solid #333333;
}
```

The navigation bar is now complete and, as you can see from the following images (which depict, from left to right, the default, hover, and active states), the buttons have a real tactile feel to them. Should this not be to your liking, it's easy to change the look of the navigation bar because everything's styled in CSS. To expand on this design, you could introduce background images for each state, thereby making the navigation bar even more graphical. However, because you didn't simply chop up a GIF, you can easily add and remove items from the navigation bar, just by amending the list created in step 1.

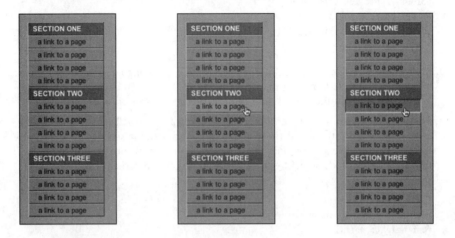

You could take this exercise further by adding a class to the relevant list item on each page of the site that such a navigation bar is used on, thereby providing users with a visual idea of where they are in the site.

Exercise: Adding a toggler

You could also combine this list with the ideas explored in the "Setting up a toggling div" exercise earlier in the chapter. The JavaScript doesn't need changing, so you're just going to make the amendments required to the list created in the previous exercise.

1. **Set up toggle links**. For each of the section links, add an onclick event. The swap value must be unique for each link, so the value for the section two link would be sectionTwoLinks, and so on.

   ```
   <a href="#" onclick="swap('sectionOneLinks');return false;">Section one</a>
   ```

2. **Amend the nested lists**. The start tag for each of the nested lists needs two additional attributes. The first is a unique id with a value correlating with that set in step 1. The second is an inline style attribute, setting display to none (leave this out if you want the lists to be visible by default).

   ```
   <ul id="sectionOneLinks" style="display: none;">
   ```

Take care in ensuring section links correlate with the relevant nested list, otherwise section links may toggle the wrong lists!

The result of this exercise is a list-based navigation bar in which the nested lists can be toggled (thereby providing you with a collapsible navigation bar; see right).

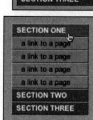

Using inline lists

Although most people use lists to set items vertically, it's possible to create horizontal lists. This might strike you as an odd thing to do, but it can be handy. For instance, if you want to stick to the semantic markup ideas we've been talking about, but require a horizontal navigation bar, you can set the list items to display inline. This example uses the following HTML list, again nested within a div with an id of navigation:

```
<div id="navigation">
  <ul>
    <li><a href="#">Latest news</a></li>
    <li><a href="#">Services</a></li>
    <li><a href="#">Customer support</a></li>
    <li><a href="#">Contact details</a></li>
  </ul>
</div>
```

All we need to set the list to display horizontally (inline) is the following CSS:

```
#navigation li {
display: inline;
}
```

Getting rid of the default bullets, padding, and margins ensures the list displays in the same way across browsers and platforms:

```
#navigation  ul {
list-style-type: none;
padding: 0;
margin: 0;
}
```

Latest news Services Customer support Contact details

As you can see from the preceding screen shot, this is pretty basic, but with some extra CSS definitions it can easily be spiced up:

LATEST NEWS   SERVICES   CUSTOMER SUPPORT   CONTACT DETAILS

> Should you set a background color on an inline list and find white gaps between items, delete the white space between the list tags in the HTML document.

5

Inline lists as breadcrumbs

Inline lists can be handy for creating **breadcrumb** links on complex websites. These are links that show the path you've taken to get to the current document. The markup is the same as in the inline lists example, but with extra padding to the left of each list item, and a nonrepeated background image that creates the familiar arrows:

```
#navigation li {
display: inline;
font: 12px Arial, sans-serif;
padding: 0 10px 0 15px;
background: url(breadcrumb_bullet.gif) left no-repeat;
}

#navigation a {
color: #000000;
}
```

```
>> Home page  >> Reviews  >> Live gigs  >> London, 2004
```

Graphical navigation with rollovers

The final exercise in this chapter concerns navigation with graphical rollovers. The following is a Photoshop mock-up of the navigation bar that we're going to build. (The vertical lines are Photoshop guides, showing the boundary of each button, and are not part of the design.)

By conventional methods, you'd export eight images from Photoshop—two for each link (twelve if you wanted to incorporate an active state). The rollovers would be applied using JavaScript. However, this process has several problems:

- Updating the rollover graphics requires a lot of work, creating and re-exporting up to a dozen new images.
- By default, there is a short pause on the hover and active states while the rollover graphic downloads.

- The hover state and active state pauses can be eradicated by using a preload script, but such scripts often don't work well with all browsers.
- Not everyone surfs the Web with JavaScript turned on.

Instead of using JavaScript, we'll use a little CSS and (drumroll) just one image, which is depicted to the right.

This image is a *single* transparent GIF that includes all three link states: link (the default), hover, and active. (What's depicted is the final image, which should be exported in one piece; this should remain a single image file, and shouldn't be chopped into three different files.) What we can do is use this as a background image for navigation links, and use CSS to display the relevant portion of the image, depending on the link action taking place.

5

As with the majority of examples in this chapter, the navigation is marked up as an unordered list. No formatting of the links of any kind is required—that's all handled by the CSS. We've again placed the list within a div tag that has an id value of navigation, so we can create CSS rules that apply only to lists within that specific div.

Exercise: Using CSS to create a graphical navigation bar

1. **Create the list**. As with previous navigation bars created in this chapter, this one consists of a simple unordered list. In a browser, this looks pretty much like you'd expect: just a plain, unordered, vertical list.

```
<div id="navigation">
  <ul>
    <li><a href="#">Latest news</a></li>
    <li><a href="#">Services</a></li>
    <li><a href="#">Customer support</a></li>
    <li><a href="#">Contact details</a></li>
  </ul>
</div>
```

- Latest news
- Services
- Customer support
- Contact details

2. **Style the list**. As done previously, browser defaults are removed.

```
#navigation ul {
margin: 0px;
padding: 0px;
list-style: none;
}
```

3. **Style list items**. Items within the list are styled to float left and display inline. The background value includes the location of the rollover image, with additional

settings being no-repeat (to stop it from tiling), then left and top, to ensure the relevant portion of the rollover image is seen by default. The margin and padding are set to 0 to override unruly browser defaults.

```
#navigation li {
float: left;
display: inline;
margin: 0px;
padding: 0px;
background: url(assets/shared/rollover.gif) no-repeat left top;
}
```

4. **Style the links**. Because you haven't set dimensions for the links yet, the backgrounds aren't sitting in the right place. You can fix this by using the following rule, which also deals with the text styles you want to put in place.

The padding and height/width settings add up to the dimensions of the area of the background image that you want to show at any one time (185px × 30px—the size of one of the link states). This is because padding is added to the element width—it's not a part of it. If you were to set the width of navigation links to 185px and then add 30px of padding to the left (which is used to indent the text), the links would take up 215px of space.

You'll again set display to block, to make the entire container the active link, thereby making this navigation bar work in the normal manner.

```
#navigation a {
font: bold 13px Arial, Helvetica, sans-serif;
text-transform: uppercase;
color: #ffffff;
text-decoration: none;
display: block;
padding: 7px 0px 0px 30px;
height: 23px;
width: 155px;
}
```

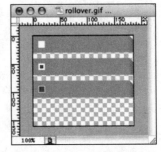

5. **Style other states**. For the hover and active states, you define which portion of the rollover graphic is supposed to be visible. This is done via background-position values. The first of these remains 0px, because you always want to see the image from its far left. The vertical reading depends on where the relevant portion of the image appears in the rollover graphic.

As you can see, the hover state is 40px from the top and the active state is 80px from the top. This means the image needs to be vertically moved –40px and –80px for the hover and active states, respectively.

Therefore, the rules for these states are as follows:

```
#navigation a:hover {
background: url(assets/shared/rollover.gif) 0px -40px;
}

#navigation a:active {
background: url(assets/shared/rollover.gif) 0px -80px;
}
```

The hover and active states are shown in the following images.

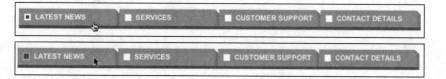

6. **Fix for Internet Explorer 5.5 for Windows**. We get more into browser hacks in Chapter 12, but we'll briefly outline one here. Internet Explorer 5.5 for Windows gets the box model wrong, incorrectly setting padding and borders within defined element dimensions. The navigation bar currently looks like this in that browser:

To deal with Internet Explorer 5.5, the width and height settings need to be the same as the dimensions of the buttons (as opposed to the measurements for compliant browsers, defined in step 4). You can set separate values for Internet Explorer 5.5 by using the box model hack. First, set the width and height for Internet Explorer 5.5 (185px width and 30px height—dimensions identical to those of one state of the rollover graphic). Then add the hack and the correct measurements for compliant browsers (as in step 4).

```
#navigation a {
font: bold 13px Arial, Helvetica, sans-serif;
text-transform: uppercase;
color: #ffffff;
text-decoration: none;
display: block;
padding: 7px 0px 0px 30px;
height: 30px;
width: 185px;
voice-family: "\"}\"";
voice-family:inherit;
height: 23px;
width: 155px;
}
```

The hack is the two voice-family rules. Internet Explorer 5.5 stops reading during the first line (it's fooled into thinking the rule terminates due to the quoted curly bracket); compliant browsers "recover" in the second voice-family line and continue to the end of the rule, with the second set of height and width values overriding the first. Everyone goes home happy—well, almost. Internet Explorer 5.5 sometimes also screws up the case of the links, ignoring the text-transform value. A workaround is to create a second #navigation a rule and put the text-transform property/value pair there:

```
#navigation a {
text-transform: uppercase;
}
```

As you can see, this fixes the navigation bar in Internet Explorer 5.5. Sadly, Internet Explorer 5 for Windows cannot deal with text-transform at all, but it manages to display everything else correctly. Still, it's only a minor thing, and that browser's market share is rapidly reducing anyway. As for obsolete browsers (Netscape 4 et al.), hide the CSS and they'll get a perfectly navigable basic list. Again, everyone goes home happy (and I mean it this time!).

> It's worth noting that many browsers permit text resizing. In such cases, users with extreme setups (text size increased a couple of settings above the default) may end up "losing" the second word of multiple-word links in this example. This will affect a minority of users, but even so, take care to ensure your navigation makes sense even if the final word is missing. For instance, contact details becoming contact still makes sense, as does help desk becoming help; however, customer support becoming customer could be problematic. Despite this issue, this method is still superior to using graphics for each link: it's easier to update, more accessible, and degrades more gracefully in alternate browsers.

Updating a graphical navigation bar

This is an extremely flexible system. Even though it has fixed-width links, it's easy to update (just create a single new rollover graphic and rework the CSS rules—such as the width settings—to accommodate the required number of links). Because there's no JavaScript, it works well with all current browsers, and because the navigation consists of semantic markup, it's logical even in browsers that don't support CSS.

Should you want to have a different image for each link (such as a unique color per tab), use CSS classes. Despite the extra work involved, the system remains beneficial compared to older methods, because there's no JavaScript, there are no preloaders, and you control everything from an external document.

Drop-down menus

A method of navigation expansion—and one that web designers often crave—is drop-down menus. It's a good idea to avoid those created by web design applications, because they tend to be composed of obsolete and invalid code. However, we're not going to create one here, because a perfectly good one exists online. Check out the excellent drop-down menu system from gazingus.org (available from www.gazingus.org/html/ Using_Lists_for_DHTML_Menus.html). It's entirely CSS-based, and although it requires JavaScript to fully function, those who surf without JavaScript are still able to access the top level of each section.

If you do decide to create drop-down menu–based navigation, avoid aping an operating system's menu style, because this may confuse visitors using that operating system and irritate visitors using a rival system. The exception to this rule is if you're creating a site that centers around nostalgia for the days where operating systems used to come on floppy disks. One such site—a Mac OS System 7 look-alike—can be found at http://myoldmac.net/ index-e.htm.

5

Dos and don'ts when designing web navigation

So, that's the end of our navigation chapter. Before we move on to working with layout, here are a few succinct tips regarding designing web navigation.

Do

- Use appropriate types of navigation.
- Provide alternate means of accessing information.
- Ensure links stand out.
- Take advantage of link states to provide feedback for users.
- Get the link state order right (link, visited, hover, active).
- Use accesskey and tabindex attributes.
- Use styled lists for navigation.
- Use CSS for rollovers.

Don't

- Add search boxes just for the sake of it.
- Use deprecated body attributes.
- Style navigation links like normal body copy.
- Use image maps unless absolutely necessary.
- Open new windows from links or use pop-ups.
- Use clunky JavaScript for rollovers.

CHAPTER 6
INTRODUCTION TO LAYOUT

In this chapter

- Looking at layout tips for the Web
- Working with grids and columns
- Examining fixed and liquid design
- Using tables, style sheets, and frames
- Placing elements logically

Layout for the Web

Although recent years have seen various institutions offer web-oriented courses, the fact remains that the majority of web designers out there are not "qualified" per se. What I mean by this is that most have come from some sort of design or technology background related to—but not necessarily a part of—the Web. Therefore, we tend to see print designers moving over to the Web through curiosity or sheer necessity and technologists dipping their toes in the field of design.

This accounts for the most common issues seen in web layouts: many designers coming from print try to shoehorn their knowledge into their website designs, despite the Web being a *very* different medium from print. Conversely, those with no design knowledge lack the basic foundations and often omit design staples. Even those of us who've worked with the Web almost from the beginning *and* who also come from a design or arts background sometimes forget that the best sites tend to be those that borrow the best ideas from a range of media, and then tailor the results to the desired output medium.

In this section, we'll take a brief look at a few layout techniques: grids and boxes, columns, and fixed versus liquid design.

Grids and boxes

Like print-oriented design, the basis of web page design tends to be formed from grids and boxes. Regardless of the underlying technology (commonly tables or CSS), web pages are formed of rectangular areas, which are then populated with content. However, unlike print design, web design tends to be horizontally and vertically oriented, with few, if any, curves. This is largely because of the limitations of technology: although text on a curve is a relatively simple thing to achieve in a desktop publishing application, doing the same thing on the Web is impossible unless you're rendering text as a graphic. Similarly, although areas of rectangular color can easily be defined in CSS, you currently need to use graphics to have curved background areas and shapes.

A good rule of thumb for web design is to keep things relatively simple. Plan the layout on paper prior to going near any design applications, and simplify the structure as much as possible. A typical web page may end up with as few as three or four structural areas (such as masthead, navigation, content, and footer areas), which can then be styled to define their relationship with each other and the page as a whole.

Working with columns

The vast majority of print media makes heavy use of columns. The main reason for this is that the eye finds it much easier to read narrow columns of text rather than paragraphs that span the width of an entire page. However, when working with print, you have a finite and predefined area within which to work and, by and large, the "user" can see the entire page at once. Therefore, relationships between page elements can be created over the entire page, and the eye can rapidly scan columns of text.

On the Web, things aren't so easy. Web pages may span more than the screen height, meaning only the top portion of the page is initially visible. Should a print page be translated directly to the Web, you may find elements lower down the page that are essential to someone's understanding of the content may not be initially visible. Furthermore, if using columns for text and content, you may end up forcing the user to scroll down and up the page several times. Finally, it's almost impossible—due to the variations in output from various browsers and platforms—to ensure text columns are the same length anyway.

Therefore, web designers tend to eschew columns, but let's not be too hasty. It's worth bearing in mind something mentioned earlier: the eye finds it tricky to read wide columns of text. Therefore, it's often good practice to limit the width of body copy on a website to a comfortable reading width. Also, if you have multiple pieces of content that you want the user to be able to access at the same time, columns can come in very handy. This can be seen in the following screenshots from the Snub Communications website.

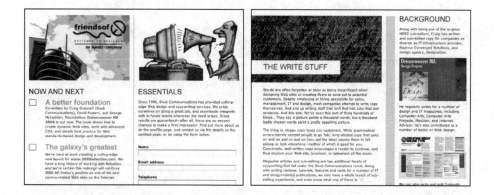

In the first shot (on the left) is the homepage. The two columns enable the reader to view both the latest news and an introduction to the organization. The second image shows part of an inner page, providing an overview of the services offered in the wider, left-hand column, and a brief background on the organization's capabilities in the other. In both cases, the text columns are a comfortable, readable width, and they enable faster access to information than if the page content were placed in a linear, vertical fashion.

Fixed vs. liquid design

As already mentioned in this book, the Web is a unique medium in that end users have numerous different systems for viewing the web page. When designing for print, the dimensions of each design are **fixed**, and although television resolutions are varied (PAL, NTSC, HDTV), those designing for screen work within a fixed frame—and regardless of the size of the screen, the picture content is always the same.

In a similar fashion, it's possible to design fixed-width sites for the Web. The earlier shots of the Snub Communications site are an example of this. Fixed-width sites are particularly beneficial in that they enable you to position elements exactly on a web page. However, because they don't expand with the browser window, fixed-width sites restrict you to designing for the lowest common screen size for your intended audience, meaning those using larger resolutions see an area of blank space (or a background pattern), as shown in the image to the right.

You can get around this limitation by creating a **liquid** web design—one that "stretches" with the web browser window. The benefit of liquid design is that it's irrelevant what resolution the end user's machine has—the design stretches to fit. The drawback is that you have to be mindful when designing that web page elements move, depending on each end user's monitor resolution and/or browser window size. You therefore cannot place elements with pixel-perfect precision.

Generally speaking, largely text-based sites tend to work best with liquid layouts, although you have to take care to ensure the content area is always readable (I've seen numerous liquid sites where the text spans the entire web page width, which is tricky enough to read at 800 × 600, let alone on larger monitor resolutions.) Sites that are largely image-based in nature (such as portfolios, many online magazines, and so on) tend to work better as fixed websites.

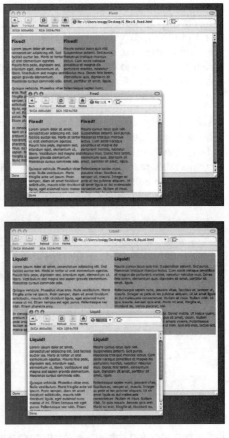

For instance, imagine the Snub Communications site as a liquid design—the images would no longer sit snugly within the columns and would instead end up "lost" among large areas of white space. (Of course, if I were to make Snub Communications a liquid design, I'd rework it considerably, but you get the point.)

Overall, though, there are no hard and fast rules and, despite what some designers might claim, neither fixed nor liquid design is "better" than the alternative. What you need to do is use whatever technique is suitable for each project you work on.

Layout technology: Tables vs. CSS

Unless you're the sort of person who favors very basic web pages, with most elements sitting underneath each other, you'll need to employ some kind of layout technology when designing your web pages. Historically, web designers have tended to use tables for doing this, combined with invisible GIFs (sometimes called **spacers** or **shims**) to stretch table cells to the required size. More recently, designers have increasingly been moving toward CSS as a means of page layout.

With few exceptions, pretty much everything you can do with a table can be done faster, better, and with a greater emphasis on accessibility when using CSS. With content and design separated, it's much easier to tweak or rework a website, because you're editing an external document that controls spacing and positioning, rather than messing around with complex tables. We discuss one of CSS's major benefits in this regard, how it encourages logical element placement, in the next section.

Tables should really be reserved for their original purpose: formatting tabular data. (Some CSS advocates suggest avoiding tables entirely, going on to show how to mark up tabular data with CSS. However, this is just as bad as telling someone to avoid CSS in favor of tables for layout.)

Logical element placement

Besides the ability to rapidly edit CSS-based layouts, the greatest benefit when using CSS is the emphasis on accessibility, partly by encouraging the designer to think about the *structure* of the document, and therefore logically place the elements within the web page (i.e., first comes the masthead, then the navigation, then the content, and so on). Each element is then styled to suit.

The use of CSS for layout instead of tables is one way of working toward this ideal. The logical placement of each element in the web page's structure results in improved document flow. And if you're scratching your head, wondering what on earth I'm talking about, let me explain. A web page should still make sense if you remove *all* formatting and "design" elements. This is how a screen reader sees the page—it simply reads from the top of the HTML page downward. Because of the way table-based layouts are created, most designers aren't concerned with how the document is structured—merely how it looks. Therefore, although one element may follow another *visually* onscreen, that may not be the case when you look at the document's code. (Also, tables tend to encourage superfluous markup, which can also hamper accessibility.) When working with CSS, the structure of the web page isn't compromised.

I realize that you might be sick of hearing about accessibility all the time, partly because it's become a buzzword among designers in recent years. This is largely due to the fact that designers are finally coming to realize not only that discrimination legislation has been around for a number of years in many countries, but also that certain organizations are now willing to take legal action to ensure websites are accessible to all. Although this doesn't affect personal websites, all commercial/service-oriented sites must ensure they at least make an attempt to be accessible.

Coming up

Over the next three chapters, we'll explore layout in depth and expand on the ideas discussed during this brief chapter. The next chapter looks at tables, primarily for the layout of tabular data, incorporating all the various underused tags that aid accessibility. The chapter also touches on general page layout with tables, but points out why this should generally be avoided.

Chapter 8 is this book's main layout chapter, and it provides a general overview of layout with CSS, along with a number of examples. By the end of that chapter, you should feel comfortable with CSS-based layouts and be able to create all manner of layouts by drawing on all the knowledge you've gained so far.

Chapter 9 takes a brief look at the third web layout technology: frames. Because the frames within a frameset are normal HTML pages (consisting of either tables or CSS-based layouts), Chapter 9 focuses mainly on creating the actual frames. Also, because the technology is considered rather dated (apart from under exceptional circumstances), Chapter 9 is succinct.

CHAPTER 7

TABLES: HOW NATURE
(AND THE W3C) INTENDED

In this chapter

- Introducing how tables work
- Using borders, padding, and spacing
- Creating accessible tables
- Enhancing tables with CSS
- Designing tables for web page layout

The great table debate

Tables were initially designed as a means of displaying tabular data online, enabling web designers to rapidly mark up things like price lists, statistical comparisons, specification lists, spreadsheets, charts, forms, and so on (the following example shows a simple table, taken from www.macuser.co.uk).

PRODUCT	SUPPLIER	PRICE	RATING
Canon Bubble Jet i9950	Pixmania.com	£446.00	5*
Canon Bubble Jet i6500	Canon	£291.00	4
Epson Stylus Photo 2100	ebuyer.com	£434.00	4
Epson Stylus Photo 1290	Simply	£273.00	3
HP Designjet 30	Dabs.com	£532.00	3
HP Deskjet 9650	Savastore.com	£329.00	3

The thing is, it wasn't long before web designers realized that you could place any web content within table cells, and this rapidly led to the now common method of chopping up Photoshop layouts and piecing them back together in tables-based web pages, often by using automated tools. CSS should have put an end to that, but plenty of web designers continue to use tables for layout because they're simple to set up—even though they cause problems (see the "Tables for layout" section later in the chapter).

The strong will of CSS advocates, who typically shout that tables are evil, often leads designers to believe that tables should be ditched entirely—however, that's not the case at all. As mentioned, tables have a specific purpose in HTML, and one that's still valid. Therefore, the bulk of this chapter is going to look at tables in the context for which they're intended: the formatting of data. By and large, we're going to leave web page layout until the next chapter, when we talk about CSS layout.

How tables work

In this section, we're going to look at how tables are structured, and some of the table element's attributes, which enable you to define the table's dimensions, borders, and spacing, padding, and alignment of its cells.

Tabular data works via a system of rows and columns, and HTML tables work in the same way. The table element defines the beginning and end of a table. Within the table element are table row elements (<tr></tr>), and nested within those are table cell elements (<td></td>). The actual content is placed inside the td elements. Therefore, a simple table with two rows containing two cells each is created like this:

```
<table>
  <tr><td>Cell one</td><td>Cell two</td></tr>
  <tr><td>Cell three</td><td>Cell four</td></tr>
</table>
```

Always ensure that you include all end tags when working with tables. If you began working with HTML way back in the mid 1990s, you may have learned that it's OK to omit the odd end tag from tables or table cells. However, not only does this result in invalid XHTML, but some browsers won't render tables accurately (or at all) when end tags are omitted.

Adding a border

You can place a border around table cells by using the border attribute and setting its value to 1 or greater. The adjacent example shows how this looks in a web browser.

| Cell one | Cell two |
| Cell three | Cell four |

Cell spacing and cell padding

In addition to amending the border size, it's possible to change the amount of padding within a table's cells, as well as the spacing between all the cells in a table. This is done with the cellpadding and cellspacing attributes, respectively. In the rather extreme example that follows, cellpadding is set to 20, cellspacing to 40, and border to 5, so that each can be differentiated with ease in the subsequent screenshot. As you can see, cellspacing not only affects the spacing between the cells, but also the distance between the cells and the table's edges.

```
<table cellpadding="20" cellspacing="40" border="5">
  <tr><td>Cell one</td><td>Cell two</td></tr>
  <tr><td>Cell three</td><td>Cell four</td></tr>
</table>
```

You might be thinking that design-wise, this example sucks, and you'd be right. The chunk-o-vision 3D border isn't particularly tasteful. Luckily, you can set the border attribute to 0, effectively turning it off, and use CSS to style borders instead (see the "Styling a table" section later on in this chapter). That section also details how to set padding in CSS, too, which provides you with site-wide control over cell padding. CSS also gives you much finer control over the individual elements in a table—whereas the inline HTML attributes impose a one-style-fits-all straightjacket.

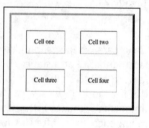

Spanning rows and cells

It's sometimes necessary for data to span multiple rows or columns. This is achieved via the rowspan and colspan attributes, respectively. In the following table, the first row has three cells. However, in the second row, the first cell spans two rows and the second cell spans two columns. This means the second row lacks a third cell, and the third row also only has two cells (whose contents align with the second and third cells of the top row). See the following screenshot of the table to help make sense of this.

```
<table border="1" cellpadding="2">
  <tr>
    <td>A cell</td>
    <td>Another cell</td>
    <td>Yet another cell!</td>
  </tr>
  <tr>
    <td rowspan="2">A cell that spans two rows</td>
    <td colspan="2">A cell that spans two columns</td>
  </tr>
  <tr>
    <td>Another cell</td>
    <td>The last cell</td>
  </tr>
</table>
```

A cell		Another cell	Yet another cell!
A cell that spans two rows		A cell that spans two columns	
		Another cell	The last cell

> In the preceding HTML, the cell elements are indented to make it easier for you to make them out. This wasn't done earlier in the chapter. Either method of writing markup is fine—it's up to you. Note, however, that if you use images within table cells, this extra white space in the HTML sometimes causes layouts to break, and must therefore be deleted.

Take care when spanning rows or columns with a cell, because it's easy to add extra cells accidentally. For instance, in the example above, it would be easy to absentmindedly add a third cell to both the second and third rows—however, doing so appends the extra cells to the end of the table (see the following example), which looks bad, and—more important—makes little structural sense. Also, some screen readers have difficulty handling such data, often assigning the wrong headers to various pieces of data (see the "Accessible tables" section later in the chapter for information on table headers).

A cell		Another cell	Yet another cell!	
A cell that spans two rows		A cell that spans two columns	This shouldn't be here	
		Another cell	The last cell	A wrongly added cell

Setting dimensions and alignment

As you can see from the examples so far, browsers by default set cell sizes to the smallest possible values that are large enough to accommodate the contents and any cell padding settings defined. Although this is suitable for the majority of purposes, designers tend to want more visual control over layouts.

Long-time designers may be well-versed in the practice of using height and width attributes to control table and cell dimensions, but beware. The width attribute is fine to use on table start tags (the possible values of which are: a number, denoting the width in pixels of the table; and a percentage, which is a percentage of the parent element's size). However, the height attribute is nonstandard and fails in the majority of web browsers (in fact, if using an XHTML DTD, it fails in every currently shipping mainstream browser), which might come as something of a shock to those people who enjoy centering content in a browser window.

As for setting widths and heights within table cells, that's something that should be avoided altogether—height and width attributes within table cells are deprecated. You might argue that this is irrelevant—after all, all major browsers support these attributes. Although this is true, deprecated attributes are not guaranteed to be supported in the future. Also, table cells always expand to accommodate the widest or tallest element in a row or column. As a result of this, defining heights and widths is often a futile attempt to control the uncontrollable.

7

Take care when using visual web design applications: many of them add deprecated elements to tables if you manually drag the cells around. Use your favored application's preferences to turn off this feature, otherwise you'll end up with obsolete and redundant markup.

The valign attribute

If you set your table's width to a small value, or if you have a lot of content in one cell and relatively little in an adjacent one, something else becomes apparent: web browsers vertically align content in the middle of cells. (Generally, horizontal alignment is, as with other text, to the left.) See the image on the right for an example.

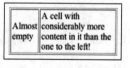

It's possible to override this vertical-centering behavior by using the valign attribute in the row or cell start tag, and setting it to top, like this: valign="top". Other values are middle (the default) and bottom, the results of which are shown in the adjacent screenshot.

It's also possible to set valign to baseline. Should a row have cells with content of different font sizes, setting valign to baseline means the baselines of all the contents will be aligned (see the top right image), which looks better than merely aligning the bottom of the characters using valign="bottom" (see the bottom right image).

The only snag is that the valign attribute is deprecated and should therefore be avoided. Maybe the logic in deprecating it has to do with the fact that the attribute is mostly used to align content to the top of table cells when using tables for layout, rather than for tabular data. CSS-based layouts align content from the top of each div rather than the middle, as you'll see in Chapter 8, meaning the valign attribute is perhaps considered redundant. However, I find the valign attribute useful when working with web-based tabular data, even though there is a CSS equivalent. . . .

The vertical-align property

The approximate CSS equivalent to the valign attribute is the vertical-align property. This property can only be applied to inline elements, and it enables you to create effects similar to valign. For instance, in HTML, you can add a class attribute with a value of valignTop to a cell, and then add the following to your CSS:

```
.valignTop {
vertical-align: top;
}
```

This results in the same effect as valign="top", as discussed in the previous section. Likewise, you can set the vertical-align property to middle, bottom, and various other values, as outlined in the CSS reference section.

And that's pretty much where the majority of web designers leave it. Most seem to think that as long as the rows and cells line up, it's a job well done, but there are several other elements and attributes that should be used when creating tables, which will be covered in the following sections.

Accessible tables

Many web designers ignore all but the most basic elements when working with tables, and in doing so they end up with output that causes problems for screen readers. By correctly and carefully structuring and formatting a table, not only will users of screen readers benefit, but you as a designer will have far more control over its *visual* appearance, too. This is something of a win-win situation, and it's therefore surprising to note how few designers bother with anything other than rows and cells in their tables.

Captions and summaries

Two seldom-used table additions that enable you to provide explanations of a table's contents are the caption element and summary attribute. The former is usually placed directly after the table start tag, and enables you to provide a means of associating the table's title with the table itself. Obviously, this also helps users—particularly those with screen readers. After hearing the caption, the screen reader will go on to read the table headers (see the section "Using table headers" later in this chapter). Without the caption, the table's contents might be relatively meaningless.

By default, most browsers center captions horizontally, and some set its contents in bold type, but these default styles can be overridden with CSS.

The summary attribute, which is invisible in browsers, is used by screen readers to give the user an overview of the table's contents prior to accessing the content. The contents of the summary attribute should be kept succinct, highlighting the most important aspects of the table contents, enabling the user to know what to anticipate.

Many suggest that summaries should be included on all tables, but this isn't necessarily the case. A summary should be used only when it performs the task for which it's designed: to make available a succinct summary of data within a table. Should you be using tables for layout, there's little point including summaries within each layout table—after all, someone using a screen reader is hardly going to jump for joy upon hearing, for the umpteenth time: "This table is used for laying out the web page." Summaries should save time, not waste it!

Using table headers

Amazingly, only a tiny fraction of data tables on the web make use of table headers, even though the majority of tables include cell data that would be better placed within headers.

The table header cell element (<th></th>) performs a similar function to the standard table cell, but is useful with regards to accessibility. Imagine a long data table comprised solely of standard cells. The first row likely contains the headers, but because they're not differentiated, a screen reader treats them as normal cells, reads them once, and then continues reading the remainder of the data. When using table headers, the data is usually read in context (header/data, header/data, and so on), enabling the user to make sense of everything.

Although headers are often at the top of a table, they may also be aligned down the left-hand side. Therefore, you also need to specify whether the header provides header information for the remainder of the row, column, row group, or column group that contains it. This is done with the scope attribute, which is added to the table header start tag and given the relevant value (row, col, rowgroup, or colgroup).

Row groups

Row group elements are almost never used, the main reason being a supposed lack of browser support. The three possible row group elements—<thead></thead>, <tbody></tbody>, and <tfoot></tfoot>—enable browsers to support the scrolling of the body area of long tables, with the head and foot of the table remaining fixed. Furthermore, when tables are printed, the aforementioned elements enable the table head and foot to be printed on each page.

Although current browser support tends to come up short in these areas, I still recommend their use, because they encourage designers to think about the structure of the tables they're creating. Also, although browsers don't do all they might with the elements, they still *recognize* them, which means they can be used as selectors in CSS, enabling you to set separate styles for the head, body, and foot data.

When using row groups, you can have one or more tbody elements and zero or one thead and tfoot elements. They should be ordered with the head first, foot second, and body/ bodies third, thereby enabling the browser to render the foot prior to receiving all of the data. Note, however, that despite this order in HTML, browsers visually render the row groups in the order you'd expect: head, body, and foot.

Building a table

We're now going to build a table, taking into account all of the information mentioned so far. While rummaging around my hard drive for some suitable data, I happened upon an iTunes playlist, which will be used as the basis of the table.

Song Name	Time	Artist	Album	Play Count
Summer Overture	2:35	Clint Mansell (Featu...	Requiem For A Dre...	8
99.9	7:42	Wire	Send	4
Dirge #2	3:40	Death In Vegas	Dirge	2
Mikki Maus	4:18	Ronnie And Clyde	Swim Team #1	3
Unreal	5:10	Unkle	Psyence Fiction	5
Emerge	4:48	Fischerspooner	Fischerspooner #1	5
Obsidian	7:05	Banco de Gaia	Igizeh	9
Jumbo	6:57	Underworld	Beaucoup Fish	3
The Box, part 4	7:36	Orbital	The Box	3
Untitled 1	6:38	Sigur Rós	( )	6
No Man's Land	6:18	David Holmes	Pi	9
Ghost Dancing	7:29	The Orb	Cydonia	6
Templates	6:07	Silo	Instar	4
In My Heart	4:36	Moby	18	4
Just Like You	4:23	Locust	Morning Light	3
Blanket head	3:31	Veer Musikal Unit	Also	4
So Easy	4:09	Röyksopp	Melody A.M.	1
Automagic	5:17	Worm Is Green	Automagic	17
Cherry Blossom	5:25	Susumu Yokota	Grinning Cat	1
Drink The Elixir	4:26	Salad	Drink Me	4

As you can see from the screenshot, the playlist lends itself well to being converted to an HTML table. At the top is the table head, which details each column's data type (song name, time, and so on). And although there's no table foot, we can simply add some information regarding whose choice of music this is—something of a signature—although the table foot can also be used to provide a succinct summary of the table's contents, akin to the value of the summary attribute discussed earlier.

Exercise: Building the table

1. **Structure the table element**. In order to emulate the structure of the iTunes playlist, set the table width to a percentage value. This means the table will stretch with the browser window. As explained earlier, you should also use the summary attribute to succinctly detail what the table's all about.

```
<table width="90%" border="1" cellpadding="2" cellspacing="0"
➥summary="Music selected by Craig Grannell, with details of song,
➥playing time, artist, album and play count.">
</table>
```

2. **Add a caption**. Immediately after the table start tag, add a caption element to provide the table with a title.

```
<caption>A playlist of great music</caption>
```

3. **Add the basic table structure**. Use row groups to provide the table with its basic structure.

```
<thead>
</thead>
<tfoot>
</tfoot>
<tbody>
</tbody>
```

7

> Remember that row groups must be added in the order outlined in the previous "Row groups" section.

4. **Add the table head content**. Using table header cell elements, add the content for the table head (the column headers) as follows:

```
<thead>
  <tr>
    <th>Song Name</th>
    <th>Time</th>
    <th>Artist</th>
    <th>Album</th>
    <th>Play Count</th>
  </tr>
</thead>
```

There's no need to add any styling—not even strong tags. By default, most browsers display table header cell content in bold (and centered) to differentiate it from table data; also, in the following section, you'll be using CSS to style everything anyway.

> *It's always best to keep your HTML as simple as possible, and do any styling in CSS. This reduces page load times, and means that you have a greater degree of control. It also means that people without the ability to view CSS see the browser defaults, which are pretty sensible and clear.*

5. **Add table foot content**. As mentioned, the footer for this table is to essentially be a signature, stating who's at fault for this selection of music. Because this is a single line of text that could potentially span the entire table width, simply include a single table cell, set to span five rows (using the colspan attribute).

```
<tfoot>
<tr><td colspan="5">Music selection by:
➥www.snubcommunications.com</td></tr>
</tfoot>
```

6. **Add table body content**. Finally, add the table's body content via the usual method, using table row and table cell elements. This table will have nearly twenty rows, so to save on trees, only the first two rows are detailed in the following code—you can add all the others in the same way. Remember that you can download the sample files from the friends of ED website (www.friendsofed.com) if you don't fancy inputting all that data yourself!

```
<tbody>
  <tr>
    <td>Summer Overture</td>
    <td>2:35</td>
    <td>Clint Mansell</td>
    <td>Requiem For A Dream</td>
    <td>7</td>
  </tr>
  <tr>
    <td>99.9</td>
    <td>7:42</td>
    <td>Wire</td>
    <td>Send</td>
    <td>4</td>
  </tr>
</tbody>
```

> *It should go without saying, but take care that your table body content aligns correctly with your table headers. Badly formed tables are one thing, but when the headers and data don't correlate, the table is useless.*

The following example shows the table so far.

A playlist of great music				
Song Name	**Time**	**Artist**	**Album**	**Play Count**
Summer Overture	2:35	Clint Mansell	Requiem For A Dream	7
99.9	7:42	Wire	Send	4
Dirge #2	3:40	Death In Vegas	Dirge	2
Mikki Maus	4:18	Ronnie And Clyde	Swim Team #1	3
Unreal	5:10	Unkle	Psyence Fiction	5
Emerge	4:48	Fischerspooner	Fischerspooner #1	5
Obsidian	7:05	Banco de Gaia	Igizeh	9
Jumbo	6:57	Underworld	Beaucoup Fish	3
The Box, part 4	7:36	Orbital	The Box	3
Untitled 1	6:38	Sigur Rós	()	6
No Man's Land	6:18	David Holmes	Pi	9
Ghost Dancing	7:29	The Orb	Cydonia	6
Templates	6:07	Silo	Instar	4
In My Heart	4:36	Moby	18	4
Just Like You	4:23	Locust	Morning Light	3
Blanket head	3:31	Veer Musikal Unit	Also	4
So Easy	4:09	Röyksopp	Melody A.M.	1
Automagic	5:17	Worm Is Green	Automagic	17
Cherry Blossom	5:25	Susumu Yokota	Grinning Cat	1
Drink The Elixir	4:26	Salad	Drink Me	4
Music selection by: www.snubcommunications.com				

Sure, it's not very pretty, but it's structurally sound, and it includes all the relevant elements to at least help make it accessible. As you can see, the addition of the caption and table header cells also makes a difference. If you don't believe it, look at the following screenshot of the same table, with plain table data cells throughout and no caption.

Song Name	Time	Artist	Album	Play Count
Summer Overture	2:35	Clint Mansell	Requiem For A Dream	7
99.9	7:42	Wire	Send	4
Dirge #2	3:40	Death In Vegas	Dirge	2
Mikki Maus	4:18	Ronnie And Clyde	Swim Team #1	3
Unreal	5:10	Unkle	Psyence Fiction	5
Emerge	4:48	Fischerspooner	Fischerspooner #1	5
Obsidian	7:05	Banco de Gaia	Igizeh	9
Jumbo	6:57	Underworld	Beaucoup Fish	3
The Box, part 4	7:36	Orbital	The Box	3
Untitled 1	6:38	Sigur Rós	()	6
No Man's Land	6:18	David Holmes	Pi	9
Ghost Dancing	7:29	The Orb	Cydonia	6
Templates	6:07	Silo	Instar	4
In My Heart	4:36	Moby	18	4
Just Like You	4:23	Locust	Morning Light	3
Blanket head	3:31	Veer Musikal Unit	Also	4
So Easy	4:09	Röyksopp	Melody A.M.	1
Automagic	5:17	Worm Is Green	Automagic	17
Cherry Blossom	5:25	Susumu Yokota	Grinning Cat	1
Drink The Elixir	4:26	Salad	Drink Me	4
Music selection by: www.snubcommunications.com				

All the information might be there, but it's harder to pick out the headers, and users will have to rely on body copy elsewhere to discover what the data in the table represents.

Styling a table

Flip back over the past few pages and you might notice that the table doesn't exactly bear a striking resemblance to the iTunes playlist as yet. But then, we're only halfway through building the table. Now it's time to start styling it using CSS.

> Note that when using CSS to style tables, there will be major issues with older browsers, such as Netscape 4. This browser also fails to correctly order rowgroup elements. The former problem can be dealt with by hiding the CSS using the @import method, but the latter is something that can't be avoided without compromising the structure of the table. Therefore, if full support for Netscape 4 is a requirement of your design, your only option is to build a table without rowgroup elements.

Adding borders to tables

As mentioned earlier, it's a good policy to avoid using the default HTML table border. It looks ugly and old-fashioned, and it's a far cry from the simple, flat, 1-pixel border used in the table-building exercise—so before working on this section, set border="0" in the table start tag.

Now, you might think it a very straightforward process to add CSS borders to a table—logically, it makes sense to simply add a border property/value pair to a grouped selector that takes care of both the table headers and table data cells.

```
th, td {
border: 1px solid #c9c9c9;
}
```

But you'd be wrong. As the screenshot to the right shows, this method results in the correct single-pixel border around the edge of the table, but creates double-thick borders everywhere else. This is because the borders don't collapse, meaning that the right-hand border of one cell sits next to the left-hand border of an adjacent cell, and so on.

Time	
2:35	Clin
7:42	Wir
3:40	Dea
4:18	Ror

You can get around this by setting the top and left borders of the table to 1px, and the bottom and right borders of the table header and data cells to 1px, thereby creating single-pixel borders throughout.

From this point, we're now going to move into exercise mode and style the remainder of the table to resemble the iTunes interface.

Time	
2:35	Clin
7:42	Wir
3:40	Dea
4:18	Ror

Exercise: Styling the playlist table

Note: From what's been worked through in the previous section, "Adding borders to tables," the CSS already contains the following:

```
table {
border-top: 1px solid #c9c9c9;
border-left: 1px solid #c9c9c9;
}

th, td {
border-bottom: 1px solid #c9c9c9;
border-right: 1px solid #c9c9c9;
}
```

Also, because padding will be set within the CSS, you no longer need the cellpadding attribute within the table start tag (although the cellspacing attribute must remain because Internet Explorer for Windows doesn't support the border-collapse property).

1. **Style the caption**. The borders have been dealt with already, so the next step is to style the caption, which currently lacks impact. The caption is effectively a title, and titles should stand out. Therefore, place some padding underneath it, set the font to bold and Arial (which, being a little blocky, is well suited to titles), and finally, set text-transform to uppercase. Note that, in the following code block, CSS shorthand is being used for three values for setting padding; as you may remember from Chapter 2, the three values set the top, horizontal (left and right), and bottom values, respectively; meaning your caption will have 0px padding everywhere except at the bottom, where padding will be 10px.

```
caption {
padding: 0 0 10px;
font: bold 120% Arial, sans-serif;
text-transform: uppercase;
}
```

A PLAYLIST OF GREAT MUSIC				
Song Name	**Time**	**Artist**	**Album**	**Play Count**
Summer Overture	2:35	Clint Mansell	Requiem For A Dream	7
99.9	7:42	Wire	Send	4

2. **Style the header**. In order to make the header stand out a bit more, you can apply the CSS rule outlined in the following code block. The url value set in the background property adds a background graphic to the table headers, which mimics the subtle metallic bas relief quality of the iTunes interface; the 0 50% values vertically center the graphic; and the repeat-x setting tiles the image horizontally.

```
th {
background: #bababa url(stripe.gif) 0 50% repeat-x;
text-align: left;
font-weight: bold;
}
```

7

185

From a design standpoint, the centered table heading text looks a bit shoddy in this case—hence setting text-align to left. Likewise, font-weight is set to bold—although bold headings are the default in most browsers, you should use this setting to account for any browsers that don't follow the normal pattern. This results in table header contents that stand out from standard data cell content.

3. **Set the font and pad the cells**. While you're at it, now's also a good time to set a better font for your table header and data cells, along with a little extra padding.

```
th, td {
border-bottom: 1px solid #c9c9c9;
border-right: 1px solid #c9c9c9;
font: 80% Verdana, Arial, sans-serif;
padding: 2px 5px;
}
```

A PLAYLIST OF GREAT MUSIC

Song Name	Time	Artist	Album	Play Count
Summer Overture	2:35	Clint Mansell	Requiem For A Dream	7
99.9	7:42	Wire	Send	4
Dirge #2	3:40	Death In Vegas	Dirge	2

4. **Styling the footer**. The footer needs to be easy to differentiate from the body cells—you can do this by reversing the foreground and background colors, using light gray text on a dark gray background.

```
tfoot {
background-color: #666666;
color: #dddddd;
font-size: 80%;
}
```

5. **Test the page**. Next, check the page in a web browser—you may notice that a couple of design issues become apparent.

A PLAYLIST OF GREAT MUSIC

Song Name	Time	Artist	Album	Play Count
Summer Overture	2:35	Clint Mansell	Requiem For A Dream	7
99.9	7:42	Wire	Send	4
Dirge #2	3:40	Death In Vegas	Dirge	2
Mikki Maus	4:18	Ronnie And Clyde	Swim Team #1	3
Unreal	5:10	Unkle	Psyence Fiction	5
Emerge	4:48	Fischerspooner	Fischerspooner #1	5
Obsidian	7:05	Banco de Gaia	Igizeh	9
Jumbo	6:57	Underworld	Beaucoup Fish	3
The Box, part 4	7:36	Orbital	The Box	3
Untitled 1	6:38	Sigur Rós	()	6
No Man's Land	6:18	David Holmes	Pi	9
Ghost Dancing	7:29	The Orb	Cydonia	6
Templates	6:07	Silo	Instar	4
In My Heart	4:36	Moby	18	4
Just Like You	4:23	Locust	Morning Light	3
Blanket head	3:31	Veer Musikal Unit	Also	4
So Easy	4:09	Röyksopp	Melody A.M.	1
Automagic	5:17	Worm Is Green	Automagic	17
Cherry Blossom	5:25	Susumu Yokota	Grinning Cat	1
Drink The Elixir	4:26	Salad	Drink Me	4

www.snubcommunications.com

The surround simply isn't strong enough, meaning the table doesn't stand out; also, the gray borders clash with the table foot's background. You can solve these problems by setting the entire table's border to the same color as the table foot's background and removing the borders from the table foot.

6. **Make the table border darker.** Amend the table rule as follows:

```
table {
border: 1px solid #666666;
}
```

The previous rule makes the table stand out, but you still need to deal with the table foot, whose light gray bottom and right borders are now even more apparent.

Cherry Blossom	5:25	Susumu Yokota	Grinning Cat	1
Drink The Elixir	4:26	Salad	Drink Me	4
www.snubcommunications.com				

7. **Edit the table foot**. You can solve this problem by setting the bottom and right borders of the cells within the table foot to 0, effectively turning them off. Do this by using the following contextual selector and declaration:

```
tfoot td {
border-bottom: 0;
border-right: 0;
}
```

Your table should now look like the following example:

A PLAYLIST OF GREAT MUSIC				
Song Name	**Time**	**Artist**	**Album**	**Play Count**
Summer Overture	2:35	Clint Mansell	Requiem For A Dream	7
99.9	7:42	Wire	Send	4
Dirge #2	3:40	Death In Vegas	Dirge	2
Mikki Maus	4:18	Ronnie And Clyde	Swim Team #1	3
Unreal	5:10	Unkle	Psyence Fiction	5
Emerge	4:48	Fischerspooner	Fischerspooner #1	5
Obsidian	7:05	Banco de Gaia	Igizeh	9
Jumbo	6:57	Underworld	Beaucoup Fish	3
The Box, part 4	7:36	Orbital	The Box	3
Untitled 1	6:38	Sigur Rós	()	6
No Man's Land	6:18	David Holmes	Pi	9
Ghost Dancing	7:29	The Orb	Cydonia	6
Templates	6:07	Silo	Instar	4
In My Heart	4:36	Moby	18	4
Just Like You	4:23	Locust	Morning Light	3
Blanket head	3:31	Veer Musikal Unit	Also	4
So Easy	4:09	Röyksopp	Melody A.M.	1
Automagic	5:17	Worm Is Green	Automagic	17
Cherry Blossom	5:25	Susumu Yokota	Grinning Cat	1
Drink The Elixir	4:26	Salad	Drink Me	4
www.snubcommunications.com				

7

Adding separator stripes

One of iTunes's best visual features is missing from the completed table: colored separator stripes. Instead of using horizontal borders to separate tabular data rows, iTunes (like many other applications) uses alternating horizontal stripes, which assist you in rapidly scanning data. Although you could conceivably add a class (setting a background color) to alternating rows, such a solution is poor when creating a static site, and would drive you crazy if you had to add another row in the middle of the table, which would require you to update all the subsequent table row start tags.

> If you're working on a dynamic site, server-side technology can enable you to automate alternating classes. See Chapter 12, pages 209–210 of Foundation Dreamweaver MX 2004 (friends of ED, ISBN: 1-59059-308-1) for more details.

David Miller's article, Zebra Tables (see www.alistapart.com/articles/zebratables/), offers a far more elegant solution. Once you attach the relevant JavaScript (downloadable from the previous URL) to your web page, you merely have to set a unique ID for the table by adding an id attribute to its start tag (for example, id="playlist"); then add an onload attribute to the web page's body tag.

```
<body onload="stripe('playlist', '#ffffff', '#dbe6fa');">
```

The table's id value is replicated for the first value; the two subsequent values are colors, defined in hex, which set the colors of the alternating stripes.

A PLAYLIST OF GREAT MUSIC

Song Name	Time	Artist	Album	Play Count
Summer Overture	2:35	Clint Mansell	Requiem For A Dream	7
99.9	7:42	Wire	Send	4
Dirge #2	3:40	Death In Vegas	Dirge	2
Mikki Maus	4:18	Ronnie And Clyde	Swim Team #1	3
Unreal	5:10	Unkle	Psyence Fiction	5
Emerge	4:48	Fischerspooner	Fischerspooner #1	5
Obsidian	7:05	Banco de Gaia	Igizeh	9
Jumbo	6:57	Underworld	Beaucoup Fish	3
The Box, part 4	7:36	Orbital	The Box	3
Untitled 1	6:38	Sigur Rós	()	6
No Man's Land	6:18	David Holmes	Pi	9
Ghost Dancing	7:29	The Orb	Cydonia	6
Templates	6:07	Silo	Instar	4
In My Heart	4:36	Moby	18	4
Just Like You	4:23	Locust	Morning Light	3
Blanket head	3:31	Veer Musikal Unit	Also	4
So Easy	4:09	Röyksopp	Melody A.M.	1
Automagic	5:17	Worm Is Green	Automagic	17
Cherry Blossom	5:25	Susumu Yokota	Grinning Cat	1
Drink The Elixir	4:26	Salad	Drink Me	4

www.snubcommunications.com

As you can see, this makes quite a difference to the table. And because of the manner in which the script works, you can add and remove as many rows as you like and the stripes will still appear in the correct manner.

There are still some final tweaks to make, though. The bottom border on table data cells is now redundant due to the stripes, so you can remove it from the relevant rule, which then ends up like this:

```
th, td {
border-right: 1px solid #c9c9c9;
font: 80% Verdana, Arial, sans-serif;
}
```

Finally, the table head could do with being more visually distinct from the data content. To do this, add a bottom border to the table headers, using the same color as the table's border:

```
th {
background: #bababa url(stripe.gif) 0 50% repeat-x;
text-align: left;
padding: 2px 5px;
font-weight: bold;
border-bottom: 1px solid #666666;
}
```

Your table should now appear as follows:

A PLAYLIST OF GREAT MUSIC				
Song Name	**Time**	**Artist**	**Album**	**Play Count**
Summer Overture	2:35	Clint Mansell	Requiem For A Dream	7
99.9	7:42	Wire	Send	4
Dirge #2	3:40	Death In Vegas	Dirge	2
Mikki Maus	4:18	Ronnie And Clyde	Swim Team #1	3
Unreal	5:10	Unkle	Psyence Fiction	5
Emerge	4:48	Fischerspooner	Fischerspooner #1	5
Obsidian	7:05	Banco de Gaia	Igizeh	9
Jumbo	6:57	Underworld	Beaucoup Fish	3
The Box, part 4	7:36	Orbital	The Box	3
Untitled 1	6:38	Sigur Rós	()	6
No Man's Land	6:18	David Holmes	Pi	9
Ghost Dancing	7:29	The Orb	Cydonia	6
Templates	6:07	Silo	Instar	4
In My Heart	4:36	Moby	18	4
Just Like You	4:23	Locust	Morning Light	3
Blanket head	3:31	Veer Musikal Unit	Also	4
So Easy	4:09	Röyksopp	Melody A.M.	1
Automagic	5:17	Worm Is Green	Automagic	17
Cherry Blossom	5:25	Susumu Yokota	Grinning Cat	1
Drink The Elixir	4:26	Salad	Drink Me	4

www.snubcommunications.com

Tables for layout

This section is going to be brief, because you should generally avoid using tables for layout whenever possible (and it usually is possible). There are exceptions—for instance, tables are an acceptable method for laying out forms (see Chapter 10). However, generally speaking, tables are less accessible than CSS, harder to maintain and update, slow to render in browsers, and don't print particularly well. More importantly, once you know how to create CSS-based layouts, you'll mostly find working with tables for layout frustrating and clunky.

A common way of creating tabular layouts is to chop up a Photoshop layout and use images to stretch table cells to the correct size. (As mentioned earlier, table cells expand to the dimensions of their content.) Many designers then use a 1-pixel invisible GIF89 (often referred to as a spacer or shim) to force content into position or stretch table cells to a certain size. Because the 1-pixel GIF is a tiny file that's cached, it can be used hundreds of times without impacting download times. However, spacer and table layout usage pretty much destroys the idea of a semantic web. Because so much of the layout is defined via inline HTML, updating it requires amendments to every page on the site (which must also be uploaded and tested in each case), rather than the simple editing and uploading of an external CSS file.

It is, of course, possible to combine CSS and tables—something that's usually referred to as a transitional layout. Such layouts are usually created to ensure layout-based backwards compatibility with obsolete devices. This direction should really only be taken when the target audience is known to include a significant number of users of obsolete browsers, and also when the layout is paramount to the working of the site (rather than just the content). When working on such a layout, there are a few golden rules:

- **Avoid nesting tables whenever possible**. Although tables can be nested like any other HTML element, doing so makes for a web page that is slow to render and nightmarish to navigate for a screen reader. (Obviously, there are exceptions, such as if you need to present a table of tabular data within your layout table.)

- **Structure the information on the page logically**. When designers use tables (particularly those exported from a graphics package), they have a tendency to think solely about how the page looks rather than its underlying code. However, it's important to look at how the information appears in the HTML, because that's how a screen reader will see it. The content should still make sense with regard to its flow and order even if the table is removed entirely. If it doesn't, you need to rework your table. You can use Opera's User mode to temporarily disable tables to find out how your information is ordered without them. Ensure that content is immediately available; if it isn't, provide a link that skips past extraneous content, such as the masthead and navigation—otherwise people using screen readers will be driven bonkers. (See www.w3.org/TR/WAI-WEBCONTENT/ for more on web content accessibility guidelines.)

- **Avoid deprecated attributes**. For instance, there's little point in setting the table's height to 100% when many web browsers ignore that rule (or need to be in "quirks" mode to support it).

- **Use CSS whenever possible to position elements**. To give an example—if you're working with a three-cell table and want the middle cell's content to begin 100 pixels from the top of the cell, don't use a spacer GIF. Instead, provide the cell with a class or unique ID, and use CSS padding.

Again, as I keep hammering home, CSS is the way to go for high-quality, modern web page layouts, and tables should be left for the purpose for which they were designed—formatting data.

In my experience, the main reason designers avoid CSS involves their not knowing how to work with it. Suitably, the next chapter deals with this very issue—creating all manner of page layouts using CSS.

7

CHAPTER 8
LAYOUTS WITH CSS

In this chapter

- Explaining CSS workflow
- Positioning web page elements with CSS
- Creating boxouts and sidebars with ease
- Examining advanced web page layout with CSS
- Creating dynamic, alternate layouts with CSS switchers
- Using CSS for printing

Introducing CSS layout

Many designers use CSS for styling fonts, but few venture further. This chapter shows how straightforward creating CSS layouts can be, so long as you carefully plan what you're going to do. Upon working through the chapter, the benefits of a CSS-based system over a table-based layout will become obvious—benefits that include the ability to rapidly edit a website's entire visual appearance from a single, external file; the ability to "skin" the site and offer alternatives; and the ability to create text-only sites and styles for print, without authoring alternate HTML documents. That last point is particularly important, because alternate devices are becoming widespread. In the past, text-only sites were fairly common, but these days CSS enables you to provide the user with various ways of presenting the same content.

Before we begin, it is worth mentioning that some browsers have problems with CSS, and this is often given as a reason to not proceed with CSS-based layouts. Of those browsers still in widespread use, Internet Explorer 5 (and the 5.5 update) for Windows causes the most frustration, although the Mac version of Internet Explorer 5 has its fair share of quirks, too. In most cases, there are simple workarounds, leading me to believe that many naysayers of CSS are negative simply because they don't know how to create such layouts. Workarounds to problems will be mentioned during the relevant portions of this chapter, and also collected and explained in depth in Chapter 12.

Workflow for CSS layouts

To use a fine art analogy, working with tables is like painting by numbers: you create a skeleton layout and then fill in the gaps with the content of choice. And, like painting by numbers, a lot of work is required to change the layout after it's completed. Working with CSS is more akin to sculpting with clay: you begin with something simple and then gradually fashion your layout. Making changes, tweaks, and even additions at a later date is simpler, and the whole process feels more organic.

Longtime web designers may feel intimidated by CSS because they don't initially have the skeleton layout of table borders to work with. In some ways, CSS sits at the extremes of web technologies, being both very graphic and designlike (in its flexibility), but also quite technical (in how it's created). Tables tend to sit in the middle of these two extremes. However, once you get the hang of CSS workflow, it soon becomes second nature.

In this section, we'll look at how to create a web page structure, and we'll recap the CSS box model.

Creating a structure

We've covered semantic markup—that is, using HTML elements for the purpose for which they were created. This theme continues when working with CSS-based layouts. With tables, cells are used to lay out a design and are merged, split, chopped, and changed until everything works visually. But when working with CSS, you need to be aware of the *structure* of your web page. That way, you can create structural elements with IDs that relate to their purpose, and then style them to suit.

For basic page structure, you mostly tend to work with the div element. This element has been around for some time, but it has historically been associated with aligning text left, right, or centrally. In CSS-based layouts, the div element's role is pivotal: a number of divs are added to the web page in logical order, creating the basic structure; each is provided with a unique ID relating to its purpose; and the divs are then styled to provide spacing, padding, backgrounds, and so on.

All this will become apparent as you continue through this chapter.

Box formatting

The box model has already been mentioned in this book, and this is a timely place for a recap, because the box model is something that tends to confuse many web designers.

In CSS, every element is considered to be within its own box, and you can define its dimensions and then add padding, a border, and a margin to each edge, as required, as shown in the following image.

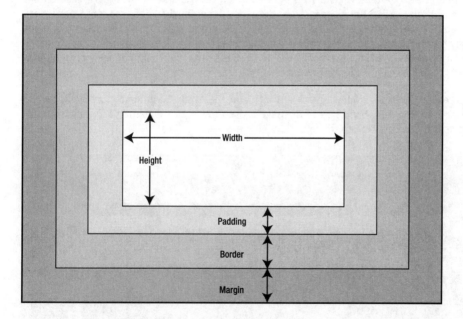

This is one of the trickiest things to understand about CSS: padding, borders, and margins are added to the set dimensions, so the sum of these elements is the overall space that they take up.

> *Note that the top and bottom margins on adjacent elements collapse, meaning that the overall box dimensions aren't necessarily fixed, depending on your design. For instance, if you set the bottom margin to 50px on an element, and you have a top margin of 100px on the element below it, the effective margin between the two elements will be 100px, not 150px.*

Some browsers—notably Internet Explorer 5 and 5.5 for Windows—don't display the box model correctly, placing padding and borders *inside* the defined dimensions of an element. This can wreck CSS-based layouts, but there are simple workarounds, as you'll see in this chapter.

Creating CSS layouts

In the remainder of this chapter, we'll walk through a number of common CSS layout techniques, which can be combined to form countless layouts. Toward the end of the chapter, we'll bring together several of the ideas discussed, to create an example of an advanced CSS-based web page layout.

Boxouts and sidebars

Boxouts and **sidebars** are design elements commonly used in magazines, but they can, in principle, also be used on the Web. A boxout is a box separate from other page content that is often used to house images, captions, and other ancillary information. Sidebars are (usually) thin bars of content that run alongside the main page content. In magazines, these may be used for supporting text, alternate features, or magazine mastheads (with contributor information). Online, both have similar uses, enabling you to immediately present content that's complementary to the main text.

For example, in the following screenshot from the Snub Communications website, the sidebar on the right-hand side of the page is used to house supplementary copy that supports the main content to the left.

And in the following screenshot of one of the reviews on the Wireviews website (www.wireviews.com), a boxout is used to house cover art, information about the album being reviewed, and links to associated content.

Creating either of these elements in CSS is done in much the same way, and the method is similar to one covered in Chapter 3. You may remember working on a drop cap in the typography section to float and style a specific character. For boxouts and sidebars, you instead float an entire div.

The float property

Mastering the float property is key to creating cutting-edge web page layouts. It enables you to float an element left or right of other web page content, which then wraps around it. This enables you to do away with ugly hacks such as fixed-width tables aligned right to create a boxout. In the previous screenshot of the Wireviews website, a div for the boxout was created and floated right of the other page content.

The benefit of using the float property over older methods is the ability to control its appearance sitewide from the external CSS file (and to control the cascade, in order to amend the appearance of elements within it; see the "Controlling the cascade" section later in this chapter). Structurally, the page is also more logical.

Creating a boxout

The first step in creating a boxout is to mark it up in HTML. The boxout itself is a div element with an `id` attribute value of boxout. The content within can take any form—here I've used an image of some artwork and a paragraph of text. The entire div should be placed prior to the content you want to float it left or right of.

```
<div id="boxout">
<img src="artwork.jpg" alt="Artwork" width="140" height="140" />
<p>Donec vitae est. Sed ligula. Aenean et nulla a velit lacinia facilisis.
➥Vesti bulum entum.</p>
</div>
<p>Lorem ipsum dolor sit amet, consectetuer adipiscing elit. Nulla blandit
➥interdum...</p>
```

Without any CSS styles, the boxout content is displayed in a standard, linear form, as shown to the right.

A few CSS styles enable us to rapidly style and position the boxout. First, we define the web page essentials, setting font, color, padding, and margins. (Padding is set to 30px so this example page doesn't hug the browser window edges.)

```
body {
font: small Verdana, sans-serif;
color: #000000;
padding: 30px;
margin: 0;
}
```

The use of keywords for defining the font size means this exercise will look different in Internet Explorer 5 and 5.5 for Windows. See Chapter 3 for information on the box model hack/Fahrner method workaround.

Then we style paragraphs based on some of the ideas explored in Chapter 3:

```
p {
margin-top: 0;
margin-bottom: 1em;
font-size: 90%;
line-height: 1.4em;
}
```

Finally, we style the boxout itself via the following rule, the results of which can be seen to the right. I've copied the style of the Wireviews site (which is fine, seeing as I designed and built it in the first place!) and used a background image to create the effect of a triangular cutout in the top-left corner. The `float` property is set to `right`, meaning the boxout floats right, with other content wrapping around it.

```
#boxout {
background: #e6e6e6 url(boxout_corner.gif) top left no-repeat;
float: right;
width: 162px;
margin-left: 30px;
margin-bottom: 20px;
padding-top: 20px;
}
```

The width of the boxout has been defined—this is vitally important. Omit this setting and the boxout spans the width of the browser window (excepting any defined body margin settings). Finally, like the drop cap created in Chapter 3, the margin settings ensure there's some space between the boxout and other page content.

Controlling the cascade

As it stands, the boxout isn't very pretty. The content hugs the boxout edges, and the text isn't differentiated from the other page copy, therefore it fails to stand out. I've already mentioned that CSS properties are often inherited. In this case, the global paragraph setting also affects paragraphs within the boxout. Earlier in the book, you saw how to control the CSS cascade, and you can do something similar here, setting specific styles for elements within the boxout by using contextual selectors.

First, we'll style the boxout images, adding a border and a bottom margin:

```
#boxout img {
border: 1px solid #818181;
margin-bottom: 1em;
}
```

Next, we'll use a grouped contextual selector to set the margins left and right of the images and paragraphs with the boxout div:

```
#boxout img, #boxout p
{
margin-left: 10px;
margin-right: 10px;
}
```

8

We'll then set some specific styles for paragraphs within the boxout, setting the font weight to bold, reducing the font size and line height from the default, and rendering it in a lighter color:

```
#boxout p {
font-weight: bold;
font-size: 80%;
line-height: 1.2em;
color: #333333;
}
```

The results of these efforts can be seen to the right. Again, seeing as this is all CSS based, every element of the boxout—size, background color and image, fonts, and so on—can be rapidly changed just by editing a few styles. (In fact, the forthcoming "From boxout to sidebar" section shows how to do just that.)

Using multiple boxouts

The use of an id in the boxout means that we're assuming only one boxout will appear on each page. However, should you want the option of using multiple boxouts, you can instead use a CSS class. Simply amend id="boxout" to class="boxout" in the HTML, and change all instances of #boxout to .boxout in the CSS.

From boxout to sidebar

In order to turn our boxout into a sidebar, we have to amend only a few things. First, we'll change the value of the id attribute to sidebar:

```
<div id="sidebar">
<img src="artwork.jpg" alt="Artwork" width="140" height="140" />
<p>Donec vitae est. Sed ligula. Aenean et nulla a velit lacinia
➥facilisis. Vesti bulum entum.</p>
</div>
```

Then, we wrap the remaining page content in a div tag of its own, which we give an id attribute with the value of content:

```
<div id="content">
<p>Lorem ipsum dolor sit amet, consectetuer adipiscing
➥elit. Nulla blandit interdum...</p>
</div>
```

In the CSS, we perform a find and replace to change #boxout to #sidebar. For the newly renamed #sidebar rule, we remove the background and top padding. Although it's fine to have a background on a sidebar, we don't want one in this example. As for the padding-top value, that is best removed, because sidebars work best when aligned with other page content.

```
#sidebar {
float: right;
width: 162px;
margin-left: 30px;
margin-bottom: 20px;
}
```

We then style the content div. The `margin-right` setting is the same as the `width` of the sidebar, and it ensures that page content doesn't wrap underneath the floated content (the image and subsequent paragraph). The border-right setting sets a vertical stripe down the page, thereby creating the sidebar, as shown to the right. (The padding setting ensures page content doesn't hug this line.)

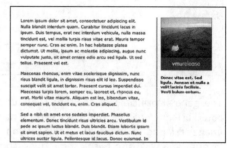

```
#content {
margin-right: 162px;
padding-right: 10px;
border-right: 1px solid #222222;
}
```

Although this method works well, it's not a perfect solution. The line is applied to the content div, which is fine when it takes up more vertical space than the sidebar. But if the sidebar content is longer than the body content, the stripe stops short. Visual examples of this and a solution can be found later in the chapter (in the "Faking column background images in CSS" section).

In general, always strive for uncluttered pages to avoid making the design feel claustrophobic. If you're using boxouts and sidebars, ensure the content isn't being crammed in and that it has enough space to "breathe." Also, if these areas are to be populated with text-based content, ensure that the widths are large enough to cater for this; it's rather pointless to set text within a sidebar that has room for only one or two words on each line.

Working with columns

Although columns of the sort found in newspapers and magazines should be avoided online, columns can be useful when you're working with various types of content. For instance, the Snub Communications homepage has two columns: the left-hand one shows current news, while the right-hand one provides an introduction to the organization and also a means to contact it. The use of columns makes both sets of information immediately available. If I had used a one-column structure, I'd have had to decide which information I wanted the user to see first and which information would initially be hidden (and perhaps never—or rarely—seen).

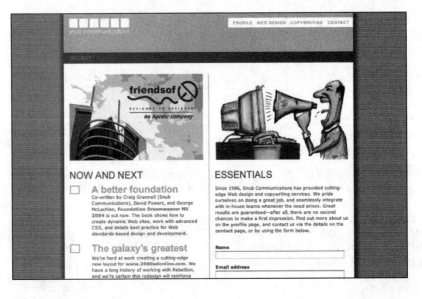

The general principle of columns is about more than written site content, though. You could use one column to house a vertical navigation bar and another to contain thumbnail images relating to an article. In this section, we're going to look at various column-based layouts, and we'll also tweak some rules along the way to show how flexible they can be.

Two-column layouts

The two-column layout is versatile and forms the basis for many CSS layouts. In fact, although it may not be immediately apparent, we've already created one during this chapter: the sidebar. However, because in that case we worked on code created for a boxout, we're going to start from scratch to make more obvious the general rules when creating column layouts.

> Although this section concentrates on two-column layouts (as its heading and the previous paragraph suggests), you should be able to take the theory presented here and apply it to a layout with any number of columns.

The basis for the columns is the following HTML:

```
<div id="newsColumn">
<h1>News</h1>
<p>(Content...)</p>
</div>

<div id="infoColumn">
<h1>Information</h1>
<p>(Content...)</p>
</div>
```

In order to save on trees, I haven't shown reams of content, but you get the idea. Two divs have been created, each of which has a unique id value that relates to the content within.

Also, before we style the divs, to create our columns, we replace the default padding and margin settings with the following:

```
body {
padding: 0;
margin: 0;
}
```

Liquid columns

Our first set of additional CSS rules creates liquid columns—that is, columns that expand with the browser window. In this case, we're going to create two of equal size, hence using a grouped selector for the width property. Setting both columns to float left places them alongside each other.

```
#newsColumn, #infoColumn {
float: left;
width: 50%;
}
```

In order to further differentiate the columns in the screenshots, I've provided each with a unique background color:

```
#newsColumn {
background-color: #cccccc;
}

#infoColumn {
background-color: #999999;
}
```

8

In some browsers, you may see a 1-pixel gap between the columns or to the right of the browser window. This happens when the window width is set to an odd number of pixels. Because we've set the column widths to 50%, some browsers cannot figure out what to do with the extra pixel and place it between or to the right of the columns. Also, Internet Explorer very occasionally has issues with two-column designs where both columns are 50% wide and floated, and have no margins or padding around them (nor are there margins and padding on the web page itself), and displays one under the other. (This is something you'll only find by thorough testing, and it's happened to me just a few times, despite the code for the pages being totally compliant.) In such cases, try reworking the page or reducing one of the column's widths to 49.99%.

Adding padding to column content

The background colors in the screenshots make it rather obvious that the column contents are hugging the column edges (and also each other). You might think adding some padding to the columns would get around this, as in the following rule:

```
#newsColumn, #infoColumn {
float: left;
width: 50%;
padding: 10px;
}
```

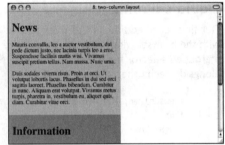

However, as you can see in the image to the right, this breaks the layout.

This happens because of the way the box model works. As mentioned previously, padding is *added* to the defined dimensions of any element. Because we set the element widths to 50%, they now take up 50% plus 10px of space. The only solution a browser has in those circumstances is to wrap the content, resulting in the "columns" appearing one under the other.

The most common solution to this is to nest divs. Within each of the columns is a second div, which houses the content.

```
<div id="newsColumn">
  <div id="newsColumnContent">
  <h1>News</h1>
  <p>(Content...)</p>
  </div>
</div>

<div id="infoColumn">
  <div id="infoColumnContent">
  <h1>Information</h1>
  <p>(Content...)</p>
  </div>
</div>
```

Instead of the padding being applied to the #newsColumn, #infoColumn rule, a new rule is created for the nested divs:

```
#newsColumnContent, #infoColumnContent {
padding: 10px;
}
```

As you can see in the images to the right, this fixes the problem and provides padding around our column content.

Some purists may argue that nesting divs in this way goes against the honing down of HTML that CSS enables, but the page retains its structural integrity. Also, it provides a method, should you require it, to offset the columns. For instance, you could set padding-top to 20px on the #infoColumn rule to push the content in that column downward.

An alternate method of creating the padding in the columns is to use contextual selectors to set the padding for each element within (such as #infoColumn p, #infoCoumn h1, etc.). However, even when you're using grouped selectors, all of the additional values you'd require would be hard to keep track of—hence my preference of the nested div approach.

Swapping sides

Every designer's been there: the clock is ticking and the deadline is threatening to zoom past your ears. Clients, however, have this knack of coming up with last-minute changes, and they rarely appreciate how major some of them are. When you use CSS, though, you can implement some of these changes almost immediately. A good example when working with two columns is the ability to switch their order. By changing the #newsColumn, #infoColumn rule's float value from left to right, the column order is immediately switched, as shown in the screenshot to the right.

```
#newsColumn, #infoColumn {
  float: right;
  width: 50%;
}
```

Try doing that with a table-based layout! Even if you were using a powerful web design application's template system, you'd still have to amend *every* page on your site, and then upload *every* changed page. With CSS, you edit and upload just *one file*.

Fixed column sizes

So far, we've looked just at liquid columns. Now we're going to switch to defining columns with fixed widths. The Snub Communications site shown earlier makes use of a fixed-width, two-column layout for its homepage's content area. This is mainly because the homepage contains large introductory images of a set width, which wouldn't work well in a liquid design.

8

In our example (going back before the column order was switched), it's simple to move the site from a liquid to a fixed design: just edit the #newsColumn, #infoColumn rule's width value.

```
#newsColumn, #infoColumn {
float: left;
width: 250px;
}
```

The clear property

Regardless of whether you're creating a liquid or a fixed design, the use of float causes problems for subsequent page content. As it stands, this appears to the right of the last floated element (if there's room) or underneath it (if there's not room). In many cases, this positioning is not appropriate to a design. For instance, if you'd like to add a footer underneath the two-column layout, to include copyright information, links, and a link to the top of the page, the footer won't appear where you want it to, because the two previous elements are floated. To achieve this design, you need to use the clear property.

The clear property defines the boundaries of an element on which no floated elements may be placed. This results in moving the element downward until the top of its box is below the bottom edge of the previous floated element. Should the value of clear be set to both, the element it's applied to moves down until it appears underneath *all* floated elements.

This concept is perhaps easier to understand with a visual example, so we'll continue working with our two-column layout. In the HTML document, after the second column, we add our footer:

```
<div id="footer">
  <p>Footer content goes here.</p>
</div>
```

Currently, this results in the display shown to the right. The gap between the content and the top of the browser window is caused by the default top margin the browser applies to the paragraph within the footer. This can be removed with the following CSS:

```
p {
margin-top: 0;
}
```

206

Creating a rule for the footer div and setting clear to both makes the footer correctly appear underneath both columns, as explained earlier.

```
#footer {
clear: both;
}
```

Faking column background images in CSS

As you can see from the previous image, a visual problem with CSS is that an element's background (both color and image) ceases with the end of the content and padding. Although you can usually work around this design-wise, often you'll want to have column backgrounds of equal height, even if they don't contain the same amount of content.

When you're working with tables, this doesn't happen, because table cells take the form of a gridlike structure rather than the "stretch to fit" boxes of CSS. The following images show a comparison with the CSS-based columns page on the left and a table-based equivalent on the right. (I've added borders to both examples to highlight the edges of the relevant CSS boxes and table cells.)

In many cases, the disparity in column heights won't be an issue, but some designs call for column backgrounds or borders that stretch the entire height of the design. There is a workaround in CSS, and although it's a bit of a hack, it involves only some basic editing of the CSS file (and, depending on your design, perhaps some small changes to the HTML file). The trick is this: rather than adding the backgrounds to the columns, you create a background image and apply it to the page.

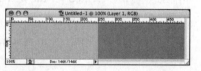

To the right is the image we created. The colors are as per our column page and, because this is flat color, the file size is less than 1KB. As mentioned earlier in the book, when creating background images for web pages, don't make them too narrow or too short. Some browsers choke when faced with a tiny background image to tile. Instead, make the image larger to reduce the strain on the browser (this image is 100px in height).

The screenshot to the right shows what happens when the image is applied to the page background, using the following CSS:

```
body {
padding: 0;
margin: 0;
background: url(two_columns.gif) repeat-y;
}
```

> The background-color *property/value pairs in the* #newsColumn *and* #infoColumn *rules are now redundant and are therefore removed.*

The image spans the entire browser window height and is displayed behind the footer, which was previously white. Although you could then apply a white background to the footer, covering up the background, if the page content isn't tall enough to span the entire browser window height, you'll see the column background continue under the footer.

For some designs, this method is appropriate, but we want to apply the image only to a specific area of the page. What we therefore have to do is wrap the elements to which the background is to be applied in a containing div and apply the background to that instead.

In HTML, we place a div with an id value of wrapper around the newsColumn and infoColumn divs. A simplified version of this code is as follows, minus the content for the divs:

```
<div id="wrapper">
  <div id="newsColumn">
    (content)
  </div>
  <div id="infoColumn">
    (content)
  </div>
</div>
```

In CSS, a style is created for the wrapper, and the background is applied to it:

```
#wrapper {
background: url(two_columns.gif) repeat-y;
}
```

The thing is, this alone isn't enough to display our background. This is because the elements within the wrapper are both floated. Technically, as far as a browser is concerned, floated elements take up no space in a web page, so the browser finds nothing to apply the background to. Therefore, we employ a simple hack. Just before the end tag of the wrapper div, we add the following:

```
<div class="separator"> </div>
```

And in CSS, we style this separator like this:

```
.separator {
clear: both;
height: 0;
}
```

This results in the intended display, shown to the right.

What happens is this: the div has a nonbreaking space as content, and because it's within the wrapper and styled to clear floated elements, it appears underneath the floated news and information divs. Because the separator div is nonfloated content, the wrapper div background appears. And to ensure the layout isn't thrown, the separator is styled to display at a height of 0 (which effectively makes it invisible).

I make no excuses—this *isn't* beautiful markup, and this *isn't* pure and semantic the way it should be. However, it *is* a method of solving a very common design issue in CSS that stops many web designers from moving away from tables. Therefore, considering the fact that the amendments are slight, it's a compromise worth making.

However, it is worth noting that this technique is suitable only for fixed-width layouts when the background is like the one shown here. There's no way of using this method to stretch a background column image over a liquid design. This is a limitation, but because you can set background positioning to a percentage value, it is feasible to use this method on simpler designs. For instance, in the "From boxout to sidebar" section earlier in the chapter, I mentioned that the vertical line ceases where the content area's content ends, making the sidebar look odd if it is taller than the main content area. Even if this were a liquid design, you could set a background image for the border, instead of setting a border on the content area. The image would take the form of a 1-pixel-wide, 50-or-so-pixel-high, flat-color GIF. It would be applied to the body tag selector like this:

```
body {
background: url(sidebar_stripe.gif) repeat-y 70% 0;
}
```

An alternative method: Absolute positioning

A combination of good planning, nested divs, float, and clear has been sufficient for even the most complex CSS-based layouts I've created over the past few years. However, there is another method of positioning that some designers use: **absolute positioning**.

If you've used Dreamweaver layers, you've already worked with absolute-positioned elements, although perhaps without realizing it. As their name suggests, absolute-positioned

209

elements are placed on a specific location on the page, bringing with them a couple of advantages:

- Elements can be placed on the page in specific locations with pixel-perfect precision and with ease.
- Elements can be positioned anywhere in an HTML document but displayed elsewhere.

That last point isn't so obvious. What I mean is that your navigation could be the last thing in your HTML document, but it could be positioned absolutely in the top-left corner. You might wonder why on earth you'd want to do such a thing, but some designers suggest this has accessibility benefits. (You have the page content as the first thing people access in screen readers.) Personally, I prefer using a skip navigation link—a link whose src is the content div (such as #content), and which is placed within an element that has a CSS style of display: none. This is invisible to CSS-enabled browsers, but accessible to screen readers. (This means that search engines that don't drill down the entire page will not miss your navigation, and will therefore visit and index linked documents.)

There also happens to be one fairly big disadvantage when using absolute positioning: the affected elements are removed entirely from the normal flow of the document. This means that, if you're not careful, those affected elements end up overlapping other elements. Some designers complain that Dreamweaver "layers" don't stay still when they try to integrate the layers with liquid table-based layouts. What's actually happening is that the layer—an absolute-positioned div—is staying put at its defined coordinates, but the rest of the page is moving, depending on the browser window width.

Setting an element to display in an absolute position is simple. In CSS, you set the position property to absolute. You can then use the top, left, bottom, or right properties with a pixel or percentage value to set the coordinates to position the element.

For instance, the following CSS sets an element with an id value of navigation to be positioned at the top of the web page and 10px from the left-hand edge (because the web page body is the element's container):

```
#navigation {
position: absolute;
top: 0;
left: 10px;
}
```

Likewise, the following CSS causes an element with an id value of photograph to be positioned 20% from the top of the web page and to hug the right-hand browser window edge:

```
#photograph {
position: absolute;
top: 20%;
right: 0;
}
```

Absolute positioning for column layouts

Absolute positioning has gained some ground in the area of CSS columns. Although floated columns are usually the way to go, it's sometimes simpler to work with absolute-positioned divs. For example, say you're working on a three-column layout that has a fixed left-hand column for navigation, a central liquid column for news, and a fixed right-hand column for information. You could achieve this design by way of floating the navigation column to the left, floating the information column to the right, and setting margins left and right on the news column, so its content doesn't appear under the floated elements. However, in order to get this to work, you must place the floated elements before the nonfloated element in the HTML, meaning you end up with a content order of navigation, information, news.

When we use absolute positioning for the navigation and information divs, they can appear anywhere in the HTML document. Here's the basic structure:

```
<div id="navColumn">
  (content)
</div>
<div id="newsColumn">
  (content)
</div>
<div id="infoColumn">
  (content)
</div>
```

We set the padding and margin on the page body to 0:

```
body {
padding: 0;
margin: 0;
}
```

We then set the navigation column to a width of 20% and position it at the top-left of the page:

```
#navColumn {
position: absolute;
top: 0;
left: 0;
width: 20%;
background-color: #cccccc;
}
```

Next, we give the information column a width of 30% and position it at the top-right of the page:

```
#infoColumn {
background-color: #999999;
position: absolute;
top: 0;
right: 0;
width: 30%;
padding: 10px;
}
```

8

If you test the page now, you'll see that the news column content appears *behind* the absolute-positioned elements. This is because anything with absolute positioning is removed from the flow of the document, as mentioned earlier. Therefore, we set margins to the left and right of the element that are equal to the widths of the absolute-positioned divs. Padding settings then ensure the news column content doesn't hug the other columns.

Because padding is added to an element's defined width, we have to take into account padding settings defined in the other columns when setting the padding for the news column. The information column has a padding setting of 10px, meaning 20px is added to its width. This is countered in the news column by setting the padding-right value to 40px, whereas the padding-left value remains at 20px. The resulting page is shown to the right.

```
#newsColumn {
background-color: #ffffff;
margin: 0 30% 0 20%;
padding: 0 40px 0 20px;
}
```

Do bear in mind, though, that subsequent content may not appear where you expect. Because the left- and right-hand columns are outside the normal document flow, subsequent content appears under the news div, as shown to the right. Should the information column be longer than the central column, as in our example, adding a footer in the normal location isn't possible.

Using z-index to control stack order

Using the z-index property on an absolute-positioned element enables you to control its position in the stack order. Should you wish to position and overlap elements on your web page, you can set the z-index value to any integer, and elements with a greater value appear in front. Note that browsers choke when too many "layers" of this sort are introduced into a web page. Also, Gecko browsers place elements with negative z-index values behind the canvas, so you can't see them. My advice regarding z-index is simple: use it sparingly.

An advanced layout with CSS

Let's now take what we've worked on so far in this book to create an advanced web page layout. To whet your appetite, here's what you'll end up with once the exercise is complete:

Exercise: Creating the structure and adding the content

You'll run through this exercise pretty quickly; refer to the relevant parts of previous chapters if you need a reminder of various aspects of XHTML and CSS.

1. **Create the default document**. Begin with a blank XHTML 1.0 Transitional document that imports the style sheet layout.css.

```
<!DOCTYPE html PUBLIC "-//W3C//DTD XHTML 1.0 Transitional//EN"
    "http://www.w3.org/TR/xhtml1/DTD/xhtml1-transitional.dtd">

<html xmlns="http://www.w3.org/1999/xhtml">
  <head>
    <meta http-equiv="content-type" content="text/html; charset=iso-8859-1" />
    <title>An advanced layout with CSS</title>
<style type="text/css" media="Screen">
/* <![CDATA[ */
@import url(layout.css);
/* ]]> */
```

```
  </style>
  </head>

  <body>

  </body>
</html>
```

2. **Create a top of page anchor**. Immediately after the body start tag, create a top of page anchor div (see the "Top of page links" section in Chapter 5).

```
<div id="topOfPageAnchor"><a name="top" id="top"></a></div>
```

3. **Create the basic document structure**. The document's structure is created from divs with unique id values.

```
<div id="wrapper">
  <div id="masthead">
    <div id="navigation"></div>
  </div>
  <div id="content"></div>
  <div id="footer"></div>
</div>
```

4. **Add navigation**. In the navigation div, add the navigation menu as a list (see the "Creating navigation bars" and "Using accesskey and tabindex" sections of Chapter 5).

```
<ul>
  <li><a href="#" accesskey="l">Latest news</a></li>
  <li><a href="#" accesskey="p">Products</a></li>
  <li><a href="#" accesskey="s">Support</a></li>
  <li><a href="#" accesskey="c">Contact details</a></li>
</ul>
```

5. **Add a separator**. After the masthead div's close tag, add the following separator div (just before the content div):

```
<div class="separatorInvisible"><!-- x --></div>
```

This separator will be used to clear floated elements, enabling subsequent content to be correctly positioned. (Remember that when we styled the navigation bar in Chapter 5, the list items were floated to display them horizontally.)

6. **Add page content and a boxout**. In the content div, add page content and a boxout. (See earlier in this chapter for boxout information; also see the "Styling semantic markup" exercise in Chapter 3 for information about text-based content.)

```
<div id="boxout">
  <img src="artwork.jpg" alt="Artwork" width="140" height="140" />
  <p>Donec vitae est. Sed ligula. Aenean et nulla a velit lacinia
➥facilisis. Vesti bulum entum.</p>
</div>
```

```
<h1>Article heading</h1>
<p>Lorem ipsum dolor sit amet, consectetuer adipiscing elit. Sed
➥aliquete lementum erat. Integer diam mi, venenatis non, cursus a,
➥hendrerit at, mi.Morbi risus mi, tincidunt ornare, tempus ut,
➥eleifend nec, risus.</p>

<h2>Curabitur sit amet risus</h2>
<p>Quisque faucibus lorem eget sapien. In urna sem, vehicula ut,
➥mattis et, venenatis at, velit. Ut sodales lacus sed eros.
➥Pellentesque tristique senectus et netus et malesuada fames ac
➥turpis egestas.</p>

<h3>Praesent rutrum</h3>
<p>Nam scelerisque dignissim quam. Ut bibendum enim in orci. Vivamus
➥ligula nunc, dictum a, tincidunt in, dignissim ac, odio.</p>

<h3>Habitant morbid</h3>
<p>Phasellus tempor felis vel molestie vehicula nibh est...</p>
```

7. **Add a visible separator**. Add another separator, which will be styled to resemble the horizontal gray bar in the mock-up.

```
<div class="separator"><!-- x --></div>
```

8. **Add some columns**. Add the three columns by creating divs with a class value of column. The first one has an inline style, which sets padding-left to 0. This is because you'll later use padding-left to add some space between the columns, and the leftmost column will be incorrectly offset if it takes on this value.

```
<div class="column" style="padding-left: 0;">
  <h1>Lorem ipsum dolor</h1>
  <p>Sit amet, consectetuer adipiscing elit. Nunc ut lorem ac nisl
➥dictum fringilla. Donec pellentesque. Aenean ac lorem malesuada erat
➥lacinia pharetra. Cras pellentesque pulvinar nunc. Praesent
➥adipiscing semper wisi. Sed laoreet pretium sapien.</p>
</div>
<div class="column">
  <h1>Suspendisse potenti</h1>
  <p>Maecenas augue orci, congue ut, ullamcorper nec, nonummy sit
➥amet, urna. Nunc et leo. Sed eu lacus id enim condimentum sagittis.
➥Sed quis leo vitae leo feugiat lacinia. Sed malesuada. Nulla nulla
➥enim, suscipit nec, tempus in, mollis eget, lorem.</p>
</div>
<div class="column">
  <h1>Fusce velit nunc</h1>
  <p>Tincidunt ac, cursus et, convallis at, elit. Quisque fermentum
➥nunc sed libero. Duis pulvinar venenatis leo. Mauris porta hendrerit
➥lectus. Vivamus sagittis. Sed consectetuer. Cum sociis natoque
➥penatibus et magnis dis parturient montes, nascetur ridiculus mus.</p>
</div>
```

8

9. **Add another separator**. These columns will be created by floating the divs left. Therefore, like under the masthead, you add an invisible separator. It should be placed after the end tag of the last column div and before the end tag of the content div.

```
<div class="separatorInvisible"><!-- x --></div>
```

10. **Add a footer**. Finally, between the content div end tag and the wrapper div end tag, add a footer. (Again, see the "Top of page links" section in Chapter 5 for more on the HTML used to accomplish this.)

```
<div id="footer">
  <p><a href="#top" onclick="javascript: scrollTo(0,0);"
➥onmouseover="window.status='Top of page'; return true;"
➥onmouseout="window.status='';">Top of page</a></p>
</div>
```

Now the document's structure and content is taken care of, but visually it won't set the world on fire, as you can see from the following image. It's time to style the page in CSS.

- Latest news
- Products
- Support
- Contact details

Donec vitae est. Sed ligula. Aenean et nulla a velit lacinia facilisis. Vesti bulum entum.

Article heading

Lorem ipsum dolor sit amet, consectetuer adipiscing elit. Sed aliquet elementum erat. Integer diam mi, venenatis non, cursus a, hendrerit at, mi. Morbi risus mi, tincidunt ornare, tempus ut, eleifend nec, risus.

Curabitur sit amet risus

Quisque faucibus lorem eget sapien. In urna sem, vehicula ut, mattis et, venenatis at, velit. Ut sodales lacus sed eros. Pellentesque tristique senectus et netus et malesuada fames ac turpis egestas.

Praesent rutrum

Nam scelerisque dignissim quam. Ut bibendum enim in orci. Vivamus ligula nunc, dictum a, tincidunt in, dignissim ac, odio.

Exercise: Styling the layout

While working through the styles, keep saving the CSS file and checking the page in a browser to see how each set of rules affects the page.

1. **Set the page essentials and font defaults**. Using the techniques discussed in Chapter 2 (in particular, see the "Drop shadows" section) and Chapter 3 (see the "Styling semantic markup" section), set the page essentials and font defaults.

```
body {
background: #ffffff url(page_background.gif) 50% 0;
color: #333333;
padding: 0; margin: 0;
font-family: Verdana, Arial, sans-serif;
}
body {
font-size: x-small;
voice-family: "\"}\"";
voice-family: inherit;
font-size: small;
}
html>body {
font-size: small;
}
```

2. **Style the wrapper**. To center the page content, set the width and margins of the wrapper div to 0 auto. Because Internet Explorer 5 for Windows doesn't understand this, the following two rules can be used to provide a workaround to center content in that browser, if you wish:

```
#wrapper {
width: 740px;
margin: 0 auto;
}
body {
text-align: center;
}
#wrapper {
text-align: left;
}
```

3. **Style the navigation and masthead**. Set the navigation div's height as per the mock-up, and then apply the masthead background image. Because the navigation is nested within the masthead, use padding-top on the masthead to push it into place. The masthead's height setting will be the same as the navigation div's. (Remember that the box model states that the box dimensions are equal to the element dimensions plus the padding, border, and margins—see the section "Box formatting" earlier in the chapter.)

```
#navigation {
height: 30px;
}
#masthead {
background-image: url(masthead.jpg);
height: 30px;
padding-top: 115px;
}
```

4. **Style the separators**. Both separators are mainly there to clear floated elements. Set the invisible separator's height to 0, for equivalent reasons as presented in the

8

"Faking column background images in CSS" section earlier in this chapter. Give the standard separator styles to make it appear as per the mock-up.

```
.separator {
height: 5px;
background-color: #a9a9a9;
clear: both;
margin-bottom: 2em;
}
.separatorInvisible {
height: 0;
clear: both;
}
```

5. **Style the columns**. Style the columns with the following rule. Use the box model hack (discussed several times already) so the columns don't appear too narrow in Internet Explorer 5 for Windows.

```
.column {
float: left;
padding-left: 10px;
width: 242px;
voice-family: "\"}\"";
voice-family:inherit;
width: 232px;
}
html>.column {
width: 232px;
}
```

6. **Style the footer**. Style the footer and footer links with the following rules. (See the "Defining link states with CSS" section in Chapter 5 for information on CSS link styling.)

```
#footer {
clear: both;
text-align: right;
padding: 20px 10px;
}
#footer a {
color: #ffffff;
}
#footer a:hover {
color: #dddddd;
}
```

7. **Style the navigation bar**. Style the navigation bar in a similar way to Chapter 5's "Using CSS to create a graphical navigation bar" exercise. There are two #navigation a rules because Internet Explorer 5.5 sometimes ignores text-transform when included in the main rule. Defining it separately ensures that browser also renders the relevant text in uppercase. (See the aforementioned exercise for more on this.)

```
#navigation ul {
list-style-type: none;
padding: 0;
margin: 0;
}
#navigation li {
float: left;
margin: 0px;
padding: 0px;
display: inline;
background: url(rollover.gif) no-repeat left top;
border-bottom: 5px solid #777777;
}
#navigation a {
font: bold 13px Arial, Helvetica, sans-serif;
text-transform: uppercase;
color: #ffffff;
text-decoration: none;
display: block;
padding: 7px 0px 0px 30px;
height: 30px;
width: 185px;
voice-family: "\"}\"";
voice-family:inherit;
height: 23px;
width: 155px;
}
html>#navigation a {
height: 30px;
width: 185px;
}
#navigation a {
text-transform: uppercase;
}
#navigation a:hover {
background: url(rollover.gif) 0px -40px;
}
#navigation a:active {
background: url(rollover.gif) 0px -80px;
}
```

8. **Style the content area**. Set the content area's background to white and define the padding so its contents don't hug the edges of the element box.

```
#content {
background-color: #ffffff;
padding: 20px 10px;
}
```

9. **Style the fonts**. Define the fonts as per Chapter 3's "Styling semantic markup" exercise.

```
p {
font-size: 85%;
line-height: 1.4em;
```

```
padding-left: 1.4em;
margin-top: 0;
margin-bottom: 1em;
}
h1, h2 {
text-transform: lowercase;
color: #555555;
font-weight: normal;
font-family: Arial, Helvetica, sans-serif;
margin: 0 0 10px 0;
padding: 0 0 2px 0;
}
h1 {
font-size: 150%;
}
h2 {
font-size: 120%;
}
h3 {
margin: 0 0 5px 0;
font-size: 90%;
color: #444444;
font-family: Arial, Helvetica, sans-serif;
font-weight: bold;
padding-left: 1.35em;
}
```

10. **Use column-specific text styles**. The default heading size is too large for the columns. Also, the paragraph offset (due to the padding-left value from the previous step) is unnecessary for the columns. These two rules deal with both issues:

```
.column h1 {
font-size: 130%;
}
.column p {
padding: 0;
}
```

11. **Style the boxout**. Style the boxout and its contents in the same way as the one earlier in this chapter. As in the previous step, set the padding value of boxout paragraphs to 0 to override the default offset.

```
#boxout {
background: #a9a9a9 url(boxout_corner.gif) top left no-repeat;
float: right;
width: 162px;
margin-left: 30px;
margin-bottom: 20px;
padding-top: 20px;
}
#boxout img {
border: 1px solid #818181;
```

```
margin-bottom: 1em;
}
#boxout img, #boxout p {
margin-left: 10px;
margin-right: 10px;
}
#boxout p {
font-weight: bold;
font-size: 80%;
line-height: 1.2em;
color: #333333;
padding: 0;
}
```

12. **Style the top of page div**. Finally, style the top of page link container, as shown in the "Top of page links" section in Chapter 5.

```
div#topOfPageAnchor {
position: absolute;
top: 0;
left: 0;
height: 0;
width: 0;
}
```

> Be aware that during this exercise, you're placing all files within the site root to keep things simple. In a proper website development, ensure your files are organized in folders as appropriate.

Again, here's the result:

This exercise shows how rapidly you can create CSS-based layouts, and how they can do everything table-based layouts can do, but with less markup and greater flexibility for later. (After all, pretty much every presentation aspect of this design can be changed by editing the CSS.)

Also, it shows the modular nature of CSS. Once you have some good code for creating a boxout, you don't need to re-create it. If a design calls for a boxout, just copy and paste in the relevant bits and amend some of the property values accordingly. The same goes for various other design elements, such as the separators, the navigation bar, and even the general layout.

Exporting layouts from graphics packages

Before closing this section, we'll cover the graphics used in the exercise. If we had created this design in an old-fashioned manner, there would be numerous chopped-up graphics for the masthead and navigation, and perhaps two graphics for the background image. This CSS-based design uses just five images—and two of those are for the boxout! Those two images are evident in the previous screenshot: the diagonal triangle (to create the angled corner) and the mesh image within the boxout.

The background image is one wide image, just like the one created in Chapter 2 (in the section "Drop shadows"). Because our navigation bar is a list and the tab text is HTML-based, it requires only a single image, which is the exact same rollover created in Chapter 5 (in the "Graphical navigation with rollovers" section). This leaves just the masthead image, which is as follows.

This screenshot was taken from a flattened version of the mock-up that had the tabs removed. You can see how it seamlessly slots into place in the layout. The reason for removing the tabs was simply to reduce download time. If we had included flattened tabs from the mock-up, the rollover graphics in our navigation bar would be overlaid anyway.

The fact that the masthead is a single image defined as a background graphic in the CSS means that it can be easily updated at any point—just upload a new image, then edit the CSS file and upload that. No messing around with editing and uploading numerous HTML documents and chopped-up graphics.

CSS switchers

The information already provided in this chapter should be enough to convince you of the power and suitability of CSS for web page layouts, but there's more to come. With careful planning and a little JavaScript, it's possible to enable users to swap the active CSS file for another by clicking a link. This system—usually referred to as a **CSS switcher**—can be used to provide variations on a layout, enable users to amend font sizes without resorting to their browser's built-in controls, or provide various contrast levels between text and background colors. In fact, anything that can be defined in CSS can be switched, and some sites go whole hog, enabling users to choose between various layouts. This is akin to applications that can be "skinned," such as the Firefox and Opera web browsers, and many Windows-based MP3 players. The most extreme (and some would argue, the best) version of this kind of website is CSS Zen Garden (www.csszengarden.com), which offers dozens of layouts, all based on the exact same underlying markup. All that changes is the CSS.

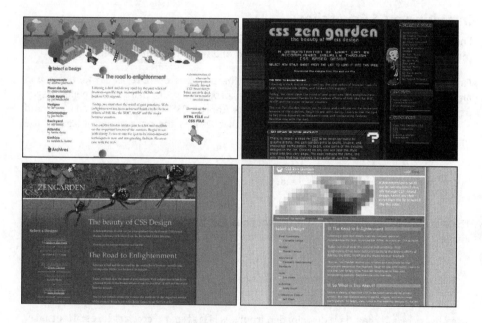

Setting up a CSS switcher is actually fairly simple, thanks to the work of Paul Snowden, whose article at A List Apart is one of the most influential to appear on the Web. The full article can be read at www.alistapart.com/articles/alternate/, but the basic principles are outlined here.

When working with a CSS switcher, you have style sheets with different relationships:

- **Persistent**: An "always on" style sheet that contains rules common to every style sheet. The rel attribute is set to stylesheet and no title attribute is set.

  ```
  <link rel="stylesheet" type="text/css" href="persistent.css" />
  ```

- **Preferred**: The style sheet that's enabled by default. Here, the rel attribute is set to stylesheet and the style sheet is named with the title attribute. Several preferred style sheets can be grouped together and enabled/disabled at once by the user by giving them identical title attributes.

```
<link rel="stylesheet" type="text/css" href="preferred.css"
➥title="preferred CSS" />
```

- **Alternate**: Style sheets that can be selected by the visitor. Here, the rel attribute is set to alternate stylesheet. As with preferred style sheets, alternate style sheets are named with the title attribute, and they can be grouped by giving them identical title attributes.

```
<link rel="alternate stylesheet" type="text/css" href="alternate.css"
➥title="alternate CSS" />
```

Installing a CSS switcher

For a quick example, we're going to use a CSS switcher to provide two options for the masthead graphic—the default and an inverted one (i.e., one with reversed colors).

First, we'll rename the style sheet created in the previous exercise as default.css and amend the #masthead rule to remove the property/value pair background-image: url(masthead.jpg);. We then create two more CSS files: preferred.css and alternate.css. The first of those has a rule that defines the background image of the masthead as it was before:

```
#masthead {
background-image: url(masthead.jpg);
}
```

The alternate.css file has a rule that defines the alternate version of the background image:

```
#masthead {
background-image: url(masthead_alt.jpg);
}
```

The file styleswitcher.js is downloaded from www.alistapart.com/articles/alternate/ and attached to the HTML document via the following code:

```
<script type="text/javascript" src="styleswitcher.js"></script>
```

The CSS files are then attached, taking into account the rules explained earlier:

```
<link rel="stylesheet" type="text/css" href="default.css" />
<link rel="stylesheet" type="text/css" href="preferred.css" title="default" />
<link rel="alternate stylesheet" type="text/css" href="alternate.css"
➥title="reversed" />
```

Finally, controls are placed on the web page to enable a user to switch the style sheet:

```
<h1>Choose a style</h1>
<p><a href="#" onclick="setActiveStyleSheet('default'); return false;">
➥default</a> | <a href="#" onclick="setActiveStyleSheet('reversed');
➥return false;">reversed</a></p>
```

Note how the onclick *attribute values correspond with those defined in the* link *elements.*

The following two screenshots show the CSS being switched.

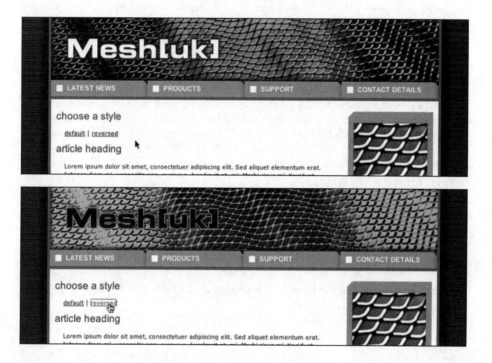

Of course, this switches only a single CSS property, but with careful planning, you should be able to picture how a CSS switcher could enable you to completely transform a site via the click of a link. Along with visual design changes, you can use a switcher to make practical changes, such as enabling the user to amend the size of the text (as www.wired.com does).

Print style sheets

This chapter's final section briefly looks at using CSS to create a printable version of a website. Printing from the Web is a hit-and-miss affair, and using CSS doesn't solve every problem in this area. However, it does increase the likelihood of getting satisfactory results when printing web pages. Designers often opt for fixed layouts when creating websites, and many sites can't be satisfactorily printed, because they're too wide for printer margins. Rather than authoring a separate, printer-friendly site for printing (a time-consuming task that requires you to continually synchronize information), it's far better to create a style sheet specifically for those that want to print content from your site.

A print style sheet is attached to web pages using the following HTML:

```
<link rel="stylesheet" type="text/css"media="print" href="print.css" />
```

The media attribute value restricts the CSS solely to print, and within the print.css style sheet, you can define styles for print, such as different fonts and margins.

> You can call a print style sheet anything you want, but print.css is a common convention, and makes it obvious to anyone maintaining the site what the style sheet is for.

For instance, for our example page, we want to define the font as a serif, because serif fonts are easier to read in print. The padding setting of the page needs to take into account printer margins, so horizontal padding is upped from 0 to 5%. Also, because we're now creating something for print, we can use points for the font size value. Finally, colors are provided with as much contrast as possible (black on white) because a lot of business users print on black-and-white laser printers, and home users with ink-jet printers will get a better result if there's more contrast.

```
body {
background: #ffffff;
color: #000000;
font: 12pt "Times New Roman", Times, serif;
padding: 0 5%;
}
```

The navigation bar is superfluous on a printed page, and it (like any other element) can be removed by setting display to none.

```
#navigation {
display: none;
}
```

Therefore, if we don't want to have images printed out, we could set img {display: none;}.

We can provide the boxout with values that make it look better in print:

```
#boxout {
float: right;
border: 1px solid #000000;
padding: 10px;
width: 200px;
margin-left: 20px;
}
```

Finally, we can give headings and paragraphs values that look better on the printed page:

```
h1, h2, h3 {
font-family: Arial, Helvetica, sans-serif;
font-weight: bold;
margin-bottom: 0.2em;
}
h1 {
font-size: 18pt;
}
h2 {
font-size: 16pt;
}
h3 {
font-size: 14pt;
}
p {
margin-top: 0;
margin-bottom: 1em;
}
```

Here's the result of our efforts in Internet Explorer's Print Preview:

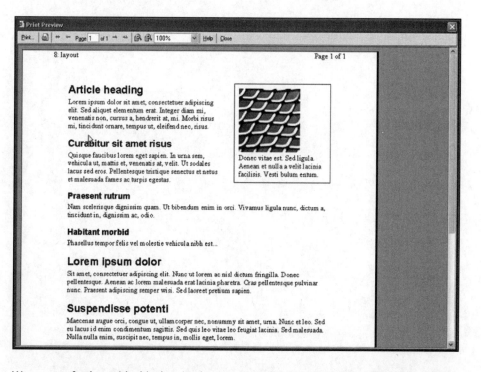

We can go further with this, but it's best to keep things simple. Print style sheets don't tend to be consistent across browsers, and you need to do a lot of testing (including actually printing out examples) in order to be sure everything works as you intend it to. For instance, although CSS2 has rules for printing in landscape, browsers (as of the time of this writing) don't support this. Also, print-specific properties such as page-break-before are rarely supported well.

It's also worth noting that in our site, the imported CSS for web browsers is set with a media attribute of screen. However, many web tools set this to all, meaning the default CSS applies to all media. If that's the case on your site, you can change the attribute value. If you don't, styles from the default CSS "leak" into the printed version, and all must be overridden in the print style sheet (mostly by zeroing values, or setting elements to display: none;).

Despite these problems, it's worth taking the time to work on a print style sheet. Just amending the fonts and page margins, and removing images that are irrelevant to the printed version of the site, not only improves your users' experience, but also makes the site seem more professional.

So, that brings us to the end of our main layout chapter. Hopefully, you're now feeling more confident about creating CSS layouts, and understand the power and potential of CSS and how straightforward CSS layouts can be to create.

CHAPTER 9
WORKING WITH FRAMES

In this chapter

- Using frames—a worthwhile endeavor, or a waste of time?
- Creating framesets
- Using iframes in web pages
- Replacing iframes with CSS

Anatomy of a frameset

Until now we've been talking about web pages that comprise single documents, whether the layouts are created with tables or CSS. Sure, external files may be attached, but the *content* is within a single file. Frames work in a different way: you have an HTML document called a **frameset**, which acts as a container for a number of **frames**. The frameset has no actual content of its own—it's literally a container, used to order and place the frames. The frames are standard HTML documents. Therefore, you essentially use a frameset to slice up the available space in a browser window and display several HTML documents simultaneously, each of which has the ability to scroll independently.

Frames: The good, the bad, and the ugly

In many ways frames are a relic, harking back to the time when the web was a sprightly young thing. Experimentation was the order of the day, as with any new medium. Unfortunately, it was also a time when some of the most hideous web elements were created, and unlike most others, frames still manage to cling on by the skin of their teeth, convincing a dwindling (but hardcore) set of web designers that they're still worth having around.

Frames: The good

To be fair, I fully acknowledge the arguments in support of frames, and yes, in very specific circumstances they can be of use. One of the most common uses for frames is to keep a site's corporate ID and navigation on display at all times. If a page has a lot of content for which the user needs to scroll, the navigation will always stay put. This, according to some, makes a site easier to use, because the navigation is always onscreen and therefore easily accessible.

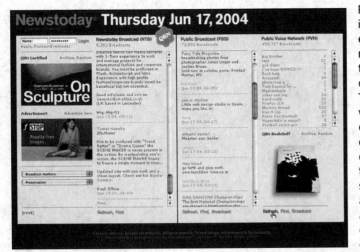

Frames can also be of use when presenting a web page with various sections that each require the ability to update and be refreshed without affecting the rest of the page. A good example of this is the designer's Mecca www.newstoday.com. This site provides a forum and news from various sources all on one page. Because each element is within its own frame, you can do things like refresh the news listings or post to the forum without refreshing the entire page. With a complex, constantly updated site such as this, frames actually make a lot of sense. You can post about news items in current view, and you don't have to wait for the entire page to download each time you post.

Similarly, frames are sometimes used within pages that have to display lengthy, regularly updated content, in order to avoid compromising the design. The Pixelsurgeon website (www.pixelsurgeon.com) is an example of this—it uses a small inline frame (see the "Internal Frames (iframes)" section later in the chapter for more information on iframes) to display a number of news items. The frame can be scrolled, enabling the site to display many dozens of items while restricting the height of the news area to that of the remaining content.

Frames: The bad

Although the prior arguments may seem compelling, frames have a dark side—and unfortunately, the bad outweighs the good. Frames disrupt the logical structure of your site because of the way they're created. Each frame is a separate HTML document, and everything is stitched together with yet another HTML document—the frameset. The result means that people using alternate devices (such as screen readers or mobile devices) may find the site difficult or impossible to use and navigate. Even those who can navigate the site may be confronted with page refresh issues, in which the entire frameset will reload rather than the content the user intended to refresh. From a design point of view, using frames also causes problems: content can't span frames—as a result, layout elements such as drop-down and fly-out menus can only be placed in frames if sufficient space is left for the entire menu to display.

Speaking of navigation, users also get frustrated when trying to bookmark pages from frames-based sites. Generally, when a frames-based site is bookmarked, the frameset itself is what's saved, not the page you're on. This inability to isolate specific pages also becomes problematic when trying to direct users to content when e-mailing or talking to them. Instead of providing a URL, you have to provide something akin to a set of directions. ("Click the products button, then scroll a bit and choose 'giant plastic artichokes,' and then click on 'blue' to see the page I'm looking at.") These issues also mean it's trickier for other sites to link to specific content on yours, which may dissuade them from linking to your site at all.

Once you do find the information you're after, you may not be able to print it. Although some browsers cope (to some extent) with printing frames-based websites, others only print the frame that's in focus (the one most recently clicked). This can result in users assuming they're printing the main page content, and then wondering why they only have a nice printout of the site's logo and navigation area.

In addition to all these points, frames-based content can cause problems for sites that use JavaScript, which require complex path information to pass instructions between pages. There's also the danger of attempting to access an element in a frame that hasn't completed downloading, or that now has alternate content within.

Search engines and frames

Search engines also trip up on frames-based sites because they index the individual pages along with the containing frameset HTML page. This results in people clicking on orphaned pages, which may contain content but no navigation. There are workarounds: you can employ JavaScript to attempt to load the frameset around the orphaned page; alternatively, you can use code that stops search engines from indexing anything other than the frameset. As you might imagine, both solutions are pretty nasty, and they often cause problems: many scripts that attempt to load framesets around orphaned pages don't work, and sometimes even crash browsers; and indexing just your frameset rather than all of the content in your site is detrimental and will mean fewer people are likely to discover your site via a search engine.

Frames for ease of development

Using frames for ease of development is also something of a red herring. The confused structure of a frames-based site hardly makes things easier, because content is spread over several separate files. Back in the old days, some developers swore by frames because they enabled a site's common areas (such as navigation and footers) to remain consistent throughout—however, today, even the most rudimentary of modern web design tools offer some kind of template facility. Additionally, frames may compromise a site in terms of its visual design (see the following section, "Frames: The ugly").

Finally, the frames-advocating web designer needs to be ever vigilant regarding copyright issues. As we'll see later, in the section entitled "Targeting links from frames-based pages," there are various values for anchor target attributes. Leaving this attribute out (or setting it to _self) opens the target document within the current frame. Should this document be someone else's website, you're entering murky copyright and intellectual property waters if the owner of the site hasn't given consent to this. External links can be set to _top, thereby loading the external document over the entire frameset. However, not all designers remember to do so.

Frames: The ugly

Aside from the problems relating to site structure, orphaned pages, and accessibility, there's one final consideration for web designers thinking about using frames: they're ugly. Frames have borders similar to tables, which create chunky, ugly dividers between the content areas of a website. You can turn these off, but you may then end up with an obvious dividing line between the static and scrolling content. And even if you manage to create a design that deals with these problems, there's still the issue of ugly scroll bars appearing at various places within your web pages. Ultimately, unless you have an astonishingly good reason for wanting to use frames, don't.

> Some people out there might be wondering about the comment on scroll bars. Sure, they may not be the prettiest things in the world, but at least you can color them, making them fit in with your design, right? Well, sort of. Although it is possible to use CSS to amend scroll bar colors, this is not part of the official CSS specification. Only Internet Explorer for Windows supports the relevant styles, and if you care enough about design to want to color scroll bars, you probably care what your design looks like in all browsers. Although Internet Explorer for Windows accounts for the majority of web users, the remainder will get something less than satisfactory, which is enough reason to avoid coloring scroll bars altogether. As such, scroll bar CSS isn't covered in this book.

9

If you're still with us, you're either a curious type or you're actually thinking about using frames. Fair enough—this is the web designer's reference after all, and I can't stop you. My personal feelings regarding frames will stop right here, and the remainder of the chapter will be technical in nature, showing you the relevant elements required to make framesets.

Creating framesets

As mentioned earlier, a frames-based website consists of a frameset and various pages placed within its frames. The frames are the same sort of documents we've already talked about, but the frameset is not. Although it's still an HTML page, it requires a specific frameset DTD, which looks like this:

```
<!DOCTYPE html PUBLIC "-//W3C//DTD XHTML 1.0 Frameset//EN"
    "http://www.w3.org/TR/xhtml1/DTD/xhtml1-frameset.dtd">
```

The frameset page lacks a body element and instead uses a frameset element, which sets the attributes for how the frames are positioned. The frameset element houses frame elements, which define the location and attribute of each frame. Note that this DTD should only be used for the frameset and not for the individual pages that will be loaded into the frameset—they should use whatever DTD is relevant to their contents (such as XHTML Transitional or XHTML Strict).

Like any XHTML document, you should also include a title element in the head of the document, otherwise your frameset page (and search engines) will proudly display Untitled (or something similarly useless) for its name. You should also state the character set, using the meta tag mentioned back in Chapter 2. Using these criteria, a basic XHTML frameset page (lacking any content) looks something like this:

```
<!DOCTYPE html PUBLIC "-//W3C//DTD XHTML 1.0 Frameset//EN"
    "http://www.w3.org/TR/xhtml1/DTD/xhtml1-frameset.dtd">
<html xmlns="http://www.w3.org/1999/xhtml">
<head>
  <meta http-equiv="content-type" content="text/html; charset=iso-8859-1" />
  <title>Document title</title>
</head>
<frameset>

</frameset>
</html>
```

A two-frame frameset

This first example shows the HTML required for a typical two-column design. The left-hand frame is typically used for a navigation area, and the right-hand frame for the main content.

```
<frameset cols="150,* ">
  <frame src="frame_one.html" />
  <frame src="frame_two.html" />
</frameset>
```

The cols attribute defines the width of each frame. This can be set to a number (for a pixel value), a percentage (to enable a liquid design), or an asterisk (*), which essentially sets its measurement to whatever available space is left.

After creating the frameset and the associated pages to load into the frames (frame_one.html and frame_two.html, which have just been populated with a heading in each case), the previous HTML results in the page shown in the following screenshot.

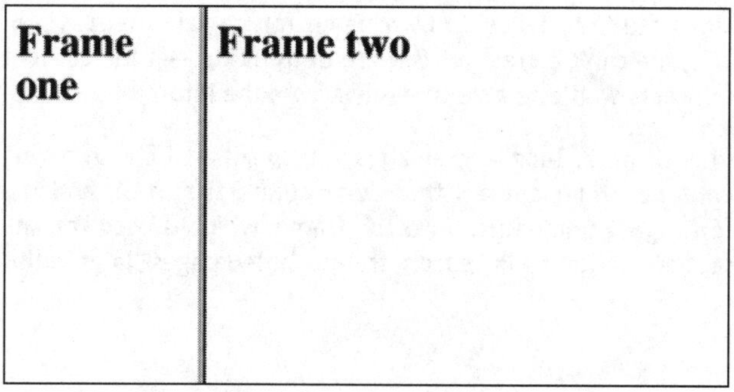

To change the alignment of the frames and split the browser window horizontally, replace the cols attribute with a rows attribute:

```
<frameset rows="150,*">
```

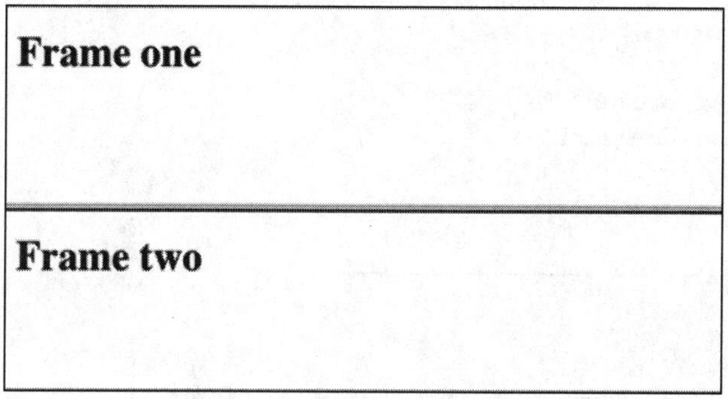

To add more frames in either case, just add more frame elements, but ensure that your cols or rows values add up (for instance, don't set values that add up to more than 100%).

Useful frame attributes

There are a number of attributes that can be added to the frame element, most of which are used to enhance the look of the frames.

- frameborder: This attribute defines whether the frame's border is displayed or not—via a value of 1 or 0, respectively. Beware: turning off the frame borders means that the user won't be able to resize the frames.

- marginheight and marginwidth: these define the margins within the frame and are best set to 0; page content padding can then be defined in CSS.

- scrolling: This attribute sets parameters for the use of scroll bars—it can be set to yes, no, or auto. If scroll bars are turned off, content that's too large for the frame may be cropped and the user won't be able to easily access it. If auto is chosen, scroll bars only appear when the content is too large for the frame.

- noresize: In XHTML, this attribute takes its own name for its value (noresize). When set, the relevant frame can't be resized. Beware of using this—if the content is too big for the frame, users won't be able to easily access the information.

Two other attributes are worthy of note: longdesc enables you to set a URL with a long description of the frame's contents (for browsers that don't support frames); and the name attribute enables you to assign a unique name to the frame, which is used for link targeting purposes (see the section "Targeting links from frames-based pages" later in this chapter).

Nesting framesets

Because each frameset only defines a set of rows *or* columns, you must nest them if you want to create more complex framesets. For instance, you can create a frameset with a masthead across the top and two columns underneath as follows:

```
<frameset rows="120,*">
  <frame src="frame_one.html" />
    <frameset cols="150,*">
      <frame src="frame_two.html" />
      <frame src="frame_three.html" />
    </frameset>
</frameset>
```

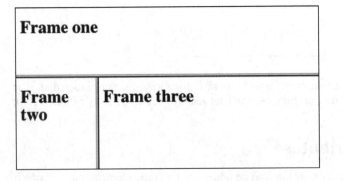

Take care when using nested framesets because things can rapidly get complicated. Also ensure that you close all frameset elements, otherwise the result will almost certainly be an incorrect display. (Also, because we're working in XHTML, the frame elements must also take a trailing slash, as shown in all the code so far.)

Targeting links from frames-based pages

By default, links open within the frame that contains them. However, there are times when this behavior is not desired. For instance, if you have a frame for navigation, you'll typically want the resulting page to open in the content area. Likewise, if you have links to external sites, chances are you'll want them to replace the entire frameset.

Both of these issues are largely dealt with by using the target attribute within anchor tags:

```
<a href="a_link.html">This link opens in the same frame</a>
<a href="a_link.html" target="_self">So does this one!</a>
<a href="a_link.html" target="_top">This link opens a page to replace the
➥frameset</a>
<a href="a_link.html" target="content">This link opens in a frame with the
➥name 'content'</a>
```

The last of the preceding code snippets is used to open a link in a frame with a specific name. It works in tandem with the name attribute, which must be added to the relevant frame. For example, the following code presents our original two-column frameset, but with name attributes for each of the frames:

```
<frameset cols="150,* ">
  <frame src="frame_one.html" name="navigation" />
  <frame src="frame_two.html" name="content" />
</frameset>
```

Should a link in the navigation frame have a target value of content (like the last of the four link examples above), it will open in place of frame_two.html (the intended content area).

Catering to non-frames-compatible browsers

The noframes element can be used to accommodate browsers that aren't frames-compatible.

```
<noframes></noframes>
```

The content of this element is displayed by non-frames-compatible browsers and ignored by those that can deal with frames. You can put whatever you like within the noframes element—it's common to include a body element, a brief explanation of why the page is there (for example, that the user's browser can't access the website because it's frames-based), and some links to the website's content, so those using browsers that can't display frames can still access everything. This content can be anything that you'd use on a normal web page.

9

In terms of placement, the noframes element should be placed inside the outermost frameset element, after all the frames:

```
<frameset cols="150,* ">
  <frame src="frame_one.html" name="navigation" />
  <frame src="frame_two.html" name="content" />
  <noframes>
    Noframes content...
  </noframes>
</frameset>
```

Internal frames (iframes)

Internal frames (sometimes referred to as floating frames) are likely to stick around for some time after the last frames-based website has long passed. This is because they're actually of some use (see the screenshot of the Pixelsurgeon website earlier in the chapter). One advantage of iframes is that they allow for simple updates of text-based information without affecting the main page, since each iframe is a separate HTML document. This means that relatively unskilled people can update a portion of a site's information easily, without affecting the rest of the design. Of course, there are better strategies for such things—SSI, content management systems, and so on—but, if you're on a budget and have to enable someone to update some specific, simple content on a site, iframes might be the way to go.

However, iframes still cause problems with regard to accessibility and search engine indexing, so they should be used in moderation and with caution. As we'll see, iframe display varies across browsers too, so thorough testing is required if you use them.

Attributes for iframes

An iframe can be placed anywhere within a web page, and the available attributes are the same as those of a standard frame (except noresize, which is absent), with the following additions:

- width and height: these define the width and height of the iframe. Set these with caution, because it's annoying if an iframe is bigger than the viewable area, or if the content of the iframe is too big for its defined dimensions. Note that these attributes can be omitted from HTML and instead defined in CSS (by way of an iframe tag selector or by applying a class to the frame).

- align: this can be set to top, middle, bottom, left, or right, and determines how to align the frame according to the surrounding content.

Creating and styling iframes

An example of the markup for creating an iframe looks like this:

```
<iframe src="internal_news.html" name="news" width="200" height="200"
➥scrolling="yes" frameborder="0"></iframe>
```

However, various browser and aesthetic problems stop us from just leaving it like that. Older browsers (such as Netscape 4) can't display iframes and so ignore them. Earlier in the chapter we looked at the noframes element, which allows viewers with non-frames-compatible browsers to see the content inside frames. There's an equivalent method for iframes, in which you include some succinct content and a link to the iframe source page between the iframe tags:

```
<iframe src="internal_news.html" name="news" width="200" height="200"
➥scrolling="yes" frameborder="0">Your browser doesn't support iframes. Please
➥<a href="internal_news.html">click here</a> to see the content.</iframe>
```

Compliant browsers will ignore this content, but browsers that can't display iframes will show it, providing users access to the content—assuming you put the relevant link in place.

Another issue is that Internet Explorer spawns both horizontal and vertical scroll bars when content is larger than the declared width or height. This means that if your iframe is 200 pixels high, but your content is 400 pixels high, you'll end up with a vertical scroll bar *and* a horizontal one, even if your iframe content is narrower than the iframe dimensions. Other browsers don't make this mistake, displaying only the relevant scroll bar.

There are ways around the problem. If you know your iframe content is always going to be too large for the iframe, set scrolling="yes" in the iframe start tag (as in the previous example); setting it to auto or omitting the attribute entirely is what causes the scroll bar problem. Alternatively, add a conditional comment in the head of the iframe content document, and experiment with the width property value until the scroll bar disappears:

```
<!--[if gte IE 5]>
<style type="text/css">
html, body {margin:0; width:180px;}
</style>
<![endif]-->
```

Styling iframes can also cause problems. Turning off the default border is a good move, because it looks clunky. Adding a border using CSS should be possible by applying it directly to the iframe (via a class or iframe tag selector); in practice, however, this fails in Internet Explorer, which bizarrely creates an ugly gap between your scroll bars and iframe borders (which happens to be the same size as the defined border).

9

The way around this is to nest the iframe in a div and provide that with a border instead. In HTML, this looks like the following:

```
<div id="iframewrapper">
<iframe src="internal_news.html" name="news" width="200" height="200"
➥scrolling="yes" frameborder="0">Your browser doesn't support iframes. Please
➥<a href="internal_news.html">click here</a> to see the content.</iframe>
</div>
```

And in CSS, something like the following can be added:

```
#iframewrapper {
width: 200px;
border: solid 3px #777777;
}
```

Replacing iframes with CSS

As mentioned, iframes can be useful for practical reasons, but many people use them for aesthetic reasons too, in order to provide a lot of information on a single page. For instance, iframes are popular for lists of news items because they enable many hundreds of lines of text to be contained in a small area. However, if this is your reason for using iframes, you may be better off replacing them with straightforward divs and then using CSS to control the overflow. If you use this method, the content will remain part of the web page, which is better for accessibility and site maintenance.

To do this, you first need to create a div with a unique id:

```
<div id="internal">
content...
</div>
```

Then style it in CSS—the rule provides the div's dimensions and determines how the div's overflow works.

```
#internal {
width: 200px;
height: 200px;
overflow: auto;
}
```

In this example, overflow:auto tends to work in the same way as setting iframe scrolling to auto, but without the pesky horizontal scroll bar issues. Other available values are hidden, scroll, and visible, which displays no scroll bar, creates permanent scroll bars, and renders content outside of the defined box, respectively. (See the CSS reference section for more details.)

And that just about wraps it up for the frames chapter (and our little diversion into CSS overflow). As mentioned, frames should only be used as a last resort—and although iframes can be useful, even they should only be used in strict moderation.

This is also the end of the layout section of this book, and you should now feel comfortable creating web page layouts. The next two chapters are going to look at some specific web page content (forms and multimedia) before the main section of this book is wrapped up with a look at testing and uploading web pages.

9

CHAPTER 10
GETTING USER FEEDBACK

In this chapter

- Creating forms, and adding fields and controls
- Styling forms in CSS
- Configuring a FormMail CGI script
- Sending forms using PHP
- Creating a layout for user feedback pages

Introducing user feedback

One of the main reasons the Web has revolutionized working life and communications is its immediacy. Unlike printed media, websites can be continually updated at relatively minimal cost and also be available worldwide on a 24/7 basis. However, communication isn't one-way, and the Web makes it very easy to enable site users to offer feedback.

Using mailto: URLs

One of the most common methods of providing immediate user feedback is by using mailto: URLs within anchor tags. Instead of the anchor tag's value being a file name or URL, it instead begins with mailto: and is immediately followed by the recipient e-mail address.

```
<a href="mailto:someone@your.domain">Click to email!</a>
```

It's possible to take this technique further. Multiple recipients can be defined using a comma-separated list, and by placing a question mark immediately after the final recipient address you can add further parameters, such as a subject and recipients to carbon copy (cc) and blind carbon copy (bcc). If using more than one parameter, you must separate them with ampersands.

```
<a href="mailto:someone@your.domain,someoneelse@your.domain?subject=Contact
➡from website&cc=bigboss@your.domain">Click to email!</a>
```

> There should be no spaces in a mailto: value, with the exception of inside the subject string. Therefore, don't place spaces before or after colons, commas, or the ? and = symbols

There are several problems with such a system. First, e-mail addresses online are often harvested by spambots. Second, a mailto: link relies on the user having a preconfigured e-mail client ready to go—something that people working on college and library machines most likely won't have. Third, not all browsers support the range of options explained earlier.

A way to combat the spambots is presented in the next section. For the second issue (the mailto: link's reliance on a preconfigured mail client), I recommend using forms for any complex website feedback. For the third issue (browser support for the more advanced mailto: options), I recommend just keeping things simple. Place your e-mail address online as a mailto: and enable the user to fill in any other details, such as the subject line.

Scrambling addresses

In my experience, having an e-mail address online for just a few days is enough to start receiving regular spam. A workaround is to encrypt any e-mail addresses using a bulletproof concoction of JavaScript. The Enkoder form from Automatic (formerly Hiveware) is perhaps the best example.

This online form at www.automaticlabs.com/products/enkoderform/ enables you to create a mailto: link that's composed of complex JavaScript. Although in time spambots will likely break this code, as they have with simpler encoders, it's the best example I've seen, and the results I've had with it have been good. Beware, though, that any users with JavaScript disabled won't see the address, so ensure you cater for them by including some other means of contacting the site owner.

The Enkoder Form

Posting your email address on a website is a sure-fire way to get an Inbox full of unsolicited email advertisements. The Enkoder protects email addresses by converting them into encrypted JavaScript code, hiding them from email-harvesting robots while revealing them to real people.

This tool is only useful for protecting an email address on a web page you've designed in HTML. It cannot be used when sending email or when posting your address into a web form, or adding your comments to a forum.

If you would like to specify your own HTML for the link, scroll down to the Advanced Form, below.

The Basic Form

Email Address:

The email address to be displayed

Link Text:

The text users will see and click

Link Title:

The "pop-up" text seen when your mouse is over the link

Subject (Optional):

An optional subject line for the email

(Enkode It »)

> *Enkoder is also available as an application for Mac OS X.*

Working with forms

In this section, we'll work through how to create a form and add controls. We'll also look at how to improve form accessibility by using the accesskey and tabindex attributes, and the label, fieldset, and legend elements.

As suggested, the best way of getting user feedback is by means of an online form, which the user fills in and submits. Fields are configured by the designer, enabling the site owner to receive specific information. However, don't go overboard: provide users with a massive, sprawling online form and they will most likely not bother filling it in and will go elsewhere.

> *Similarly, although you can use JavaScript to make certain form fields required, I'm not a fan of this technique, because it annoys users. For instance, I've been on several sites where providing an e-mail address was mandatory, but what if the user doesn't have e-mail and is accessing the form from a library? The user would have to either submit a fake e-mail address, which helps no one, or give up, which certainly doesn't help you.*

So, keep things simple and use the fewest fields possible. In the vast majority of cases, you should be able to simply create name, e-mail address, and phone number fields, and include a text area that enables users to input their query.

10

Creating a form

Form controls are housed within a form element, whose attributes also determine the location of the script used to parse it (see the section "Sending feedback" later in the chapter). Other attributes define the encoding type used and the method by which the browser sends the form's data to the server. A typical start tag for a form therefore looks like this:

```
<form action=http://www.yourdomain.com/cgi-bin/FormMail.cgi
➥method="post">
```

> This form tag includes attributes that point at a CGI script, but alternative methods of sending forms include PHP, ASP, and ColdFusion. Check with your hosting company about what methods are available for sending forms, and use the support offered by your ISP.

Adding controls

Form controls are largely added using the input element. The type attribute declares what kind of control the element is going to be. The most common controls are text, which produces a single-line text input field; checkbox and radio, which are used for multiple-choice options; and submit, which is used for the all-important Submit button.

Drop-down option lists can be created using the select, option, and optgroup elements, while the textarea element provides a means for the user to offer a multiple-line response (this is commonly used in online forms for a questions or query area). A form's HTML may therefore look like the following, producing the page depicted to the right.

```
<form action="http://www.yourdomain.com/cgi-bin/FormMail.cgi"
➥method="post">
<p><strong>Name</strong><br />
<input type="text" name="realname" size="30" /></p>
<p><strong>Email address</strong><br />
<input type="text" name="email" size="30" /></p>
<p><strong>Telephone</strong><br />
<input type="text" name="phone" size="30" /></p>
<p><strong>Are you a Web designer?</strong><br />
<input type="radio" name="designer" value="yes" />Yes |
➥<input type="radio" name="designer" value="no" />No</p>
<p>What platform do you favor?<br />
<select name="platform">
<option selected="selected">Windows XP</option>
<option>Windows 2000</option>
<option>Mac OS X</option>
<option>Linux</option>
<option>Other</option>
</select></p>
```

```
<p><strong>Message</strong><br />
<textarea name="message" rows="5" cols="30"></textarea></p>
<p><input type="submit" name="SUBMIT" value="SUBMIT" /></p>
</form>
```

> *Paragraphs in forms often cause problems for Netscape 4, so thoroughly check your pages if authoring with that browser in mind.*

The bulk of the HTML is pretty straightforward. In each case, the name attribute value labels the control, meaning you end up with the likes of Name: Craig in your form results, rather than just a bunch of answers. For multiple option controls (check boxes and radio buttons), this attribute is identical, and an individual value attribute is set in each start tag.

By default, controls of this type—along with the select list—are off, but you can define a default option. We've done this for the select list by setting selected="selected" on the Windows XP option. You'd do the same on a radio button to select it by default, and with a check box you'd set checked="checked".

Some of the attributes define controls: the input element's size attribute sets a character width for the fields, while the textarea's rows and cols attributes set the number of rows and columns, again in terms of characters. It's also worth noting that any content within the textarea element is displayed, so if you want it to start totally blank, you must ensure there's nothing—not even white space—between the start and end tags. (Some applications that reformat your code, such as Tidy and some website editors, place white space here, which some browsers subsequently use as the default value/content of the textarea. This results in the textarea's content being partially filled with spaces, and anyone trying to use it may then find their cursor's initial entry point is partway down the text area, which can be off-putting.)

Longtime web users may have noticed the omission of a Reset button in this example. This button used to be common online, enabling the user to reset a form to its default state. However, I've never really seen the point in having it there, hence its absence.

> *A full list of controls is in the reference section of this book.*

Improving form accessibility

Although there's an onscreen visual relationship between form label text and the controls, they're not associated in any other way. This sometimes makes forms tricky to use for those people using screen readers and other assistive devices. Also, by default, the *TAB* key cycles through various web page elements in order, rather than jumping to the first form field (and continuing through the remainder of the form before moving elsewhere). Both of these issues are dealt with in this section.

10

The label, fieldset, and legend elements

The `label` element enables you to define relationships between the text labeling a form control and the form control itself. In the following example, the Name text has been surrounded in a `label` element with the `for` attribute value of `realname`. This corresponds to the `name` and `id` values of the form field associated with this text.

```
<p><strong><label for="realname">Name</label></strong><br />
<input type="text" name="realname" id="realname" size="30" /></p>
```

Most browsers won't visually display this (although you can, if you wish, style the `label` element in CSS), but most apply an important accessibility benefit: if you click the label, it gives **focus** to the corresponding form control (in other words, it selects the form control related to the label). Note that the `id` attribute—absent from the form example earlier in the chapter—is required for this. If it's absent, clicking the text within the `label` element won't cause the browser to do anything.

The `fieldset` element enables you to group a set of related form controls to which you apply a label via the `legend` element. Neither has any required attributes, although the latter accepts the `accesskey` attribute (see the section "Adding accesskey and tabindex attributes" later in the chapter).

```
<fieldset>
<legend>Personal information</legend>
<p><strong><label for="realname">Name</label></strong><br />
<input type="text" id="realname" name="realname" size="30" /></p>
<p><strong><label for="email">Email address</label></strong><br />
<input type="text" id="email" name="email" size="30" /></p>
<p><strong><label for="phone">Telephone</label></strong><br />
<input type="text" id="phone" name="phone" size="30" /></p>
</fieldset>
```

As you can see from the preceding screenshot, these elements combine to surround the relevant tags with a border and provide the group of labels and fields with an explanatory title. Each browser deals with the visual presentation in its own way—the default look is certainly not consistent (and the depicted one from Internet Explorer 6 on Windows is by far the most visually appealing). However, as always, the visual appearance can be controlled using CSS. For instance, the following CSS updates the appearance shown in the previous screenshot to that shown to the right.

```
fieldset {
border: 1px dashed #555555;
}
legend {
padding: 0 10px;
font: 12px Verdana, Arial, sans-serif;
color: #000000;
background-color: #ffffff;
text-transform: uppercase;
}
```

> When styling form elements, be sure to rigorously test across browsers, because the display of form elements is not consistent. For instance, omitting the background-color definition from the legend rule makes the line appear behind the legend in Internet Explorer, but this doesn't happen in most other browsers.

Adding accesskey and tabindex attributes

These attributes were first mentioned in Chapter 5 (in the section "Using accesskey and tabindex"). The accesskey attribute can be used to provide keyboard access to focus an element by means of its value (which is case sensitive) and the operating system's modifier key (usually *ALT* on Windows and *CTRL* on Mac).

The tabindex attribute is used to define the page's element tab order, and its value can be set as anything from 0 to 32,767. Because the tabindex values needn't be sequential, they can be set in increments of ten, enabling you to "slot in" others later, without reworking every value on the page. With that in mind, we could set tabindex="11" on the realname field, tabindex="21" on the email field, and tabindex="31" on the phone field (these field names are based on their id/name values from the previous example). Assuming no other tabindex attributes with a lower value are elsewhere on the page, the realname field is the first element highlighted when the *TAB* key is struck, and then (in order) the cycle would continue with the email and phone fields.

> The reason we started with 11 rather than 1 was because if we then ignore the last digit, the tabindex values become standard integers, starting with 1. In other words, remove the final digits from 11, 21, and 31, and you end up with 1, 2, and 3.

In my experience, accesskey is perhaps of more use for site navigation than form controls, but you can easily apply accesskey values to form controls (and legend elements also) via the means explained in Chapter 5.

10

Layout for forms

Earlier, we covered how to lay out a form using paragraphs and line breaks. In this section, we'll see how we can also use tables and CSS to produce a more advanced page. Previously, we also touched upon styling form elements with CSS, and here we'll expand on this idea to ensure the forms fully integrate with your website's visual design.

Adding styles

Form fields can be styled, enabling you to get away from the rather clunky default look offered by most browsers. Although the default appearance isn't very attractive, it does make obvious which elements are fields and which are buttons. Therefore, if you do choose to style forms in CSS, ensure that the elements are still easy to make out.

A simple, elegant style to apply to text input fields and text areas is as follows:

```
.formField {
border: 1px solid #333333;
background-color: #dddddd;
}
```

This replaces the default 3D border with a solid, dark gray border, and it also sets the background color as a light gray, thereby drawing attention to the form input fields. Be wary of adding padding to these elements—Gecko and Internet Explorer apply the values as you'd expect, but Opera and Safari ignore them entirely. Because the border is defined using a class, it can be applied to multiple elements. The reason we don't use a tag selector and apply this style to all input fields is that radio buttons and check boxes look terrible with rectangular borders around them. However, applying this style to the select element tends to work well.

> Depending on the number of input fields, radio buttons, and check boxes you have, it may be simpler to apply the border and background-color properties to the input tag (i.e., replace .formField with input in the previous rule) and then override the settings in a class that's subsequently applied to radio buttons and check boxes.

The default Submit button style can also be amended in a similar fashion, and padding can also be applied to it. This is usually a good idea, because it enables the button to stand out and draws attention to the text within.

> At the time of this writing, Safari ignores form styles, instead using the Mac OS X "Aqua" look and feel. Form functionality is not affected by this, but layouts could be, so ensure you test styled forms in that browser, even if they look fine in every other browser.

Should you desire a more styled Submit button, you can instead use an image.

```
<input type ="image" src="submit.gif" height="20" width="100"
➥alt="Submit form" />
```

A final style point worth bearing in mind is that you can define the form itself. You might wonder why on earth you'd want to do that, but it can be useful to control the margins above and below the form, and also to set its width. The second of those points should be obvious to any of you who've worked through the code in this chapter: the fieldset border stretches to the entire window width, which looks very odd if the form labels and controls take up only a small area of the browser window. Reducing the form's width to specifically defined dimensions enables you to get around this.

Form layout with tables

A common way of laying out forms is to use a table to line up the labels and form controls. For our first three fields, we may have something like this:

```
<fieldset>
<legend>Personal information</legend>
<table cellpadding="0" cellspacing="0" border="0"
➥summary="A contact details form.">
<tr>
<td class="formLabel">
<label for="realname">Name</label></td>
<td><input class="formField" type="text" id="realname" name="realname"
➥size="30" /></td>
</tr>
<tr>
<td class="formLabel"><label for="email">Email address</label></td>
<td><input class="formField" type="text" id="email" name="email"
➥size="30" /></td>
</tr>
<tr>
<td class="formLabel"><label for="phone">Telephone</label></td>
<td><input class="formField" type="text" id="phone" name="phone"
➥size="30" /></td>
</tr>
</table>
</fieldset>
```

> Note that the fieldset and legend elements must surround the table containing the relevant fields. If using these elements, you may need multiple tables for your form.

Because we've added a class to each cell containing the labels, we can amend the text-align property in all of them, along with other CSS properties such as font-weight, the latter of which negates the need for the strong elements used earlier. Applying a padding-right value to these cells also produces a gap to the right of the label cells. We'll call this class formLabel. If we also apply a class to the table itself (formTable), we can use a contextual selector to add some padding at the bottom of each cell (see the image at right).

```
.formTable td {
padding: 0 0 5px 0;
}
td.formLabel {
padding-right: 10px;
text-align: right;
font-weight: bold;
}
```

Name	
Email address	
Telephone	

Form layouts with CSS

The previous table-based layout can be emulated in CSS. A structure is built of divs and spans that replaces the table rows and cells, although it can prove a little code-heavy and be of dubious quality with regard to semantic markup. However, CSS does bring with it the benefit of being able to rapidly restyle and move elements.

Here, the form width needs defining, which we do via a class (formContact) whose only property value is width: 350px;.

```
<form action="http://www.yourdomain.com/cgi-bin/FormMail.cgi"
➥method="post" class="formContact" >
<fieldset>
<legend>Personal information</legend>

<div class="row">
<span class="formLabel"><label for="realname">Name</label></span>
<span class="formControl"><input class="formField" type="text"
➥id="realname" name="realname" size="30" /></span>
</div>

<div class="row">
<span class="formLabel"><label for="email">Email address</label></span>
<span class="formControl"><input class="formField" type="text" id="email"
➥name="email" size="30" /></span>
</div>

<div class="row">
<span class="formLabel"><label for="phone">Telephone</label></span>
<span class="formControl"><input class="formField" type="text" id="phone"
➥name="phone" size="30" /></span>
</div>

<div class="spacer"><!-- spacer --></div>
</fieldset>
</form>
```

> *This isn't a complete form—it's just a guide regarding how to use this method. This example lacks, for instance, a* Submit *button and many of the controls in the example from earlier in the chapter.*

Because all of the spans will be floated, a spacer div is placed after the final form control, which will be set to clear floated elements. The various classes are then defined in CSS.

The spans containing the labels (class: formLabel) are floated left, the text is aligned right, and font-weight is set to bold. The width setting is more than large enough to contain the largest of the text labels.

```
.formLabel {
float: left;
text-align: right;
font-weight: bold;
width: 120px;
}
```

The spans containing the form controls (class: formControl) are floated right. The width setting is 10px less than the sum of the form's width minus the formLabel width setting, thereby creating a 10px gap between form labels and controls.

```
.formControl {
float: right;
width: 220px;
}
```

The row class is set to clear floated elements, and padding-top is set to 5px. This results in the rows sitting underneath each other and having gaps between them.

```
.row {
clear: both;
padding-top: 5px;
}
```

Finally, the spacer is defined, to clear the previous row (thereby enabling subsequent content to be positioned underneath). height is set to 10px, to produce a gap beneath the final field.

```
.spacer {
clear: both;
height: 10px;
}
```

Although this works fine in Opera and Internet Explorer, Safari and Gecko apparently apply a default padding within the fieldset, and so need an amendment to that rule to correctly lay out the form:

```
fieldset {
border: 1px dashed #555555;
padding: 0;
margin: 0;
}
```

The jury's out regarding whether this is a better solution than using tables. It could be argued that forms comprise tabular data, and tables certainly enable you to structure forms in a way that seems logical. The CSS example is riddled with span tags, increasing page weight. However, as mentioned earlier, because of the way the CSS layouts are marked up, it would be simple later on to rapidly restyle the form (and also to move the elements around).

10

Sending feedback

In this section, we'll check out how to send form data using a CGI script and PHP.

Once users submit information, it needs to go somewhere and a method of getting there. Several techniques are available for parsing forms, but we're first going to cover the most common: a server-side CGI script. Essentially, this script collects the information submitted, formats it, and delivers it to the addresses you configure within the script.

FormMail, available from Matt's Script Archive (www.scriptarchive.com), is probably the most common, and a number of web hosts preconfigure this script in their web space packages. However, FormMail does have flaws, and it hasn't kept up with current technology. Therefore, I recommend using *nms* FormMail (available from http://nms-cgi.sourceforge.net/ and described next), a script that emulates the behavior of FormMail but takes a more modern and bug-free approach.

Configuring *nms* FormMail

The thought of editing and configuring scripts gives some designers the willies, but *nms* FormMail takes only a couple of minutes to get up and running. First, you need to add some more input elements to your web page, after the form start tag:

```
<input type="hidden" name="subject" value="Contact form from website" />
<input type="hidden" name="redirect"
➥value="http://www.yourdomain.com/contact_thanks.html" />
```

Obviously, the values in the preceding elements need changing for your page. The subject value can be whatever you like—just make it obvious, so you or your clients can use an e-mail package to filter website form responses efficiently.

The redirect value isn't required, but it's good to provide positive feedback to users, not only to confirm that their form's been sent, but also to communicate that their query will be dealt with as soon as possible. Many "thank you" pages online tend to look a little barren, with a single paragraph of text. That's why I tend to make this page a duplicate of my standard contact page, but with the confirmation paragraph above the form. The script itself needs only minimal editing. Because CGI scripts tend to break with slight errors, I highly recommend editing them in a text editor that doesn't affect document formatting, such as NoteTab for Windows (www.notetab.com) or BBEdit for Mac (www.barebones.com).

The first line of the script defines the location of Perl on your web host's server. Your hosting company can provide this, so you can amend the path accordingly.

```
#!/usr/bin/perl -wT
```

Elsewhere, you only need to edit some values in the user configuration section. The $mailprog value defines the location of the sendmail binary on your web host's server. You can find this out from your web host's system admin.

```
$mailprog = '/usr/lib/sendmail -oi -t';
```

The $postmaster value is the address that receives bounced messages if e-mails cannot be delivered. It should be a different address from that of the intended recipient.

```
$postmaster =  'someone@your.domain';
```

The @referers value lists IP addresses or domain names that can access this script, thereby stopping just anyone from using your script and your server resources. For instance, the Snub Communications mail form has snubcommunications.com and the site's IP address for this value (as a space-delimited list).

```
@referers = qw(dave.org.uk 209.207.222.64 localhost);
```

The @allow_mail_to value contains the addresses to which form results can be sent, again as a space-delimited list. If you include just a domain here, then any address on that domain is valid as a recipient. If you're using only one address, set the $max_recipients value to 1, to increase security.

```
@allow_mail_to = qw(you@your.domain some.one.else@your.domain localhost);
```

Multiple recipients

You can also use the script to e-mail multiple recipients. To do so, an additional hidden input element is needed in the HTML:

```
<input type="hidden" name="recipient" value="emailgroup" />
```

And in the script itself, two lines are changed. The @allow_mail_to value is removed, because it's catered for by the newly amended %recipient_alias. Both are shown here:

```
@allow_mail_to   = ();
%recipient_alias = ('emailgroup =>
➥'your-name@your.domain,your-name@somewhere-else.domain',);
```

Should a script be used for multiple groups of recipients, you need a unique value for each in the HTML and to amend the %recipient_alias value accordingly:

```
%recipient_alias   = (
➥'emailgroup1' => 'your-name@your.domain,your-name@somewhere-else.domain',
➥'emailgroup2'  => 'foo@your.domain');
```

10

Script server permissions

Upload the script to your site's `cgi-bin`. Once there, the script's permissions must be set. Exactly how this is achieved depends on what FTP client you're using. Some enable you to right-click and "get info," while others have a permissions or `CHMOD` command buried among their menus. Consult your documentation and find out which your client has. If you can `CHMOD` the script file, set it to 755. If you have to manually set permissions, do so as per the screenshot shown to the right. Finally, check that the script's file extension matches that in your form element's action attribute (`.pl` or `.cgi`—the latter is usually preferred by servers).

Sending form data by PHP

If your hosting company offers support for PHP, the most widely used server-side technology, there is no need to install a CGI script such as FormMail. Everything can be done with PHP's built-in `mail()` function. The function requires three pieces of information:

- The address the mail is being sent to
- The subject line
- The message itself

An optional fourth argument to `mail()` permits you to send additional information in the e-mail headers, such as `from`, `cc`, and `bcc` addresses, and to specify a particular character encoding (if, for instance, you need to include accented characters or an Asian language in the e-mail). Although the PHP script can be put in a separate page, the most convenient method is to use a self-processing form. This displays the feedback page as normal when the user first visits the page, but it contains all the necessary PHP code to process the form and simply displays an acknowledgment at the top of the form once the mail has been sent. The code is straightforward. Even if you have no experience working with PHP, the following instructions should have you up and running very quickly.

1. Save the page containing the form with a PHP extension—for instance, `feedback.php`. Amend the opening form tag like this:

```
<form action="<?php echo $_SERVER['PHP_SELF']; ?>" method="post">
```

2. At the top of the page, insert the following PHP code block above the DOCTYPE. Although I've warned you elsewhere in the book never to place any content above the DOCTYPE, it's perfectly safe to do so in this case, because the PHP code doesn't produce any HTML output.

```
<?php
if ($_POST) {
  if (get_magic_quotes_gpc()) {
    foreach ($_POST as $key => $value) {
      $temp = stripslashes($value);
      $_POST[$key] = $temp;
```

```
        }
      }
    $to = 'me@example.com';
    $subject = 'Feedback from website';
    // message goes here
    // headers go here
    $sent = mail($to, $subject, $message, $headers);
    }
  ?>
```

3. The script begins by checking whether the POST array has been set. This happens only when a user clicks the form's Submit button, so this entire block of code will be ignored when the page first loads. It then makes sure the content from the form is in the right format to send by e-mail. The only lines you have to change are those beginning with $to and $subject. You will also need to replace the lines indicating where the message and headers go.

4. Replace me@example.com with the e-mail address that the feedback is to be sent to. Make sure the address is in quotes, and that the line ends with a semicolon.

5. Replace the content inside the quotes in the following line with whatever you want the subject line to say.

6. Next, build the message. To do this, retrieve the value of each form field and add any extra text you want. Say, for instance, you have three fields in your form: name, email, and address. PHP stores their values as $_POST['name'], $_POST['email'], and $_POST['address']. In other words, the field's name goes in quotes inside the square brackets of $_POST[].

   Surrounding text is put in quotes, and each part is joined together by using a period. You insert new lines by typing \n inside double quotes. To build a message from the three fields, you would use the following code:

```
$message = "From: " . $_POST['name']) . "\n";
$message .= "Email: " . $_POST['email'] . "\n";
$message .= "Address: " . $_POST['address'];
```

   Note that there is a period before the equal sign in the second and third rows. This adds the value of the previous line to the message.

7. There are many additional headers you can add to an e-mail. The following example shows how to add a from address, a reply-to address, a cc address, and UTF-8 encoding (for messages that require accents or Asian languages):

```
$headers = "From: feedback@example.com\n";
$headers .= "Reply-To: " . $_POST['email'] . "\n";
$headers .= "Cc: copycat@example.com\n";
$headers .= "Content-type: text/plain; charset=UTF-8";
```

   As with the message, the headers are built using the period to join text in quotes and form variables. Each of these headers (except the last one) must be followed by the PHP new line character (\n). Lines 1 and 3 don't contain any values from the form, so the \n simply goes before the closing double quote. On line 2, the \n follows a form value, so the two are joined by a period, and the new line character goes inside its own set of double quotes.

10

One nice little touch in this script is that the second line of the headers puts the user's e-mail address in the Reply-to field of the e-mail, so all you have to do is click Reply in your e-mail program to send a message back to the right person.

If you want to use a special encoding, such as UTF-8, for your e-mails, make sure the web page containing the form uses the same encoding in its meta tag.

You don't need to use all these headers. Just remove the complete line for any that you don't want.

8. Insert the code from steps 6 and 7 at the points indicated in step 2.

9. The final line of code sends the e-mail and sets a variable called $sent.

10. Immediately above the form in the main part of your page, insert the following code:

```php
<?php
if (isset($sent)) {
    echo '<p>Thank you, your details have been sent.</p>';
    }
?>
```

This text will display only if the $sent variable has been set. Put whatever message you like in place of the one shown here.

11. Save the page, upload it to your hosting company, and test it. In a few moments, you should receive the test message in your inbox. That's all there is to it!

> Although these instructions should be sufficient to help you get a PHP form working successfully, server-side coding can seem intimidating if you've never done it before. If you would like to learn more about working with PHP and Dreamweaver, see Foundation Dreamweaver MX 2004 by Craig Grannell, David Powers, and George McLachlan (friends of ED, ISBN: 1-59059-308-1) or PHP Web Development with Dreamweaver MX 2004 by Allan Kent and David Powers, with Rachel Andrew (Apress, ISBN: 1-59059-350-2). Also check the Apress online catalog at www.apress.com for non-Dreamweaver-specific books on PHP and other server-side technologies.

Using e-mail to send form data

In rare cases, it may not be possible to set up a form to send form data (although even most free web hosts tend to provide users with some kind of form functionality, even if it's a shared script). If you find yourself in this sticky situation, it's possible to use a mailto: URL for the form's action attribute value. This causes browsers to e-mail the form parameters and values to the specified address.

```
<form method="post"  action="mailto:anemailaddress@somewhere.com"
➥enctype="text/plain">
```

This might seem a simpler method than messing around with CGI scripts, but it has major shortfalls:

- Some browsers don't support `mailto:` as a form action.

- The resulting data may arrive in a barely readable (or unreadable) format, and you have no control over this.

- This method isn't secure.

- The user won't be redirected and may therefore not realize data has been sent.

That last problem can be worked around by adding a JavaScript alert to the form start tag:

```
<form method="post" action="mailto:anemailaddress@somewhere.com"
➥enctype="text/plain" onsubmit="window.alert('This form is being sent by
➥email. Thank you for contacting us.')">
```

Of course, this relies on JavaScript being active on the user's browser—but, then, this is a last resort.

A layout for contact pages

Once you've completed a form, you need to integrate it into your site in a way that most benefits the site's visitors. I've always been of the opinion that it's a good idea to offer users multiple methods of contact on the same page. This makes it easy for them to contact you, as it requires fewer clicks than the fairly common presentation of a form and link to other contact details.

The following screenshot of the Snub Communications site shows what I reckon is a good layout.

10

On the left is the form, with the fewest fields needed to be able to respond to someone effectively. On the right-hand side of the page are other contact details, such as a mailing address and telephone numbers (along with a brief disclaimer confirming that Snub Communications uses personal details collected via the site only for the purpose of getting in touch with clients as appropriate, and that under no circumstances will any details be passed on to third-party organizations).

Here, everything is in one place, which makes sending feedback to and/or getting in contact with the organization convenient for the end user. The Snub Communications site doesn't require a map, but if it did, a link to it would appear on this page, too. The map page itself would likely resemble this one, but with the map in place of the form—after all, it's frustrating to have a map to an organization's location, get lost, and then discover you don't have the organization's full address and telephone number. Therefore, make it easy on your website's users and provide maps with other contact details on the same page.

We're not going to get into how to create this layout, because we've already covered the techniques earlier in the book (see the section "From boxout to sidebar" in Chapter 8). We've covered plenty of ground here, so now it's time to leave the subject of collecting user feedback behind and progress to the next chapter, which explores the delicate art of adding multimedia to websites.

CHAPTER 11
ADDING MULTIMEDIA

In this chapter

- Introducing plug-ins
- Examining popular multimedia plug-ins
- Embedding Flash and QuickTime movies in a web page

Multimedia and the Web

Every now and again, the Web makes a technological quantum leap that further pushes the boundaries of what's possible in online design and media. **Plug-ins** were perhaps the greatest of these, enabling all manner of technologies to work in cooperation with browsers and opening the Internet up to streaming movies, online gaming, and more.

Of all the available plug-ins, the most important can be broken down into the following two camps: plug-ins that provide the means for immersive and highly interactive contents, and plug-ins that provide the means to play audio and video.

Unfortunately, unlike the core browser standards we've explored elsewhere in this book, plug-ins largely rely on proprietary technology, which is often not installed by default on PCs and Macs. Technology that works well on one platform may work less well on others, and you must also be mindful that users don't tend to keep up to date with regard to the latest available version of each plug-in.

Also, you should ensure that whenever you use plug-ins for important and essential content (such as navigation), you provide an alternative for those that don't have the plug-in installed. In addition, you should be mindful of the accessibility issues that plague much plug-in–oriented content (in that it's mostly not accessible unless extreme care is taken when creating the elements to be embedded in the web page). For instance, although a Flash-based navigation bar may be beautiful, if you don't offer an alternative, it will be closed to a portion of your visitors.

Popular multimedia plug-ins

The only plug-in that can almost (but not quite) justify itself as a "standard" is Macromedia Flash. The technology is open to other manufacturers to use in their products, and the plug-in tends to be installed by default on both Macs and PCs. Statistics seem to suggest that Flash's reach is almost total, but you should be wary of believing that Flash-based web page elements will work on all machines—some companies and institutions forbid the installation of plug-ins, and many users will have an older version of the Flash plug-in that may not be compatible with the features of more recent Flash releases. However, it is possible to target older versions of the player when exporting movies (see right).

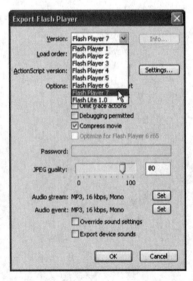

At its most basic level, Flash is a package for vector-based animation and, as mentioned earlier in the book, it's long been abused on the Web, with countless designers using it to create pointless website introductions. But, when used with care, Flash can bring life to a website, and it's an effective and efficient means of creating embedded animation. You can also use it to create high-quality headings and display copy. And because Flash output is vector-based, it tends to be more detailed than bitmap-based GIF images and usually produces smaller files. Also, because basic animation has been a core feature of Flash for several years, you can usually save animations to target earlier versions of the plug-in, thereby maximizing your audience.

However, Flash has evolved, and it's now far more than a means of creating website animations. At the application's heart is a powerful scripting language, ActionScript, and many online games are now entirely Flash-based, such as the excellent Yeti Sports (www.yetisports.org).

In many ways, Flash is well suited to online gaming. The vector-based format means that low-bandwidth, quality graphics can be created, and ActionScript enables you to make complex interactions within the games. The only problem with Flash is that—at the time of this writing, at least—the Mac player is sluggish, playing back animations considerably more slowly than the Windows version. Therefore, if working heavily with Flash, ensure that you thoroughly test on both platforms.

Another way Flash has evolved is in the area of accessibility. A major drawback of Flash is that all content is presented through a binary file, locking away any text and making it difficult to create a website that is accessible to the disabled. Flash MX introduced some limited accessibility features, and Flash MX 2004 made further improvements, such as enabling the use of tabindex and accesskey for some interface components.

Making a Flash site accessible is much more complex than with a text-based medium, such as XHTML, but it's a skill developers have to acquire if they want to make extensive use of Flash. The subject of Flash accessibility as a whole is too complex and off-topic to discuss here. However, Macromedia provides an online guide to Flash's features and general accessibility, which is a good place to start: www.macromedia.com/macromedia/accessibility/.

11

> For more on authoring quality Flash projects, check out the following books: Foundation Flash MX 2004 by Kristian Besley and Sham Bhangal (friends of ED, ISBN: 1-590559-303-0), Foundation PHP 5 for Flash by David Powers (friends of ED, ISBN: 1-59059-466-5), and Foundation ActionScript for Flash MX 2004 by Sham Bhangal, (friends of ED, ISBN: 159059-305-7).

Another of Macromedia's plug-ins has made less of an impact than Flash, but is nonetheless worthy of mention. Often mistaken for Flash, Shockwave is actually more powerful (although Flash continues to close the gap), providing a means to create 3D gaming environments akin to early PlayStation games, immersive product demonstrations, and more. Shockwave content is typically authored in Macromedia Director and plays back in a web browser via the Shockwave plug-in, which is rather weightier than the Flash plug-in and again proves more sluggish on the Mac. Because Shockwave's reach is less than Flash's, only use it when you know your target audience is likely to have the plug-in installed (such as for advanced online games), and not for anything critical to the usability of your website. A good place to discover what Shockwave can do is www.shockwave.com.

Although Macromedia plug-ins seemingly have web animation and gaming pretty much sewn up, online movie playback has a number of companies competing for market share. Apple's QuickTime Player, Real's RealPlayer, and Microsoft's Windows Media Player, along with their associated technologies, battle it out for the online video market. Unfortunately, the formats associated with these players tend to be mutually incompatible, and if you cater for only one, you run the risk of leaving out a large section of your potential audience or forcing them to download a new player.

I've seen so many conflicting sets of figures now that I'm not even going to guess at which player is the market leader, or which has the most potential. Also, the market has a habit of changing with speed—Apple's QuickTime was once the definite underdog, but with iTunes installing QuickTime by "stealth" methods, the technology is now available on considerably more Windows PCs than it was prior to iTunes' arrival. Therefore, many Windows users can now play QuickTime movies without having downloaded the plug-in on its own.

A general rule when authoring video for the Web is to offer multiple download formats, in order to cater for the widest possible audience. Even though Windows Media Player, QuickTime Player, and RealPlayer are all available on Windows and Mac, performance varies considerably (with Windows Media Player being particularly poor on Mac). Furthermore, some codecs (compression formats) aren't available on both platforms, so always ensure you thoroughly test your movies before putting them online.

11

Embedding multimedia

Over the years, the Web has been a battleground, with browser developers going up against open standards in an effort to grab market share. Numerous extensions to HTML were created by browser developers, which gained widespread acceptance but never made it into the recognized standards. Many of these have since disappeared and, by and large, browsers today adhere to standards set by the W3C. However, there is a major exception: the embed element.

Browser developers considered the embed element to be the logical follow-up to img, but the W3C already catered for embedded objects with its object element. Therefore, the

W3C never included embed in any official HTML specification, despite it being used on millions of websites. Matters were further complicated by Internet Explorer later dropping support for Netscape-style plug-ins, thereby requiring the use of object for embedding multimedia content.

Unfortunately, support for object in general is very poor—even in Internet Explorer, which, for instance, doesn't correctly deal with showing fallback elements that should appear when the embedded object cannot be displayed for some reason—and most other browsers still require embed when embedding multimedia content. Therefore, web designers are left with a problem: do they try to work toward total standards-compliance, thereby compromising their sites and perhaps creating a solution that fails to work in some browsers, or do they create a workable solution that works in every modern browser, but means the page doesn't validate?

Apple's developer guidelines suggest the following code soup to embed a QuickTime movie in a web page:

```
<object classid="clsid:02BF25D5-8C17-4B23-BC80-D3488ABDDC6B"
➥width="320" height="256"
➥codebase="http://www.apple.com/qtactivex/qtplugin.cab">
<param name="SRC" value="movie.mov">
<param name="AUTOPLAY" value="true">
<param name="scale" value="2">
<param name="loop" value="false">
<embed src="movie.mov" width="320" height="256" scale="2"
➥autoplay="true" loop="false" pluginspage="http://www.apple.com/
➥quicktime/download/"/>
</embed>
</object>
```

This works fine in all browsers (and the preceding code sets scale to 2, exploiting a feature of QuickTime that enables you to scale small movies, thereby avoiding postage stamp–sized movies when catering for low-bandwidth users). However, due to the inclusion of the embed element, the page this code is included on will not validate.

Likewise, the typical code that the latest version of Flash kicks out when publishing a movie is bloated and invalid:

```
<object classid="clsid:d27cdb6e-ae6d-11cf-96b8-444553540000"
➥codebase="http://download.macromedia.com/pub/shockwave/cabs/flash/
➥swflash.cab#version=7,0,0,0" width="550" height="400" id="animation"
➥align="middle">
<param name="allowScriptAccess" value="sameDomain" />
<param name="movie" value="movie.swf" />
<param name="quality" value="high" />
<param name="bgcolor" value="#ffffff" />
<embed src="movie.swf" quality="high" bgcolor="#ffffff" width="550"
➥height="400" name="animation" align="middle"
➥allowScriptAccess="sameDomain" type="application/x-shockwave-flash"
➥pluginspage="http://www.macromedia.com/go/getflashplayer" />
</object>
```

Nevertheless, it *works*, and designers the world over are therefore content to use it.

There have been efforts to buck the trend and replace this code soup with lean, valid markup. A well-known example is Drew McLellan's Flash Satay, detailed in full at www.alistapart.com/stories/flashsatay/. McLellan's experiment replaces the default Flash code with something like this:

```
<object type="application/x-shockwave-flash" data="c.swf?path=movie.swf"
➥width="550" height="400">
<param name="movie" value=" c.swf?path=movie.swf" />
<img src="noflash.gif" width="550" height="400" alt="" />
</object>
```

This code validates, but movies fail to stream in Internet Explorer. McLellan got around this issue by using a small Flash movie to load a larger one, but still problems occurred, with a random portion of web users not being able to see embedded content added to a web page when using this method. Although most users could see the content, "most" is never really enough in web design.

Ultimately, we have to admit that the world of web design is not perfect, and sometimes hacks and workarounds are unavoidable. Ultimately, it's up to you which path you choose, but you should remember that you're creating websites for an audience, and the most important thing is that as many people as possible can access the content. In the vast majority of cases, this can be achieved with lean, standards-compliant code but, unfortunately, embedded multimedia is the one area where this ideal is still some way off.

11

CHAPTER 12

TESTING, TWEAKING,
AND UPLOADING

In this chapter

- Creating a browser test suite
- Banishing common browser bugs
- Working with legacy and alternate devices
- Validating web pages

The final test

The one time web designers tend to envy designers in other fields is when it comes to testing their sites. Although we're a long way from the "design a site for each browser" mentality that afflicted the medium in the late 1990s, we've still not quite reached the holy grail of "author once, display anywhere."

The methods outlined in this book take you most of the way there, providing a solid foundation for websites that should need little tweaking to get them working across all web browsers. However, to say such sites will never need *any* amendments is naïve. Therefore, unless authoring for an internal corporate environment where everyone uses the same browser, designers must always ensure they thoroughly test their sites in a range of browsers.

A browser test suite

The browsers used to test websites and as a basis for development vary from designer to designer. Ultimately, it comes down to personal taste in many ways, but I tend to use the Gecko engine as a starting point. This engine is the guts of Mozilla, Firefox, and other projects available at www.mozilla.org. The reason I tend to use it as a starting point is because it's a very standards-compliant rendering engine, with few quirks, and it generally doesn't permit sloppy errors (which Internet Explorer is far more likely to let you get away with).

Once the basic site structure and layout is up and running, I tend to test in a range of alternate browsers, typically in the following order:

1. **Internet Explorer 6 for Windows**: Because it's the most used browser on the face of the planet, if your site doesn't work in it—even if you've used compliant markup and CSS, and your pages validate—you must make changes to ensure the majority of web users can use the site.

2. **Internet Explorer 5.5 for Windows**: Despite poor press, Internet Explorer 5.5 isn't too hard to deal with, if you know its quirks. I've already mentioned its problems with the box model in this book, and the box model hack (or an equivalent) is a way of dealing with this.

3. **Opera**: It's rapidly gaining in popularity (in fact, because it's set to identify itself as Internet Explorer by default, there may be many more Opera users out there than most people realize), so it makes sense to test sites in this browser. Generally speaking, layouts that work in Gecko browsers work fine in Opera, with the odd exception here and there.

4. **Safari for Mac**: Apple's Safari is the default browser for Mac OS X. Although Mac users comprise only a relatively small percentage of web users, they tend to be pretty vocal when things don't work on their machines, so testing in Safari is a good idea. Also, as more users migrate to Mac OS X (from earlier versions of the Mac OS, and perhaps from Windows), this browser is likely to gain some ground. Generally, it performs well, although not quite as well as Opera and Gecko.

5. **Internet Explorer 5 for Mac**: It's been cancelled, but plenty of people still use this ex-default Mac browser. Back in its day (it was released in Spring 2001), this was not only the bee's knees of web browsers, but the bee's legs, and perhaps its wings, too. It was the first truly "standards-compliant" web browser, and the one that set the bar for those that followed. Sadly, it's now seriously showing its age, and although it correctly supports the box model, it has numerous quirks that tend to drive web designers bonkers. Luckily, there is a CSS hack that enables you to set rules specifically for Internet Explorer 5 for Mac, as we'll see later in the chapter.

6. **Internet Explorer 5 for Windows**: Seeing as this pile of junk was released way back in 1999, it's unsurprising that it has quite a few omissions with regard to CSS standards. This is the point in testing where we begin to seriously push the "good enough" angle: if a site more or less looks as it should in this browser, and if users can access the content, fine. However, never compromise the site in other browsers just so it works in this one, seeing as Internet Explorer 5's market share is rapidly diminishing as a result of superior subsequent releases.

7. **Netscape 4**: Test in this browser more as a sanity check than anything else. I almost always use @import these days to attach style sheets, so I boot up Netscape 4 to check that the CSS is hidden, and that the site's content is navigable and accessible.

And that's it. Sure, there are other browsers out there, but you could go insane endlessly testing sites in all of them. Most are pretty niche anyway. For instance, iCab is a Mac browser that's been in development since Mac OS X was first announced. At the time of this writing, its CSS support still makes Internet Explorer 5 for Windows look like a class browser. There's no way of catering for iCab without seriously compromising your site, but seeing as such a minority of a minority use it anyway (and choose to use it—they're using neither a browser welded to their operating system, nor something that's been preinstalled), we can choose to ignore it.

At each stage of testing, I recommend that you save test HTML and CSS files *a lot*. If something fails in a browser, another copy is created and a fix made. (Don't continually overwrite files, because it's sometimes useful—and, indeed, necessary—to go back to previous versions.) The page must then be confirmed in all previous browsers. It might sound like a lot of work, but in most cases, this takes only minutes. However, there have been times when I've sat there yelling like an idiot at my computer screen, wondering why my compliant and validated web pages that worked perfectly in every other browser suddenly and unceremoniously fall to bits in Internet Explorer for Mac.

That, in essence, is what the first part of this chapter is about: collecting some tales of woe with regard to browser quirks, and telling you how to get around them.

Overcoming browser quirks

I must point out that this section is not exhaustive. If I were to list a fix for every browser quirk out there, you may need a small truck to transport this book—and such a thing is likely to be fairly inconvenient in the typical design studio. ("Pass me the book for a

12

minute." "Brrrrrmmmm.") However, it does collect common errors mentioned during this book and the fixes that I've come across over the years.

Gaps in graphical layouts

If you've created a layout with tables or CSS that has unexplained gaps in it, the likelihood is that they're the result of white space appearing in the HTML. Although browsers should ignore white space, they sometimes don't. A common example of this is with the list-based navigation bar created in Chapter 5. If you find gaps between the tabs when you test the page in a browser, remove any white space within the list elements, and then from between the list elements, and the problem should be fixed.

> Don't remove all white space from your page. Although some designers still advocate this practice, largely due to it shaving a few bytes off your HTML file, it results in web pages that are a major pain to edit.

Internet Explorer and the XML declaration

Even if your code is perfect, you may find the site doesn't display properly in Internet Explorer for Windows. The most likely reason is the inclusion of the XML declaration:

```
<?xml version="1.0" encoding="ISO-8859-1"?>
```

This throws Internet Explorer into quirks mode, and removing the declaration entirely fixes the problem (see the section "What about the XML declaration?" in Chapter 2).

Box model hacking for Internet Explorer 5 on Windows

Prior to version 6, Internet Explorer for Windows got the box model wrong, placing padding and borders within defined element dimensions rather than outside them. Therefore, an element with a 200px width, 20px of padding at each edge, and a 5px border has a box width of 250px in a compliant browser (5 + 20 + 200 + 20 + 5), but only 200px in Internet Explorer 5 and 5.5 for Windows (thereby leaving only 150px for content). In some designs, this isn't a problem, but for many CSS layouts, this wrecks things—especially when pixel-perfect placement is involved.

Tantek Çelik's box model hack, which is explained in depth at www.tantek.com/CSS/Examples/boxmodelhack.html, enables you to provide "false" values for Internet Explorer 5 and then an accurate value for compliant browsers.

```
div#example {
padding: 20px;
border: 5px solid #000000;
width: 250px;
voice-family: "\"}\"";
voice-family:inherit;
```

```
width: 200px;
}
html>body #example {
width: 200px;
}
```

The first value is set for Internet Explorer 5 and 5.5. The voice-family lines cause that browser to quit reading the rule. Other browsers continue, and the second value overrides the first. The second rule deals with Opera 5, which suffers from the same bug that enables us to use the box model hack, but gets the box model right. This is largely included for completeness, but with that browser's market share being so small, and Opera users tending to rapidly upgrade, you may wish to omit this rule.

Conditional comments for Internet Explorer on Windows

Although the box model hack is in very common usage, it is a hack, and some designers prefer their CSS to be kept pure from such things. It's still possible to work around the failings of earlier versions of Internet Explorer by using **conditional comments**. Here, you create a style sheet with no workarounds, and then a separate style sheet just with workarounds for each version of Internet Explorer that you want to target. The Internet Explorer–specific style sheet or style sheets are then applied by the use of one or more conditional comments, which are specially formatted comment tags that only Internet Explorer recognizes.

To target Internet Explorer in general (including version 6), you use the following conditional comment:

```
<!--[if IE]>
<link rel="stylesheet" type="text/css" href="ie.css" />
<![endif]-->
```

To target by specific version number, you amend the opening comment:

```
<!--[if IE 5.0]>
<link rel="stylesheet" type="text/css" href="ie5.css" />
<![endif]-->
```

To emulate the box model hack, you could use either of the following two examples. The first targets all version 5 releases of Internet Explorer, and the second targets Internet Explorer releases prior to version 6.

```
<!--[if IE 5]>
<link rel="stylesheet" type="text/css" href="hack.css" />
<![endif]-->

<!--[if IE lt 6]>
<link rel="stylesheet" type="text/css" href="hack.css" />
<![endif]-->
```

Note that the code order is extremely important when using conditional comments. If you don't want your standard CSS rules to override those in the Internet Explorer–specific style sheets, the conditional comments must come *after* where your default CSS is attached in the head of the HTML document.

12

Internet Explorer for Mac issues

Although great at the time of release, Internet Explorer for Mac is showing its age and has many problems. One common—and infuriating—problem affects CSS layouts that have columns that add up to 100% of the window width. Italicized text on the edge of a column sometimes causes Internet Explorer 5 to make the column wider than it should be, thereby making the page larger than the window width. If these elements are floated, as is often the way for columns, one then appears underneath the other. Short of rewriting the copy to get around Internet Explorer 5's bug—a ludicrous thing to have to do—it's usually best to use a CSS hack to set specific widths for Internet Explorer for Mac.

Again, this hack was discovered by Tantek Çelik, and it enables you to import rules for Internet Explorer 5 for Mac only. It should be positioned after where your default CSS is attached in the head of your HTML file:

```
/*\*//*/
@import "ie5mac.css";
/**/
```

This browser has numerous other float bugs, too, most of which are detailed in full at www.macedition.com/cb/ie5macbugs/. Chances are, if you're having problems with Internet Explorer 5 for Mac, that's where you'll find a fix.

> Many more CSS hacks for a whole range of browsers can be found online at http://centricle.com/ref/css/filters/.

Opera quirks regarding body and list styling

Unlike other browsers, Opera sets default padding on the page body. Therefore, you must override this in CSS to ensure the page displays the same as in other browsers (see the section "Content margins and padding in CSS" in Chapter 2).

Opera also sets margins under list elements, which you can override by setting margin to 0 using a list tag selector (see the section "List margins and padding" in Chapter 3).

Common errors

If your site still isn't working, work through the following list:

- Ensure your page has the correct DOCTYPE (see Chapter 2).
- Validate your HTML and CSS to eradicate errors (see the next section, "Useful online services").
- Use comments to isolate elements and CSS styles to discover what is causing the problems.

- Ensure the code you're using is supported by all target browsers (everything within this book should be fine in all currently shipping browsers).

- Ensure your browser is set to its default setup. For instance, it's very easy to think your fonts are incorrectly sized and then to realize that your browser's fonts are set to display larger than the default.

And, if all else fails, rebuild the page in small steps, checking after each one.

Useful online services

Web designers rely on the Internet for a living, and they can also use it to assist them in their work via a number of useful online services. Many of them are free, and all the ones mentioned here should take up permanent residence in your bookmarks folder.

W3C Markup Validation Service

Although you may be meticulous in crafting your web pages and studious with regard to markup, everyone makes mistakes. The W3C Markup Validation Service, available at http://validator.w3.org/, helps to catch them.

Put a page through the service, and it either passes the test, in which case you see the depicted screenshot, or the service provides a list of error messages and makes suggestions regarding what you can do to fix the page. It's an invaluable tool when creating those initial template web pages, and it should be bookmarked by every web designer.

W3C Link Checker

Part of the aforementioned service is the W3C Link Checker, which can be accessed directly at http://validator.w3.org/checklink. With most web design packages providing some sort of link checker, you might wonder why you should bother using a service such as this. Rather than just checking to see whether links are broken or not, W3C's service makes suggestions for improvements. For instance, it flags instances of JavaScript use in links, linking to the organization's page on alternate techniques, and it also notifies you of things like directory redirects lacking a trailing slash.

Tidy

Created by Dave Raggett and now maintained by a group of volunteers over at http://tidy.sourceforge.net/, Tidy is a must-have utility for web designers. While the W3C's validation services are very handy, Tidy flags errors and also attempts to fix them. Although it's not perfect, and the offline versions require careful configuration to get the best results, it can be a godsend for finding and fixing missing end tags, omitted attributes, and more. A lengthy introduction to the tool can be found at www.w3.org/People/Raggett/tidy/ and an online version is available at http://cgi.w3.org/cgi-bin/tidy.

W3C CSS Validation Service

Many web design applications come bundled with versions of Tidy, but few have an effective means of testing and validating CSS. Seeing as you usually have few CSS files, there's really no excuse for not ensuring they're totally valid. The service is free, it enables you to test online files or to upload them from your computer, and it provides plenty of options for tweaking output. Point your browser at http://jigsaw.w3.org/css-validator/ to use the service.

Multiple Internet Explorer installs for Windows

The top reason I hear for why web designers don't test their sites in Internet Explorer 5.5 (despite that browser still commanding a fair chunk of the market) is that you can only install one version of Internet Explorer on a PC. Well, that's fair enough—after all, many solo designers can hardly afford to buy a new PC for every version of Internet Explorer they wish to test on. One oft-mooted solution is Microsoft's Virtual PC, which enables you to run multiple PC-based operating systems on a single machine (and, therefore, a different version of Internet Explorer on each). Available for Mac and Windows, it seems the perfect solution (indeed, many Mac users swear by it). However, even if you've got a powerful machine, it's tough to emulate an entire operating system of such complexity as Windows, and things frequently grind to a halt.

Until fairly recently, this was what I decided to do: my PC ran Internet Explorer 6, and Internet Explorer 5.5 and 5.0 were on an iBook, running at a snail's pace in Virtual PC. And then I discovered something rather exciting over at the Insert Title Web Design website (http://labs.insert-title.com/labs/article.aspx?ID=795). Joe Maddalone had noticed the version of Internet Explorer distributed due to the Eolas patent lawsuit ran alongside his standard build of Internet Explorer 6. He decided to craft earlier versions of the browser, to see if he could get those up and running, too. It worked.

Over at the URL in the previous paragraph is an explanation of how he did it, along with links to package downloads of earlier versions of Internet Explorer. At the time of this writing, I have Internet Explorer 5.5 and 5.0 installed alongside 6, and it took something in the region of two minutes to get them working. There are minor issues—using bookmarks crash these versions of the browser, and conditional comments don't work—but otherwise, they prove to be a great way of testing websites in different versions of Internet Explorer. The following image is a screenshot of Internet Explorer 6 and Internet Explorer 5.5 running on the same PC, both displaying Tantek Çelik's box model hack page.

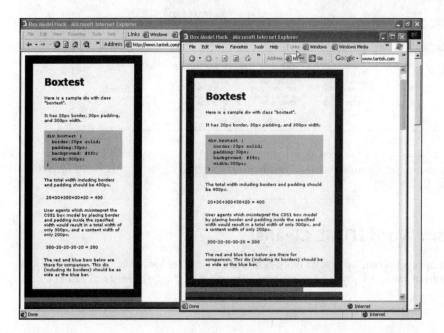

iCapture

It tends to vanish from the Web every now and again, but Daniel Vine's iCapture site (www.danvine.com/icapture/) is well worth checking out for those of you who don't have access to Safari. Using some old Macs and clever programming, it enables you to submit a URL to the site, whereupon a screen capture of the page in Safari is then placed online for a limited amount of time. A sister site, ieCapture (www.danvine.com/iecapture/), aims to cater for Mac users, providing them with a means to take screenshots in various Windows-based browsers.

> If you use the iCapture service regularly, don't forget to donate, to help with the site's bandwidth costs.

Textism Word HTML Cleaner

Most designers come up against Word-originated HTML files sooner or later. Stripping junk code from them is a joyless process, and although it might seem easier to just copy and paste the text and reformat the documents, there is another way. Textism's Word HTML Cleaner (www.textism.com/wordcleaner/) strips the junk, but leaves basic formatting intact, which you can then style using CSS (well, assuming whoever created the original Word document used headings. . . .).

Favelets

Designers tend to have large monitors, but the majority of those surfing the Web do so at 1024×768 or 800×600. Constantly changing your monitor resolution to test sites in those resolutions takes time and tends to mess up other application settings. Some people end up creating desktop patterns with the various resolutions drawn on and then manually drag their browser windows around to fit, but I much prefer using **favelets** (also sometimes referred to as **bookmarklets**).

I first found out about these useful things from Tantek Çelik's site www.tantek.com/favelets/. Essentially, favelets are JavaScript bookmarks that enable you to affect the browser window and perform various operations. Some of the more esoteric favelets don't tend to perform well in all browsers, but the most basic (and, in my opinion, most useful) ones do, such as those that resize the browser window with the click of a mouse.

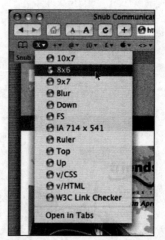

Favelets can be installed just by dragging them to your browser's toolbar, and they can be filed just like any other type of link (see the screenshot to the right). I've edited the screen size ones to "snap" to the top-left of the screen as well as resize the browser window. The JavaScript is

```
javascript:moveTo(0,0);window.resizeTo(800,600)
```

In order to change the snap position and browser window size, just amend the values within the brackets.

That's a wrap!

And so, with a lump in my throat, I say farewell. I hope you've enjoyed reading through this book and feel inspired to create all manner of exciting, standards-compliant websites. Relevant source code for some of the chapters can be found at the friends of ED website (www.friendsofed.com), as can any errata correcting errors that may have crept in. And the friends of ED forums (www.friendsofed.com/forums) provide lively discussions where you can talk about topics covered in this book and all other aspects of web design.

XHTML REFERENCE

This section of the reference guide details, in alphabetical order, generally supported elements and associated attributes. This is not intended as an exhaustive guide; rather, its aim is to list those elements important and relevant to current web design. Archaic deprecated elements such as `font` and `layer` are therefore ignored, as well as many attributes once associated with the `body` element, but the guide includes still occasionally useful deprecated and nonstandard elements and attributes such as `embed` and `target`.

Note that in the following pages, various styles are used for the attribute names and values. For the sake of clarity, quote marks have been omitted, but never forget that XHTML attributes must be quoted. Therefore, where you see the likes of id=name *in this reference section, the final output would be* id="name".

Standard attributes

Standard attributes are common to many elements. For brevity, they are listed in full here rather than in the XHTML element table later in the chapter. For each element in the forth-coming table, I simply state which groups of standard attributes are applicable to the element.

Core attributes

Attribute	Description
class=*classname*	Specifies a CSS class to define the element's visual appearance.
id=*name*	Defines a unique reference ID for the element.
style=*style* (deprecated)	Sets an inline style. Deprecated in XHTML 1.1, so it should be used sparingly and with caution.
title=*string*	Specifies the element's title. Often used with links to provide a tooltip expanding on the link's purpose or the target's content.

Not valid in these elements: base, head, html, meta, param, script, style, *and* title.

Keyboard attributes

Attribute	Description
accesskey=*character*	Defines a keyboard shortcut to access an element. The short-cut must be a single character. Most commonly used with navigation links. See also Chapter 5, "Using accesskey and tabindex."
tabindex=*number*	Defines the tab order of an element. Most commonly used with form input elements. Setting the value to 0 excludes the element from the tabbing order. The maximum value allowed is 32767. The tabindex values on a page needn't be consecutive (for instance, you could use multiples of 10, to leave space for later additions). See also Chapter 5, "Using accesskey and tabindex."

Language attributes

Attribute	Description
dir=*dir*	Specifies the text rendering direction: left-to-right (ltr, the default) or right-to-left (rtl).
lang=*language* (deprecated)	Specifies the language for the tag's contents, using two-letter primary ISO639 codes and optional dialect codes. Included for backward compatibility with HTML. Used together with xml:lang (see below) in XHTML 1.0, but deprecated in XHTML 1.1.
	Examples: lang="en" (English) lang="en-US" (US English) ISO639 codes include the following: ar (Arabic), zh (Chinese), nl (Dutch), fr (French), de (German), el (Greek), he (Hebrew), it (Italian), ja (Japanese), pt (Portuguese), ru (Russian), sa (Sanskrit), es (Spanish), and ur (Urdu).
xml:lang=*language*	Replaces lang in XHTML 1.1, but both should be used together in XHTML 1.0 to ensure backward compatibility with HTML and older browsers. xml:lang takes precedence if set to a different value.

Not valid in these elements: base, br, frame, frameset, hr, iframe, param, *and* script.

Event attributes

As of HTML 4.0, it's been possible to trigger browser actions by way of HTML events. Again, these are listed in full here and referred to for the relevant elements of the XHTML element table. In XHTML, all event names must be in lowercase (e.g., onclick, not onClick).

Core events

Attribute	Description
onclick=*script*	Specifies a script to be run when the user clicks the element's content area
ondblclick=*script*	Specifies a script to be run when the user double-clicks the element's content area

continues

Attribute	Description
onkeydown=*script*	Specifies a script to be run when the user presses a key while the element's content area is focused
onkeypress=*script*	Specifies a script to be run when the user presses and releases a key while the element's content area is focused
onkeyup=*script*	Specifies a script to be run when the user releases a pressed key while the element's content area is focused
onmousedown=*script*	Specifies a script to be run when the user presses down the mouse button while the cursor is over the element's content area
onmousemove=*script*	Specifies a script to be run when the user moves the mouse cursor in the element's content area
onmouseout=*script*	Specifies a script to be run when the user moves the mouse cursor off the element's content area
onmouseover=*script*	Specifies a script to be run when the user moves the mouse cursor onto the element's content area
onmouseup=*script*	Specifies a script to be run when the user releases the mouse button on the element's content area

Not valid in these elements: base, bdo, br, frame, frameset, head, html, iframe, meta, param, script, style, *and* title.

Form element events

These events are generally restricted to form elements, although some other elements accept some of them.

Attribute	Description
onblur=*script*	Specifies a script to be run when the element loses focus
onchange=*script*	Specifies a script to be run when the element changes
onfocus=*script*	Specifies a script to be run when the element is focused

Attribute	Description
onreset=*script*	Specifies a script to be run when a form is reset
onselect=*script*	Specifies a script to be run when the element is selected
onsubmit=*script*	Specifies a script to be run when a form is submitted

Window events

These events are valid only in the following elements: body and frameset.

Attribute	Description
onload=*script*	Specifies a script to be run when the document loads
onunload=*script*	Specifies a script to be run when the document unloads

> *Although* onresize *is part of DOM2, it's not recognized by the XHTML specification. If an* onresize *event is required, it cannot be applied directly to the* body *element. Instead, you must declare it in the document head using* window.onresize=functionName.

XHTML elements and attributes

The following pages list XHTML elements, associated attributes, and descriptions for all. Unless otherwise stated, assume an element is allowed in pages with XHTML Strict, XHTML Transitional, or XHTML Frameset DTDs. Do not use elements or attributes with DTDs that don't allow them. For instance, the target attribute cannot be used with XHTML Strict—doing so renders the page invalid.

Some elements are shown with a trailing forward slash. These are empty tags. Instead of having a start tag, content, and an end tag, these elements have a combined form. This takes the form of a start tag with an added trailing forward slash. Prior to the slash, a space is usually added. For instance, <br /> denotes a line break.

Element	Attribute	Description	Standard attributes
`<!-- … -->`		Defines a comment. See also Chapter 2, "Commenting your work."	No attributes
`<!DOCTYPE>` *(required)*		Specifies a DTD for the document. This is required for a valid XHTML document. See also Chapter 2, "DOCTYPE declarations explained."	No attributes
`<a>`		Defines an anchor. Can link to another document by using the `href` attribute, or create an anchor within a document by using the `id` or `name` attributes. Despite the number of available attributes, some aren't well supported. Generally, `href`, `name`, `title`, and `target` are commonly used. See also Chapter 5, "Anchors (creating links)."	Core attributes, keyboard attributes, language attributes Core events, `onblur`, `onfocus`
	`href=URL`	Defines the link target.	
	`name=name` *(deprecated)*	Names an anchor. Due to be replaced by `id` in future versions of XHTML.	
	`rel=relationship`	Specifies the relationship from the current document to the target document. Common values include next, prev, parent, child, index, toc, and glossary.	
	`rev=relationship`	Specifies the relationship from the target document to the current document. Common values include next, prev, parent, child, index, toc, and glossary.	

Element	Attribute	Description	Standard attributes
	target=_blank/ _parent/ _self/_top/[name] (deprecated)	Defines where the target URL opens. Primarily of use with frames, stating which frame a target should open in. Commonly used in web pages to open external links in a new window—a practice that should be avoided, because it breaks the browser history path. *Cannot be used in XHTML Strict. Unavailable in XHTML 1.1.*	
	type=MIME type	Specifies the MIME type of the target. For instance, if linking to a plain text file, you might use the following: `<a href="document.txt" ➥type="text/plain">`	
`<abbr>`		Identifies the element content as an abbreviation. This can be useful for nonvisual web browsers. For example: `<abbr ➥title="Doctor">Dr.</abbr>` See also Chapter 3, "Acronyms and abbreviations."	Core attributes, language attributes Core events
`<acronym>`		Identifies the element content as an acronym. This can be useful for nonvisual web browsers. For example: `<acronym title="North ➥Atlantic Treaty ➥Organization">NATO </acronym>` See also Chapter 3, "Acronyms and abbreviations."	Core attributes, language attributes Core events

continues

Element	Attribute	Description	Standard attributes
`<address>`		Used to define addresses, signatures, or document authors. Typically rendered in italics, with a line break above and below (but no additional space).	Core attributes, language attributes Core events
`<applet>` *(deprecated)*		Adds an applet to the web page. Deprecated in favor of the object element, but still required for embedding some Java applets. *This element cannot be used with an XHTML Strict DOCTYPE. Likewise, all of the element's attributes are deprecated and cannot be used with the XHTML Strict DOCTYPE.*	Core attributes, keyboard attributes, language attributes. Core events
	align=*position*	Defines text alignment around the element. Possible values are left, right, top, middle, and bottom.	
	alt=*string*	Alternate text for browsers that don't support applets.	
	archive=*URL*	Defines a list of URLs with classes to be preloaded.	
	code=*URL* *(required)*	Defines the class name of the code to be run. This attribute is *required*.	
	codebase=*URL*	Base URL of the applet.	
	height=*number* *(required)*	Pixel height of the applet. This attribute is *required*.	
	hspace=*number*	Sets horizontal space around the applet.	
	name=*name*	Sets a unique name for this instance of the applet, which can be used in scripts.	
	object=*name*	Defines a resource's name that contains a serialized representation of the applet.	
	vspace=*number*	Sets vertical space around the applet.	

Element	Attribute	Description	Standard attributes
	width=*number* (required)	Pixel width of the applet. This attribute is *required*.	
<area />		Defines a clickable area within a client-side image map. Should be nested within a map element (see separate <map> entry). See also Chapter 5, "Image maps."	Core attributes, keyboard attributes, language attributes Core events, onblur, onfocus
	alt=*string* (required)	Provides alternate text for nonvisual browsers. This attribute is *required*.	
	coords= *coordinates list*	Specifies coordinates for the clickable image map area. Values are defined as a comma-separated list. The number of values depends on the shape attribute value: For rect, four values are required, defining the coordinates on the x and y axes of the top-left and bottom-right corners. For circle, three values are required, with the first two defining the x and y coordinates of the hotspot's center, and the third defining the circle's radius. For poly, each pair of x and y values defines a point of the hotspot.	
	href=*URL*	The link target.	
	nohref=*nohref*	Enables you to set the defined area to have no action when the user selects it. nohref is the only possible value of this attribute.	

continues

Element	Attribute	Description	Standard attributes
	shape=*rect*|*circle*|*poly*|*default*	Defines the shape of the clickable region.	
	target=*_blank*|*_parent*|*_self*|*_top*|*[name]* (deprecated)	Defines where the target URL opens. *Cannot be used in XHTML Strict.*	
\<b\>		Renders text as bold. This element is a physical style, which defines what the content looks like (presentation only), rather than a logical style, which defines what the content is (which is beneficial for technologies like screen readers). It's recommended to use the logical element \<strong\>\</strong\> in place of \<b\>\</b\> (see separate \<strong\> entry). See also Chapter 3, "Logical and physical styles."	Core attributes, language attributes Core events
\<base /\>		Specifies a base URL for relative URLs on the web page	
	href=*URL* (required)	Defines the base URL to use. This attribute is *required*.	
	target=*_blank*|*_parent*|*_self*|*_top*|*[name]* (deprecated)	Defines where to open page links. Can be overridden by inline target attributes. *Cannot be used in XHTML Strict.*	
\<bdo\>		Overrides the default text direction.	Core attributes, language attributes
	dir=*ltr*|*rtl* (required)	Defines text direction as left to right (ltr) or right to left (rtl). This attribute is *required*.	

Element	Attribute	Description	Standard attributes
`<big>`		Increments text size to the next size larger as compared to surrounding text. Because the size differential is determined by the browser, precise text size changes are better achieved via span elements and CSS. Some browsers misinterpret this tag and render text as bold. See also Chapter 3, "The big and small elements."	Core attributes, language attributes Core events
`<blockquote>`		Defines a lengthy quotation. To validate as XHTML Strict, enclosed content must be set within a block-level element (such as `<p></p>`). Although it is common for web designers to use this element to indent content, the W3C strongly recommends using CSS for such things.	Core attributes, language attributes Core events
	cite=*URL*	Defines the online location of quoted material.	
`<body>` *(required)*		Defines the document's body and contains the document's contents. This is a *required* element for web pages.	Core attributes, language attributes Core events, onload, onunload
` `		Inserts a single line break.	Core attributes

continues

Element	Attribute	Description	Standard attributes

`<button>`		Defines a push button element within a form. Works similarly to buttons created with the `input` element, but offers greater rendering scope. This is because all content becomes the content of the button, enabling the creation of buttons with text and images. For example:
		
		`<button type="submit">`
		`Order now! <img`
		`➥src="go.gif" alt="Go" />`
		`</button>`
			Core attributes, keyboard attributes, language attributes
			
			Core events, onblur, onfocus

	disabled=*disabled*	Disables the button. disabled is the only possible value of this attribute.	
	name=*name*	Defines the button's name.	
	type=*button|reset|submit*	Identifies the button's type.	
	value=*string*	Defines the button's initial value.	
`<caption>`		Defines a caption for a table. Seldom used, but recommended because it enables you to associate a table's title with its contents. Omitting the caption may mean the table's contents are meaningless out of context. See also Chapter 7, "Captions and summaries."	Core attributes, language attributes Core events
`<cite>`		Defines content as a citation. Usually rendered in italics. See also Chapter 3, "Citations and definitions."	Core attributes, language attributes Core events

Element	Attribute	Description	Standard attributes
`<code>`		Defines content as computer code sample text. Usually rendered in a monospace font. See also Chapter 3, "Logical styles for programming-oriented content."	Core attributes, language attributes Core events

`<col />`		Defines properties for a column or group of columns within a colgroup. Attributes defined within a col element override those set in the containing colgroup element. col is an empty element that contains attributes only. The following example sets the column widths of the table's first three columns to 10, 30, and 50 pixels, respectively:
		
		`<colgroup span="3">`
		`    <col width="10" /></col>`
		`    <col width="30" /></col>`
		`    <col width="50" /></col>`
		`</colgroup>`
			Core attributes, language attributes
			
			Core events

	align=*left*|*right*| *justify*|*center* *(deprecated)*	Defines the horizontal alignment of table cell content. It's recommended that you instead use the CSS text-align property (see its entry in the CSS reference) to do this.	

	span=*n*	Defines how many successive columns are affected by the col tag. Use only when the surrounding colgroup element does not specify the number of columns.
		
		The following example creates a colgroup with five columns, with each of the middle three columns 30 pixels wide:
		
		`<colgroup>`
		`    <col width="10" />`
		`    <col width="30" span="3" />`
		`    <col width="50" />`
		`</colgroup>`	

continues

Element	Attribute	Description	Standard attributes
	valign=*top*/*middle*/ *bottom*/*baseline* *(deprecated)*	Specifies the vertical alignment of table cell content. It's recommended that you instead use the CSS vertical-align property (see its entry in the CSS reference) to do this.	
	width=*percentage*/ *number*	Defines the width of the column. Overrides the width settings in colgroup.	
<colgroup>		Defines a column group within a table, enabling you to define formatting for the columns within. See <cols> entry for examples.	Core attributes, language attributes Core events
	align=*left*/*right*/ *justify*/*center* *(deprecated)*	Defines the horizontal alignment of the table cell content within the colgroup. It's recommended that you instead use the CSS text-align property (see its entry in the CSS reference) to do this.	
	span=*number*	Defines how many columns the colgroup should span. Do not use if any of the col tags within the colgroup also use span. Otherwise, the col definitions will be ignored.	
	valign=*top*/*middle*/ *bottom*/*baseline* *(deprecated)*	Specifies the vertical alignment of the table cell content within the colgroup. It's recommended that you instead use the CSS vertical-align property (see its entry in the CSS reference) to do this.	

Element	Attribute	Description	Standard attributes
	width=*percentage/number*	Defines the width of columns within the colgroup. Can be overridden by the width settings of individual col elements.	
<dd>		Defines a definition description within a definition list. See the <dl> entry for an example. See also Chapter 3, "Definition lists."	Core attributes, language attributes Core events
<del>		Indicates deleted text. Usually appears in strikethrough format. See also Chapter 3, "Emulating tracking features with logical styles."	Core attributes, language attributes Core events
	cite=*URL*	Defines the URL of a document that explains why the text was deleted.	
	datetime=*date*	Defines the date and time that the text was amended. Various formats are possible, including YYYY-MM-DD and YYYY-MM-DDThh:mm:ssTZD (where TZD is the time zone designator). See www.w3.org/TR/1998/NOTE-datetime-19980827 for more date and time formatting information.	
<dfn>		Defines enclosed content as the defining instance of a term. Usually rendered in italics. See also Chapter 3, "Citations and definitions."	Core attributes, language attributes Core events

continues

Element	Attribute	Description	Standard attributes
`<div>`		Defines a division within a web page. Perhaps one of the most versatile but least understood elements. Used in combination with an id or class, the div tag element allows sections of a page to be individually styled and is the primary XHTML element used for the basis of CSS-based web page layouts. See also Chapter 8, "Workflow for CSS layouts."	Core attributes, language attributes Core events

`<dl>`		Defines a definition list. Contains pairs of term and definition elements, as follows:
		
		`<dl>`
		`  <dt>Windows</dt>`
		`  <dd>Operating system`
		`➥made by Microsoft.</dd>`
		`  <dt>Mac OS</dt>`
		`  <dd>Operating system`
		`➥made by Apple.</dd>`
		`</dl>`
		
		See also Chapter 3, "Definition lists."
			Core attributes, language attributes
			
			Core events

`<dt>`		Defines a definition term within a definition list. See the `<dl>` entry for an example. See also Chapter 3, "Definition lists."	Core attributes, language attributes Core events
`<em>`		Defines enclosed content as emphasized. Generally renders as italics in a browser and is preferred over the use of `<i></i>` element. See also Chapter 3, "Logical and physical styles."	Core attributes, language attributes Core events

Element	Attribute	Description	Standard attributes
<embed> *(nonstandard)*		Embeds an object. Nonstandard and not supported by any XHTML DOCTYPE. If this is included in a web page, the page will not validate. Poor browser support for the W3C preferred alternative, object, leaves developers with little choice other than to use this nonstandard tag when embedding Flash or other multimedia into a web page.	
		See also Chapter 11, "Embedding multimedia."	
	align=*left/right/ top/bottom*	Defines the alignment of the embedded object in relation to the surrounding text.	
	height=*number*	Defines the height of the object in pixels.	
	hidden=*yes/no*	Hides the player or media file when set to yes. Defaults to no.	
	hspace=*number*	Sets horizontal space around the object.	
	name=*name*	Sets a name for the object.	
	pluginspage=*URL*	Defines a URL for information on installing the relevant plug-in.	
	src=*URL* *(required)*	Provides the location of the object to be embedded. This attribute is *required*.	
	type=*MIME type*	Specifies the MIME type of the plug-in required to run the file.	
	vspace=*number*	Sets vertical space around the object.	
	width=*number*	Defines the width of the object in pixels.	

continues

Element	Attribute	Description	Standard attributes
`<fieldset>`		Creates a group of related form elements by nesting them within the `fieldset` element. Usually used in tandem with the `legend` element to enhance form accessibility (see the `<legend>` entry for more information).	Core attributes, language attributes Core events
		See also Chapter 10, "Improving form accessibility."	
	accesskey=*character*	Defines a keyboard shortcut to access an element.	
`<form>`		Indicates the start and end of a form. Cannot be nested within another form element. Generally, the method and action attributes are most used.	Core attributes, language attributes Core events, onreset, onsubmit
		See also Chapter 10, "Working with forms."	
	accept=*content-type list*	Specifies a comma-separated list of MIME types that the server processing the form can handle correctly.	
	accept-charset=*charset list*	Specifies a comma-separated list of character sets for form data.	
	action=*URL* (required)	The URL of the form processing application where the data is sent once the form is submitted. This attribute is *required*.	

Element	Attribute	Description	Standard attributes
	enctype=*encoding*	The MIME type used to encode the form's content before it's sent to the server, so it doesn't become scrambled. Defaults to application/x-www-form-urlencoded. Other options are multipart/form-data, which can be used when the user is able to upload files, and text-plain, which can be used when using a mailto: value for the action instead of a server-side script to parse the form data.	
	method=*get|post*	Specifies the http method used to submit the form data. The post value is most commonly used.	
	name=*name* (deprecated)	Defines the form's name. *Cannot be used in XHTML Strict.*	
	target=*_blank| _parent|_self| _top|[name]* (deprecated)	Defines where the target URL is opened. *Cannot be used in XHTML Strict.*	
<frame>		Defines a frame. *This element and its attributes must only be used with the XHTML Frameset DTD, and not with XHTML Strict or XHTML Transitional.* See also Chapter 9, "Creating framesets."	Core attributes
	frameborder=*0|1*	Defines whether frame borders are present (frameborder="1") or not (frameborder="0").	
	longdesc=*URL*	Defines a URL for a long description of the frame contents for non-frames-compatible browsers.	

continues

Element	Attribute	Description	Standard attributes
	marginheight= *number*	The vertical space between the frame edges and its contents (measured in pixels).	
	marginwidth= *number*	The horizontal space between the frame edges and its contents (measured in pixels).	
	name=*name*	Defines a name for the frame.	
	noresize=*noresize*	Stops the user from resizing the frame. The only available value is noresize.	
	scrolling=*auto| no|yes*	Specifies whether scroll bars appear when the frame contents are too large for the visible area. The yes value mean permanent scroll bars are shown; no means scroll bars don't appear, even if the content is too large for the frame; and auto means scroll bars appear when the content is too large for the frame.	
	src=*URL*	Defines the location of the frame's default HTML document.	

`<frameset>`		Defines a frameset. Must have either a cols *or* a rows attribute. *This element and its attributes must only be used with the XHTML Frameset DTD, and not with XHTML Strict or XHTML Transitional.*
		
		`<frameset cols="150,* ">`
		`<frame src=`
		➥`"frame_one.html" />`
		`<frame src=`
		➥`"frame_two.html" />`
		`</frameset>`
		
		See also Chapter 9, "Creating framesets."
			Core attributes onload, onunload

Element	Attribute	Description	Standard attributes
	cols=*percentage/number"**	Defines the number and sizes of columns (vertical frames). When setting the value to *, the frame it's applied to takes up all remaining browser window space for that dimension. If more than one value is *, the remaining space is split between those frames the * value is assigned to.	
	rows=*percentage/number"**	Defines the number and sizes of rows (horizontal frames). See preceding entry for an explanation of how the * value works.	
<h*n*>		Defines enclosed contents as a heading. Available levels are 1 to 6. Note that although h4 through h6 tend to be displayed smaller than body copy by default, they are not a means to create small text; rather, they are a way to enable you to structure your document. This is essential, because headings help with assistive technology, enabling the visually impaired to efficiently surf the Web. See also Chapter 3, "Paragraphs and headings."	Core attributes, language attributes Core events
<head> *(required)*		Defines the header of the HTML file. Houses information-based elements, such as base, link, meta, script, style, and title. This is a *required* element for web pages.	Language attributes
	profile=*URL*	The location of a metadata profile for this document. Not commonly used.	

continues

Element	Attribute	Description	Standard attributes
`<hr />`		Inserts a horizontal rule.	Core attributes, language attributes Core events
`<html>` *(required)*		Defines the start and end of the HTML document. This is a *required* element for web pages. No HTML content should be placed before the html start tag or after the html end tag.	Language attributes
	`xmlns=namespace`	Defines the XML namespace (e.g., `http://www.w3.org/1999/xhtml`). See also Chapter 2, "Document defaults."	
`<i>`		Renders text as italic. This element is a physical style, which defines what the content looks like (presentation only), rather than a logical style, which defines what the content is (which is beneficial for technologies like screen readers). It's generally preferable to use the logical element `<em></em>` in place of `<i></i>`. See also Chapter 3, "Logical and physical styles."	Core attributes, language attributes Core events
`<iframe>`		Defines an inline frame. Content within the element is displayed only in browsers that cannot display the iframe. *This element and its attributes cannot be used in XHTML Strict.* See also Chapter 9, "Internal frames (iframes)" and "Creating and styling iframes."	

Element	Attribute	Description	Standard attributes
	frameborder=*0*/*1*	Defines whether a frame border is present (frameborder="1") or not (frameborder="0").	
	height=*percentage/ number*	Defines the iframe's height.	
	longdesc=*URL*	Defines a URL for a long description of the iframe's contents for non-frames-compatible browsers.	
	marginheight= *number*	The vertical space (in pixels) between the iframe's edges and its contents.	
	marginwidth= *number*	The horizontal space (in pixels) between the iframe's edges and its contents.	
	name=*name*	Defines a name for the iframe.	
	scrolling=*auto/ no/yes*	Specifies whether scroll bars appear when the iframe's contents are too large for the visible area. The yes value means permanent scroll bars are shown; no means scroll bars don't appear, even if the content is too large for the frame; and auto means scroll bars appear when the content is too large for the frame.	
	src=*URL*	Defines the location of the iframe's default HTML document.	
	width=*percentage/ number*	Defines the iframe's width.	

continues

Element	Attribute	Description	Standard attributes
`<img />`		Inserts an image. Both the `src` and `alt` attributes are required; although many web designers omit the `alt` attribute, it's essential for screen readers. The `height` and `width` values are recommended, too, in order to assist the browser in rapidly laying out the page. The `border` value, despite common usage, is deprecated and should be avoided. Use CSS to determine whether images have borders. See also Chapter 4, "Working with images in XHTML."	Core attributes, language attributes Core events
	`alt=text` *(required)*	Provides alternate text for nonvisual browsers. Should provide an indication of an image's content or, if it's a link, its function. When an image has no visual significance, use `alt=""`. This attribute is *required*. See also Chapter 4, "Using alt text for accessibility benefits."	
	`border=number` *(deprecated)*	Defines a border. Despite its common usage, this attribute is deprecated and cannot be used in XHTML Strict. Instead, use CSS to set borders on images. See also Chapter 4, "Applying CSS borders to images."	
	`height=number`	Defines the image's height in pixels.	
	`ismap=URL`	Defines the image as a server-side image map. The image must be contained within an anchor tag. Server-side image maps require specialized setup and are rarely used. Do not confuse this attribute with usemap (see the upcoming usemap entry).	

Element	Attribute	Description	Standard attributes
	longdesc=*URL*	Provides the location of a document containing a long description of the image.	
	src=*URL* *(required)*	The URL of the image to be displayed. This attribute is *required.*	
	usemap=*URL*	Defines the image as a client-side image map. See also Chapter 5, "Image maps."	
	width=*number*	Defines the image's width in pixels.	
`<input />`		Defines a form input field. See also Chapter 10, "Adding controls."	Core attributes, keyboard attributes, language attributes Core events, onblur, onchange, onfocus, onselect
	accept=*list*	A list of MIME types that can be accepted by this element. *Only used with type="file".*	
	alt=*text*	Provides alternate text for nonvisual browsers. *Only used with type="image".*	
	checked=*checked*	Sets input element's default state to checked. The only value for this attribute is checked. *Only used with type="checkbox" and type="radio".*	
	disabled=*disabled*	Disables the input element. The only value for this attribute is disabled. *Cannot be used with type="hidden".*	
	maxlength=*number*	Defines the maximum number of characters allowed. *Only used with type="text".*	

continues

Element	Attribute	Description	Standard attributes
	name=*name* (required*)	Defines a name for the input element.	
		Required for the following types: button, checkbox, file, hidden, image, password, text, and radio.	
	readonly=*readonly*	Indicates the input element is read-only and cannot be modified. The only value for this attribute is readonly. *Only used with type="text".*	
	size=*number*	Defines in characters (*not* pixels) the size of the input element. (For pixel-defined widths, use CSS.)	
		Cannot be used with type="hidden".	
	src=*URL*	Defines the URL of the image to be displayed. *Only used with type="image".*	
	type=*button| checkbox|file| hidden|image| password|radio| reset|submit|text*	Defines the input element type. Defaults to *text*.	
	value=*string* (required when type=*checkbox* and type=*radio*)	When type="button", type= "reset", or type="submit", it defines button text.	
		When type="checkbox" or type="radio", it defines the result of the input element; the result being sent when the form is submitted.	
		When type="hidden", type="password", or type="text", it defines the element's default value.	
		When type="image", it defines the result of the field passed to the script. *Cannot be used with type="file".*	

Element	Attribute	Description	Standard attributes

`<ins>`		Defines inserted text. Usually appears in underline format, which can be confusing because links are also underlined. It's therefore recommended that you use CSS to change the underline color.
		
		`ins {`
		`text-decoration: none;`
		`border-bottom: 1px solid red;`
		`}`
		
		See also Chapter 3, "Emulating tracking features with logical styles."
			Core attributes, language attributes
			
			Core events

	`cite=URL`	Defines the URL of a document that explains why the text was inserted.	
	`datetime=date`	Defines the date and time that the text was amended. Various formats are possible, including YYYY-MM-DD and YYYY-MM-DDThh:mm:ssTZD (where TZD is the time zone designator). See www.w3.org/TR/1998/NOTE-datetime-19980827 for more date and time formatting information.	
`<kbd>`		Defines "keyboard" text (text inputted by the user). Usually rendered in a monospace font. See also Chapter 3, "Logical styles for programming-oriented content."	Core attributes, language attributes Core events

continues

Element	Attribute	Description	Standard attributes
`<label>`		Assigns a label to a form control, enabling you to define relationships between text labels and form controls. For example: `<p><strong><label for=` ➥`"realname">Name</label><` ➥`/strong> ` `<input type="text"` ➥`name="realname"` ➥`id="realname" size="30"` ➥`/></p>` See also Chapter 10, "The label, fieldset, and legend elements."	Core attributes, language attributes Core events, onblur, onfocus
	`accesskey=` *character*	Defines a keyboard shortcut to access an element.	
	`for=`*text*	Defines the form element that the label is for.	

`<legend>`		Defines a caption for a fieldset. Must be nested within a fieldset element. For example:
		
		`<fieldset>`
		`<legend>Caption for this fieldset</legend>`
		`form labels and controls…`
		`</fieldset>`
		
		See also Chapter 10, "The label, fieldset, and legend elements."
			Core attributes, language attributes
			
			Core events

	`accesskey=` *character*	Defines a keyboard shortcut to access an element.	
`<li>`		Defines a list item. Must be nested within `<ol>` or `<ul>` elements (see the separate `<ol>` and `<ul>` entries). See also Chapter 3, "Working with lists."	Core attributes, language attributes Core events

Element	Attribute	Description	Standard attributes
	type=*format* *(deprecated)*	Specifies the list type for the list item. (See the `<ol>` and `<ul>` entries for possible values.) *Cannot be used in XHTML Strict.*	
	value=*number* *(deprecated)*	Defines the number of the item in an ordered list. *Cannot be used in XHTML Strict.*	
`<link />`		Defines the relationship between this document and another. Must be placed in the head section of a document. Mainly used for attaching an external style sheet to a document. See also Chapter 2, "Attaching external CSS files: The link method."	Core attributes, language attributes Core events
	charset=*charset*	Defines the character set of the target document.	
	href=*URL*	The URL of the target.	
	hreflang=*language code*	Defines the language of the linked document.	
	media=*media type list*	Defines the target medium for the linked document (all, aural, braille, handheld, print, projection, screen, tty, or tv). More than one medium can be combined in a comma-delimited list.	
	rel=*relationship*	Specifies the relationship from the current document to the target document (alternate, appendix, bookmark, chapter, contents, copyright, glossary, help, index, next, prev, section, start, stylesheet, or subsection). More than one relationship can be combined in a space-separated list.	

continues

Element	Attribute	Description	Standard attributes
	rev=*relationship*	Specifies the relationship from the target document to the current document (see the preceding entry for values).	
	target=*_blank|* *_parent|_self|* *_top|[name]* *(deprecated)*	Defines where the target URL opens. *Cannot be used in XHTML Strict.*	
	type=*MIME type*	Specifies the target's MIME type, such as text/css or text/javascript.	
<map>		Contains client-side image map specifications. Contains one or more area elements.	Core attributes, keyboard attributes, language attributes
		See also Chapter 5, "Image maps."	Core events, onblur, onfocus
	id=*name* *(required)*	Defines a unique name for the map. This attribute is *required*.	
	name=*name* *(deprecated)*	Defines a unique name for the map. (Superseded by id, but used for backward compatibility.)	
<meta />		Provides meta information about the document. Must be placed inside the HTML page's head section. Each meta element requires a content attribute and also an http-equiv or a name attribute. Most commonly used to define the character set, and to set keywords and descriptions for search engines (increasingly ineffective, as search engines now pay more attention to page content and links than to meta tags).	Language attributes
		See also Chapter 2, "Meta tags," "What about the XML declaration?" and "Keywords and descriptions."	

Element	Attribute	Description	Standard attributes
	content=*string* (required)	Defines the value of the meta tag property.	
	http-equiv=*string*	Specifies the http equivalent name for the meta information. Examples are content-type, expires, refresh, and set-cookie.	
	name=*string*	Specifies a name for the meta information. Examples are author, description, generator, and keywords.	
	scheme=*string*	Specifies the metadata profile scheme.	
<noembed> *(nonstandard)*		Nested within embed elements and displayed only when the browser cannot display the embedded object. Nonstandard and not supported by any XHTML DOCTYPE. If this is included in a web page, the page will not validate.	
<noframes>		Defines content to be displayed in non-frames-compatible browsers. Should be placed inside a frameset element. *Intended for use with XHTML Frameset DOCTYPE only.* See also Chapter 9, "Catering for non-frames-compatible browsers."	Core attributes, language attributes
<noscript>		Defines content to be displayed in browsers that don't support scripting. This is considered a "block-level" element, so it cannot be nested in an element that accepts only inline content, such as a paragraph, heading, or preformatted text. Can be used inside a div, form, or list item.	Core attributes, language attributes

continues

Element	Attribute	Description	Standard attributes
<object>		Defines an embedded object. See also Chapter 11, "Embedding multimedia."	Core attributes, keyboard attributes, language attributes Core events
	archive=*URL*	Defines a list of URLs to resources used by the object.	
	border=*number* *(deprecated)*	Sets the object's border width. *Cannot be used in XHTML Strict.*	
	classid=*URL*	Defines the URL of the object.	
	codebase=*URL*	Defines the base URL of the object.	
	codetype=*MIME type*	Defines the object's MIME type.	
	data=*URL*	Defines the URL of the object's data.	
	declare=*declare*	Declares an object but does not download it until the object is used. The only value for this attribute is declare.	
	height=*number*	Defines the object's height in pixels.	
	name=*name*	Sets a unique name for this instance of the object, which can be used in scripts.	
	standby=*text*	Defines text to display while the object is downloading.	
	type=*MIME type*	Defines the object data's MIME type.	
	usemap=*URL*	Specifies the client-side image map to use with the object.	
	width=*number*	Defines the object's width in pixels.	
<ol>		Defines the start and end of an unordered list. Contains one or more li elements.	Core attributes, language attributes Core events
	start=*number* *(deprecated)*	Starts the list numbering at the defined value instead of 1. *Cannot be used in XHTML Strict.*	

Element	Attribute	Description	Standard attributes
	type=1|A|a|I|I *(deprecated)*	Specifies the list numbering system (1=default numerals, A=uppercase letters, a=lowercase letters, I=uppercase Roman numerals, and i=lowercase Roman numerals). *Cannot be used in XHTML Strict.*	
`<optgroup>`		Defines a form option group, enabling you to group related options in a select element. Beware: display output varies between browsers. Most italicize optgroup label values to highlight them, while others (such as Opera) highlight them by inverting the optgroup label value. Others display them as per option values.	Core attributes, language attributes Core events
		`<select name=">` `<optgroup label="fruits">` `<option value="Apple">` ➡Apple`</option>` `<option value="Pear">` ➡Pear`</option>` `</optgroup>` `<optgroup label="vegetables">` `<option value="Carrot">` ➡Carrot`</option>` `<option value="Turnip">` ➡Turnip`</option>` `</optgroup>` `</select>` See also Chapter 10, "Adding controls."	
	disabled=*disabled*	Disables the option group. The only value for this attribute is disabled.	
	label=*string* *(required)*	Defines a label for the optgroup. This attribute is *required*.	
	tabindex=*number*	Defines the tab order of an element.	

continues

Element	Attribute	Description	Standard attributes
`<option>`		Defines an option within a drop-down list. Nested within a select element and can be placed within optgroup elements. (See separate `<select>` and `<optgroup>` entries.) See also Chapter 10, "Adding controls."	Core attributes, language attributes Core events
	`disabled=disabled`	Disables the option. The only value for this attribute is `disabled`.	
	`label=string`	Defines a label for this option.	
	`selected=selected`	Sets the option as the default. The only value for this attribute is `selected`.	
	`value=string`	Defines the value of the option to be sent when the form is submitted.	
`<p>`		Defines a paragraph. See also Chapter 3, "Paragraphs and headings."	Core attributes, language attributes Core events
`<param>`		Supplies parameters for applets and objects. Must be enclosed within an applet or object element, and must come at the start of the content of the enclosing element.	
	`id=name`	Defines a unique reference ID for the element.	
	`name=name`	Defines a unique name for the element.	
	`type=MIME type`	Specifies the MIME type for the element.	
	`value=string`	Defines the element's value.	
	`valuetype=data| object|ref`	Specifies the MIME type of the value as data, ref (the value of a URL pointing to the data), or object (the value of an object within the document).	

Element	Attribute	Description	Standard attributes
`<pre>`		Defines enclosed contents as preformatted text, thereby preserving the formatting from the HTML document. Usually displayed in a monospace font. Cannot contain images, objects, or any of the following tags: big, small, sub, and sup.	Core attributes, language attributes Core events
	width=*number* *(deprecated)*	Defines the maximum number of characters per line. This attribute is deprecated; use CSS to define the element width instead. *Cannot be used in XHTML Strict.*	
`<q>`		Defines enclosed content as a short quotation. Some browsers automatically insert quote marks.	Core attributes, language attributes Core events
	cite=*URL*	Defines the location of quoted online material.	
`<s>` *(deprecated)*		Defines strikethrough text. This element is deprecated and cannot be used in XHTML Strict. It's recommended to use CSS to define strikethrough text instead (via text-decoration: line-through).	Core attributes, language attributes Core events
`<samp>`		Defines enclosed content as a computer code sample. Usually rendered in a monospace font. See also Chapter 3, "Logical styles for programming-oriented content."	Core attributes, language attributes Core events
`<script>`		Inserts a script into the document.	
	charset=*charset*	Defines the script's character set.	

continues

Element	Attribute	Description	Standard attributes
	defer=*defer*	Indicates the script doesn't generate document content. This attribute's only value is defer. This allows the browser to delay parsing the script until after the page has loaded. Although this may speed up loading, it will generate script errors if user interaction results in a call to a script that still hasn't been parsed. Use with care.	
	language=*encoding* (*deprecated*)	Specifies the scripting language. Superseded by the type attribute, and no longer required. *Cannot be used in XHTML Strict.*	
	src=*URL*	Provides the URL of an external script.	
	type=*MIME type* (*required*)	Defines the MIME type of the scripting language, such as text/javascript or text/vbscript. This attribute is *required*.	
<select>		Creates a drop-down menu or scrolling list (depending on whether multiple has been set). This element is a container for option and optional optgroup elements. See also Chapter 10, "Adding controls."	Core attributes, keyboard attributes, language attributes Core events, onblur, onchange, onfocus
	disabled=*disabled*	Disables the element. The only value for this attribute is disabled.	
	multiple=*multiple*	Specifies that multiple items can be selected. If absent, only single options can be selected. If included, the select element displays as a scrolling list rather than a drop-down menu. The only value for this attribute is multiple.	
	name=*name*	Defines a name for the element.	
	size=*number*	Sets the element to a pop-up menu when the value is 1, or a scrolling list when the value is greater than 1.	

Element	Attribute	Description	Standard attributes
`<small>`		Reduces text size as compared to the surrounding text. Because the browser determines the size differential, precise text size changes are better achieved via span elements and CSS. See also Chapter 3, "The big and small elements."	Core attributes, language attributes Core events

`<span>`		Identifies a span of inline elements for applying styles to. For example:
		
		`<p>Use span elements to create`
		`➥<span class="stylename">styled`
		`➥inline text</span>.</p>`
			Core attributes, language attributes
			
			Core events

`<strike>` *(deprecated)*		Defines strikethrough text. This element is deprecated and cannot be used in XHTML Strict. It's recommended to use CSS to define strikethrough text instead (via `text-decoration: line-through`).	Core attributes, language attributes Core events
`<strong>`		Defines enclosed contents as strongly emphasized. Generally renders as bold text in browsers and is preferred over `<b></b>`. See also Chapter 3, "Logical and physical styles."	Core attributes, language attributes Core events

`<style>`		Used to embed CSS rules in the head of a web page or to import CSS files.
		
		`<style type="text/css"`
		`➥media="all">`
		`@import url(stylesheet.css);`
		`.thisPageOnly {`
		`color: #de3de3;`
		`}`
		`</style>`
		
		See also Chapter 2, "Attaching CSS files: The @import method."
			Language attributes

continues

Element	Attribute	Description	Standard attributes
	media=*list* (required)	Defines target media on which this style can be rendered. Possible values are all, aural, braille, handheld, print, projection, screen, tty, and tv.	
	title=*string*	Specifies the element's title.	
	type=*MIME type* (required)	Defines the MIME type of the style's contents. The only currently viable value is text/css, although this may change in future.	
<sub>		Defines contents as subscript text. See also Chapter 3, "Teletype, subscript, and superscript."	Core attributes, language attributes Core events
<sup>		Defines contents as superscript text. See also Chapter 3, "Teletype, subscript, and superscript."	Core attributes, language attributes Core events
<table>		Defines the start and end of a table. See also Chapter 7, "How tables work."	Core attributes, language attributes Core events
	border=*number*	Defines the table border width.	
	cellpadding= *percentage|number*	Defines the space between cell edges and contents.	
	cellpadding= *percentage\number*	Defines the space between table cells.	
	summary=*string*	Provides a summary of the table contents for nonvisual browsers.	
	width=*percentage| number*	Defines the table's width in pixels.	
<tbody>		Defines the table body. See also Chapter 7, "Row groups" and "Building a table."	Core attributes, language attributes Core events
	align=*left|right| justify|center* (deprecated)	Defines the horizontal alignment of table cell content. It's recommended that you instead use the CSS text-align property (see its entry in the CSS reference) to do this.	

Element	Attribute	Description	Standard attributes
	valign=*top*|*middle*|*bottom*|*baseline* (deprecated)	Specifies the vertical alignment of table cell content. It's recommended that you instead use the CSS `vertical-align` property (see its entry in the CSS reference) to do this.	
`<td>`		Defines a table cell. See also Chapter 7, "How tables work" and "Building a table."	Core attributes, language attributes Core events
	abbr=*string*	Provides an abbreviation of the cell's contents. Browsers can then choose to use this if they are short on space or to aid accessibility. Not commonly used, but particularly potentially useful for screen readers.	
	align=*left*|*right*|*justify*|*center* (deprecated)	Defines the horizontal alignment of table cell content. It's recommended that you instead use the CSS `text-align` property (see its entry in the CSS reference) to do this.	
	axis=*name*	Provides a name for a related group of cells. Not commonly used.	
	colspan=*number*	Defines how many columns the cell spans. See also Chapter 7, "Spanning rows and cells."	
	headers=*id list*	A list of cell IDs that provide header information for this cell, thereby enabling nonvisual browsers to associate header information with the cell. If more than one value is used, values are space separated. Example: `<th id="theTitle" ↪scope="col">The title</th> <th id="price" ↪scope="col">Price</th> … <td headers="theTitle">A new ↪book</td> <td headers="price">$29.99</td>`	

continues

Element	Attribute	Description	Standard attributes
	height=*number* (deprecated)	Defines the height of a cell in pixels. This attribute is deprecated—use CSS to define cell dimensions. *Cannot be used in XHTML Strict.*	
	nowrap=*nowrap* (deprecated)	Disables text wrapping. The only value for this attribute is nowrap. *Cannot be used in XHTML Strict. (Use CSS white-space instead.)*	
	rowspan=*number*	Defines how many rows the cell spans. See also Chapter 7, "Spanning rows and cells."	
	scope=*col|colgroup |row|rowgroup*	States whether the cell provides header information for the rest of the row, column, rowgroup, or colgroup that contains it. (See the headers description.)	
	valign=*top|middle| bottom|baseline* (deprecated)	Specifies the vertical alignment of table cell content. It's recommended that you instead use the CSS vertical-align property (see its entry in the CSS reference) to do this.	
	width=*number* (deprecated)	Defines the width of a cell in pixels. This attribute is deprecated—use CSS to define cell dimensions. *Cannot be used in XHTML Strict.*	
<textarea>		Defines a text area within a form. Any element content is displayed as the textarea's default value, and that includes spaces. Therefore, if you want a blank textarea, avoid having any spaces between the start and end tags. Although the cols and rows attributes are required, you can override these settings by using CSS. See also Chapter 10, "Adding controls."	Core attributes, language attributes Core events, onblur, onchange, onfocus
	cols=*number* (required)	Specifies the visible width in characters of the textarea. This attribute is *required*.	

Element	Attribute	Description	Standard attributes
	disabled=*disabled*	Disables the element. The only value for this attribute is disabled.	
	name=*name*	Defines a name for the element.	
	readonly=*readonly*	Indicates the textarea is read-only and cannot be modified. The only value for this attribute is readonly.	
	rows=*number* (*required*)	Specifies the visible height (expressed as a number of rows) of the textarea. This attribute is *required*.	
`<tfoot>`		Defines a table footer. See also Chapter 7, "Row groups" and "Building a table."	Core attributes, language attributes Core events
	align=*left*|*right*| *justify*|*center* (*deprecated*)	Defines the horizontal alignment of table cell content. It's recommended that you instead use the CSS text-align property (see its entry in the CSS reference) to do this.	
	valign=*top*|*middle*| *bottom*|*baseline* (*deprecated*)	Specifies the vertical alignment of table cell content. It's recommended that you instead use the CSS vertical-align property (see its entry in the CSS reference) to do this.	
`<th>`		Defines a table header cell. See the `<td>` entry for attributes. See also Chapter 7, "How tables work" and "Building a table."	Core attributes, language attributes Core events
`<thead>`		Defines a table header. See also Chapter 7, "Row groups" and "Building a table."	Core attributes, language attributes Core events
	align=*left*|*right*| *justify*|*center* (*deprecated*)	Defines the horizontal alignment of table cell content. It's recommended that you instead use the CSS text-align property (see its entry in the CSS reference) to do this.	

continues

Element	Attribute	Description	Standard attributes
	valign=*top|middle| bottom|baseline* *(deprecated)*	Specifies the vertical alignment of table cell content. It's recommended that you instead use the CSS vertical-align property (see its entry in the CSS reference) to do this.	
`<title>` *(required)*		Defines the title of a document. This is a *required* element for web pages.	Core attributes, language attributes
`<tr>`		Defines a table row. See also Chapter 7, "How tables work" and "Building a table."	Core attributes, language attributes Core events
	align=*left|right| justify|center* *(deprecated)*	Defines the horizontal alignment of table cell content. It's recommended that you instead use the CSS text-align property (see its entry in the CSS reference) to do this.	
	valign=*top|middle| bottom|baseline* *(deprecated)*	Specifies the vertical alignment of table cell content. It's recommended that you instead use the CSS vertical-align property (see its entry in the CSS reference) to do this.	
`<tt>`		Renders as teletype (monospaced) text. See also Chapter 3, "Teletype, subscript, and superscript."	Core attributes, language attributes Core events
`<ul>`		Defines the start and end of an unordered list. Contains one or more li elements. See also Chapter 3, "Unordered lists."	Core attributes, language attributes Core events
`<var>`		Defines contents as a variable name. Usually rendered in italics. See also Chapter 3, "Logical styles for programming-oriented content."	Core attributes, language attribute Core events

WEB COLOR REFERENCE

This section of the reference guides provides an overview of how to write color values for the Web, as well as a full list of supported color names.

Color values

On the Web, colors are displayed by mixing red, green, and blue light (RGB). Values range from 0 to 255 and can be written as such (e.g., rgb(5,233,70)), but they are more commonly written in hexadecimal. Colors written in hex consist of a hash sign (#) followed by six digits. The six digits are made up of pairs, representing the red, green, and blue color values, respectively.

- #XXxxxx: Red color value
- #xxXXxx: Green color value
- #xxxxXX: Blue color value

Hexadecimal notation is a numbering system that has 16, rather than 10, as its base. Digits range from 0 to F, with 0 to 9 representing the same value as ordinary numbers, and the letters A to F representing 10 to 15. The letters can be either uppercase or lowercase. If we set the first two digits to their highest value (ff) and the others to null, we get #ff0000, which is the hex color value for red. If we write #00ff00, we get green, and #0000ff is blue. If all are set to full, we get white (#ffffff), and if all are null values, we get black (#000000).

Hexadecimal can also be written in shorthand if the six-digit value is composed of pairs in which both numbers are the same. For instance, #ff6600 (orange) can be written as #f60, and #ffffff (white) can be written as #fff. All three pairs must consist of equal numbers. For instance, you cannot use shorthand for #ffff01. Also, although hexadecimal can be written in shorthand, many designers choose not to do so, because when all color values are written in full, it tends to be easier to scan CSS files for specific values.

Web-safe colors

The 216-color web-safe palette uses hex combinations of the following hex value pairs only: 00, 33, 66, 99, cc, and ff—for example, #cc6699, #33ff66, and #ff0000.

Using these pairs provides us with 216 colors that are said to not dither on Macs and Windows PCs that have 8-bit monitors (256 colors).

Color names

Although a significant number of HTML color names are supported by major browsers, the CSS standard only recognizes the following 17.

Color name	Color hex value
Aqua	#00ffff
Black	#000000
Blue	#0000ff
Fuchsia	#ff00ff
Gray	#808080
Green	#008000
Lime	#00ff00
Maroon	#800000
Navy	#000080
Olive	#808000
Orange	#ffa500
Purple	#800080
Red	#ff0000
Silver	#c0c0c0
Teal	#008080
White	#ffffff
Yellow	#ffff00

Although each color name in the preceding table begins with a capital letter (for book style purposes), color names are case insensitive, and lowercase is most commonly used. However, most designers ignore color names entirely, using hex all the time for consistency's sake—a practice that the W3C recommends.

ENTITIES REFERENCE

Generally speaking, characters not found in the normal alphanumeric set must be added to a web page by way of **character entities**. These take the form &#n;, with n being a two- to four-digit number. Many entities also have a name, which tends to be more convenient and memorable; these are also listed. However, entities are case sensitive, so take care when adding them to your web pages.

Although some browsers display nonalphanumeric characters, it's better to use entities to ensure your page displays as intended across a large range of machines.

Most reference guides tend to list entities in numerical order, but I find it more useful to browse by grouped items, so I list entities alphabetically within sections such as "Common punctuation and symbols" and "Characters for European languages." (The exception is for Greek characters, which I've listed in the order of the Greek alphabet, rather than in alphabetical order from an English language perspective.)

Characters used in XHTML

The less-than and ampersand characters are used in XHTML markup, and to avoid invalid and broken pages, these should be added to your web pages as entities. It's also common (although not required) to add greater-than and quotation marks as entities.

The ampersand character is commonly used in URL query strings (particularly when working with server-side languages), and in such cases, the & must be replaced by the entity name or number (it will still be correctly interpreted by the browser).

Character	Description	Entity name	Entity number
"	Quotation mark (straight)	&quot;	&#34;
&	Ampersand	&amp;	&#38;
<	Less-than sign	&lt;	&#60;
>	Greater-than sign	&gt;	&#62;

Punctuation characters and symbols

Although many web designers tend to get around punctuation character limitations by using double hyphens (--) in place of em dashes (—), triple periods (. . .) in place of an ellipsis (...), and straight quotation marks ("") instead of "smart" quotes (""), XHTML supports many punctuation characters as character entities. Likewise, plenty of symbols are supported in XHTML, so you needn't write (c) when the copyright symbol is available.

This section lists all such characters and is split into four subsections: quotation marks, spacing and nonprinting characters, punctuation characters, and symbols.

Quotation marks

Character	Description	Entity name	Entity number
'	Left single	&lsquo;	&#8216;
'	Right single	&rsquo;	&#8217;
"	Left double	&ldquo;	&#8220;
"	Right double	&rdquo;	&#8221;
‹	Single left angle	&lsaquo;	&#8249;
›	Single right angle	&rsaquo;	&#8250;

Character	Description	Entity name	Entity number
«	Double left angle	«	«
»	Double right angle	»	»
‚	Single low-9	‚	‚
„	Double low-9	„	„

Spacing and nonprinting characters

Character	Description	Entity name	Entity number
	Em space		
	En space		
Nonprinting	Left-to-right mark	‎	‎
	Nonbreaking space		
	Overline	‾	‾
Nonprinting	Right-to-left mark	‏	‏
	Thin space		
Nonprinting	Zero-width joiner	‍	‍
Nonprinting	Zero-width nonjoiner	‌	‌

Punctuation characters

Character	Description	Entity name	Entity number
¦	Broken vertical bar	¦	¦
•	Bullet point	•	•
†	Dagger	†	†
‡	Double dagger	‡	‡

continues

Character	Description	Entity name	Entity number
″	Double prime, seconds, inches	&Prime;	&#8243;
…	Ellipsis	&hellip;	&#8230;
—	Em dash	&mdash;	&#8212;
–	En dash	&ndash;	&#8211;
/	Fraction slash	&frasl;	&#8260;
¡	Inverted exclamation mark	&iexcl;	&#161;
¿	Inverted question mark	&iquest;	&#191;
′	Prime, minutes, feet	&prime;	&#8242;
-	Soft hyphen	&shy;	&#173;

Symbols

Character	Description	Entity name	Entity number
ℑ	Blackletter capital I, imaginary part	&image;	&#8465;
ℜ	Blackletter capital R, real part	&real;	&#8476;
©	Copyright symbol	&copy;	&#169;
ª	Feminine ordinal	&ordf;	&#170;
º	Masculine ordinal	&ordm;	&#186;
¬	Not sign	&not;	&#172;
¶	Paragraph sign	&para;	&#182;
‰	Per mille symbol	&permil;	&#8240;
®	Registered trademark symbol	&reg;	&#174;

Character	Description	Entity name	Entity number
§	Section sign	&sect;	&#167;
™	Trademark symbol	&trade;	&#8482;
℘	Script capital P, power set	&weierp;	&#8472;

Characters for European languages

For any characters that have accents, circumflexes, or other additions, entities are available. However, many of these entities have their roots in the days when ASCII was the only available encoding method. These days, as long as you use the appropriate input method, and the page is correctly encoded, you may not need to use these entities. They are still listed here, though, for times when you just want to be on the safe side.

Take care when adding these, because case is important. In most cases, capitalizing the first letter of the entity name results in an uppercase character, but this isn't always so (notably the Icelandic characters "eth" and "thorn," the uppercase versions of which require the entire entity name to be in uppercase).

Character	Description	Entity name	Entity number
´	Acute accent (no letter)	&acute;	&#180;
¸	Cedilla (no letter)	&cedil;	&#184;
ˆ	Circumflex spacing modifier	&circ;	&#710;
¯	Macron accent	&macr;	&#175;
·	Middle dot	&middot;	&#183;
˜	Tilde	&tilde;	&#732;
¨	Umlaut	&uml;	&#168;
Á	Uppercase A, acute accent	&Aacute;	&#193;
á	Lowercase a, acute accent	&aacute;	&#225;

continues

Character	Description	Entity name	Entity number
Â	Uppercase a, circumflex accent	&Acirc;	&#194;
â	Lowercase a, circumflex accent	&acirc;	&#226;
À	Uppercase A, grave accent	&Agrave;	&#192;
à	Lowercase a, grave accent	&agrave;	&#224;
Å	Uppercase A, ring	&Aring;	&#197;
å	Lowercase a, ring	&aring;	&#229;
Ã	Uppercase A, tilde	&Atilde;	&#195;
ã	Lowercase a, tilde	&atilde;	&#227;
Ä	Uppercase A, umlaut	&Auml;	&#196;
ä	Lowercase a, umlaut	&auml;	&#228;
Æ	Uppercase AE ligature	&AElig;	&#198;
æ	Lowercase ae ligature	&aelig;	&#230;
Ç	Uppercase C, cedilla	&Ccedil;	&#199;
ç	Lowercase c, cedilla	&ccedil;	&#231;
É	Uppercase E, acute accent	&Eacute;	&#201;
é	Lowercase e, acute accent	&eacute;	&#233;
Ê	Uppercase E, circumflex accent	&Ecirc;	&#202;
ê	Lowercase e, circumflex accent	&ecirc;	&#234;
È	Uppercase E, grave accent	&Egrave;	&#200;

Character	Description	Entity name	Entity number
è	Lowercase e, grave accent	&egrave;	&#232;
Ë	Uppercase E, umlaut	&Euml;	&#203;
ë	Lowercase e, umlaut	&euml;	&#235;
Ð	Uppercase eth	&ETH;	&#208;
ð	Lowercase eth	&eth;	&#240;
Í	Uppercase I, acute accent	&Iacute;	&#205;
í	Lowercase i, acute accent	&iacute;	&#237;
Î	Uppercase I, circumflex accent	&Icirc;	&#206;
î	Lowercase i, circumflex accent	&icirc;	&#238;
Ì	Uppercase I, grave accent	&Igrave;	&#204;
ì	Lowercase i, grave accent	&igrave;	&#236;
Ï	Uppercase I, umlaut	&Iuml;	&#207;
ï	Lowercase i, umlaut	&iuml;	&#239;
Ñ	Uppercase N, tilde	&Ntilde;	&#209;
ñ	Lowercase n, tilde	&ntilde;	&#241;
Ó	Uppercase O, acute accent	&Oacute;	&#211;
ó	Lowercase o, acute accent	&oacute;	&#243;
Ô	Uppercase O, circumflex accent	&Ocirc;	&#212;

continues

Character	Description	Entity name	Entity number
ô	Lowercase o, circumflex accent	&ocirc;	&#244;
Ò	Uppercase O, grave accent	&Ograve;	&#210;
ò	Lowercase o, grave accent	&ograve;	&#242;
Ø	Uppercase O, slash	&Oslash;	&#216;
ø	Lowercase o, slash	&oslash;	&#248;
Õ	Uppercase O, tilde	&Otilde;	&#213;
õ	Lowercase o, tilde	&otilde;	&#245;
Ö	Uppercase O, umlaut	&Ouml;	&#214;
ö	Lowercase o, umlaut	&ouml;	&#246;
Œ	Uppercase OE ligature	&OElig;	&#338;
œ	Lowercase oe ligature	&oelig;	&#339;
Š	Uppercase S, caron	&Scaron;	&#352;
š	Lowercase s, caron	&scaron;	&#353;
ß	Lowercase sz ligature	&szlig;	&#223;
Þ	Uppercase thorn	&THORN;	&#222;
þ	Lowercase thorn	&thorn;	&#254;
Ú	Uppercase U, acute accent	&Uacute;	&#218;
ú	Lowercase u, acute accent	&uacute;	&#250;
Û	Uppercase U, circumflex accent	&Ucirc;	&#219;

Character	Description	Entity name	Entity number
û	Lowercase u, circumflex accent	û	û
Ù	Uppercase U, grave accent	Ù	Ù
ù	Lowercase u, grave accent	ù	ù
Ü	Uppercase U, umlaut	Ü	Ü
ü	Lowercase u, umlaut	ü	ü
Ý	Uppercase Y, acute accent	Ý	Ý
ý	Lowercase y, acute accent	ý	ý
Ÿ	Uppercase Y, umlaut	Ÿ	Ÿ
ÿ	Lowercase y, umlaut	ÿ	ÿ

Currency signs

Although the dollar sign is supported in XHTML, other common currency symbols are not. However, several can be added by way of entities, as shown in the following table.

Character	Description	Entity name	Entity number
¢	Cent	¢	¢
¤	General currency sign	¤	¤
€	Euro	€	€
£	Pound	£	£
¥	Yen	¥	¥

Mathematical, technical, and Greek characters

This set of entities combines mathematical and technical symbols and the Greek alphabet (which is commonly used in scientific work). For ease of use, this section is divided into three subsections: common mathematical characters (fractions and the most commonly used mathematical symbols), advanced mathematical and technical characters (characters of interest to those marking up technical documents or anything other than basic mathematical text), and Greek characters.

Common mathematical characters

Character	Description	Entity name	Entity number
°	Degree sign	°	°
÷	Division sign	÷	÷
½	Fraction—one half	½	½
¼	Fraction—one quarter	¼	¼
¾	Fraction—three quarters	¾	¾
>	Greater-than sign	>	>
≥	Greater-than or equal to sign	≥	≥
<	Less-than sign	<	<
≤	Less-than or equal to sign	≤	≤
−	Minus sign	−	−
×	Multiplication sign	×	×
¹	Superscript one	¹	¹
²	Superscript two	²	²
³	Superscript three	³	³

Advanced mathematical and technical characters

Character	Description	Entity name	Entity number
ℵ	Alef symbol, first transfinite cardinal	&alefsym;	&#8501;
≈	Almost equal to, asymptotic to	&asymp;	&#8776;
∠	Angle	&ang;	&#8736;
≅	Approximately equal to	&cong;	&#8773;
∗	Asterisk operator	&lowast;	&#8727;
⊕	Circled plus, direct sum	&oplus;	&#8853;
⊗	Circled times, vector product	&otimes;	&#8855;
∋	Contains as member	&ni;	&#8715;
.	Dot operator	&sdot;	&#8901;
∈	Element of	&isin;	&#8712;
∅	Empty set, null set, diameter	&empty;	&#8709;
∀	For all	&forall;	&#8704;
ƒ	Function, florin (Latin small f with hook)	&fnof;	&#402;
≡	Identical to	&equiv;	&#8801;
∞	Infinity	&infin;	&#8734;
∫	Integral	&int;	&#8747;
∩	Intersection, cap	&cap;	&#8745;
⌈	Left ceiling	&lceil;	&#8968;

continues

Character	Description	Entity name	Entity number
⌊	Left floor	&lfloor;	&#8970;
∧	Logical and, wedge	&and;	&#8743;
∨	Logical or, vee	&or;	&#8744;
μ	Micro sign	&micro;	&#181;
∇	Nabla, backward difference	&nabla;	&#8711;
∏	N-ary product, product sign	&prod;	&#8719;
∑	N-ary summation	&sum;	&#8721;
∉	Not an element of	&notin;	&#8713;
⊄	Not a subset of	&nsub;	&#8836;
≠	Not equal to	&ne;	&#8800;
∂	Partial differential	&part;	&#8706;
±	Plus-minus sign, plus-or-minus sign	&plusmn;	&#177;
∝	Proportional to	&prop;	&#8733;
⌉	Right ceiling	&rceil;	&#8969;
⌋	Right floor	&rfloor;	&#8971;
√	Square root, radical sign	&radic;	&#8730;
⊂	Subset of	&sub;	&#8834;
⊆	Subset of or equal to	&sube;	&#8838;
⊃	Superset of	&sup;	&#8835;
⊇	Superset of or equal to	&supe;	&#8839;
∃	There exists	&exist;	&#8707;

Character	Description	Entity name	Entity number
∴	Therefore	&there4;	&#8756;
~	Tilde operator, varies with, similar to	&sim;	&#8764;
∪	Union, cup	&cup;	&#8746;
⊥	Up tack, orthogonal to, perpendicular	&perp;	&#8869;

Greek characters

Character	Description	Entity name	Entity number
Α	Uppercase alpha	&Alpha;	&#913;
α	Lowercase alpha	&alpha;	&#945;
Β	Uppercase beta	&Beta;	&#914;
β	Lowercase beta	&beta;	&#946;
Γ	Uppercase gamma	&Gamma;	&#915;
γ	Lowercase gamma	&gamma;	&#947;
Δ	Uppercase delta	&Delta;	&#916;
δ	Lowercase delta	&delta;	&#948;
Ε	Uppercase epsilon	&Epsilon;	&#917;
ε	Lowercase epsilon	&epsilon;	&#949;
Ζ	Uppercase zeta	&Zeta;	&#918;
ζ	Lowercase zeta	&zeta;	&#950;
Η	Uppercase eta	&Eta;	&#919;

continues

Character	Description	Entity name	Entity number
η	Lowercase eta	&eta;	&#951;
Θ	Uppercase theta	&Theta;	&#920;
θ	Lowercase theta	&theta;	&#952;
I	Uppercase iota	&Iota;	&#921;
ι	Lowercase iota	&iota;	&#953;
Κ	Uppercase kappa	&Kappa;	&#922;
κ	Lowercase kappa	&kappa;	&#954;
Λ	Uppercase lambda	&Lambda;	&#923;
λ	Lowercase lambda	&lambda;	&#955;
Μ	Uppercase mu	&Mu;	&#924;
μ	Lowercase mu	&mu;	&#956;
Ν	Uppercase nu	&Nu;	&#925;
ν	Lowercase nu	&nu;	&#957;
Ξ	Uppercase xi	&Xi;	&#926;
ξ	Lowercase xi	&xi;	&#958;
Ο	Uppercase omicron	&Omicron;	&#927;
ο	Lowercase omicron	&omicron;	&#959;
Π	Uppercase pi	&Pi;	&#928;
π	Lowercase pi	&pi;	&#960;
Ρ	Uppercase rho	&Rho;	&#929;
ρ	Lowercase rho	&rho;	&#961;
ς	Lowercase final sigma	&sigmaf;	&#962;
Σ	Uppercase sigma	&Sigma;	&#931;

Character	Description	Entity name	Entity number
σ	Lowercase sigma	&sigma;	&#963;
T	Uppercase tau	&Tau;	&#932;
τ	Lowercase tau	&tau;	&#964;
Y	Uppercase upsilon	&Upsilon;	&#933;
υ	Lowercase upsilon	&upsilon;	&#965;
Φ	Uppercase phi	&Phi;	&#934;
φ	Lowercase phi	&phi;	&#966;
X	Uppercase chi	&Chi;	&#935;
χ	Lowercase chi	&chi;	&#967;
Ψ	Uppercase psi	&Psi;	&#936;
ψ	Lowercase psi	&psi;	&#968;
Ω	Uppercase omega	&Omega;	&#937;
ω	Lowercase omega	&omega;	&#969;
ϑ	Small theta symbol	&thetasym;	&#977;
ϒ	Greek upsilon with hook	&upsih;	&#978;
ϖ	Greek pi symbol	&piv;	&#982;

Arrows, lozenge, and card suits

Character	Description	Entity name	Entity number
↵	Carriage return	&crarr;	&#8629;
↓	Down arrow	&darr;	&#8595;
⇓	Down double arrow	&dArr;	&#8659;

continues

Character	Description	Entity name	Entity number
←	Left arrow	←	←
⇐	Left double arrow	⇐	⇐
↔	Left-right arrow	↔	↔
⇔	Left-right double arrow	⇔	⇔
→	Right arrow	→	→
⇒	Right double arrow	⇒	⇒
↑	Up arrow	↑	↑
⇑	Up double arrow	⇑	⇑
◊	Lozenge	◊	◊
♣	Clubs suit	♣	♣
♦	Diamonds suit	♦	♦
♥	Hearts suit	♥	♥
♠	Spades suit	♠	♠

Converting the nonstandard Microsoft set

The final table in this section lists the nonstandard Microsoft set and modern equivalents. Some older HTML editors, such as Dreamweaver 4, insert nonstandard entity values into web pages, causing them to fail validation. Here, we present the outdated nonstandard value and its corresponding approved alternatives (entity name and entity number, either of which can be used).

Character	Description	Nonstandard value	Entity name	Entity number
,	Single low-9 quote	&#130;	&sbquo;	&#8218;
ƒ	Lowercase Latin f with hook (florin)	&#131;	&fnof;	&#402;
„	Double low-9 quote	&#132;	&bdquo;	&#8222;
…	Ellipsis	&#133;	&hellip;	&#8230;
†	Dagger	&#134;	&dagger;	&#8224;
‡	Double dagger	&#135;	&Dagger;	&#8225;
ˆ	Circumflex spacing modifier	&#136;	&circ;	&#710;
‰	Per mille symbol	&#137;	&permil;	&#8240;
Š	Uppercase S, caron	&#138;	&Scaron;	&#352;
<	Less-than sign	&#139;	&lt;	&#60;
Œ	Uppercase OE ligature	&#140;	&OElig;	&#338;
'	Left single quote	&#145;	&lsquo;	&#8216;
'	Right single quote	&#146;	&rsquo;	&#8217;
"	Left double quote	&#147;	&ldquo;	&#8220;
"	Right double quote	&#148;	&rdquo;	&#8221;
•	Bullet point	&#149;	&bull;	&#8226;
–	En dash	&#150;	&ndash;	&#8211;
—	Em dash	&#151;	&mdash;	&#8212;
~	Tilde	&#152;	&tilde;	&#732;
™	Trademark symbol	&#153;	&trade;	&#8482;

continues

Character	Description	Nonstandard value	Entity name	Entity number
š	Lowercase s, caron	&#154;	&scaron;	&#353;
>	Greater-than sign	&#155;	&gt;	&#62;
œ	Lowercase oe ligature	&#156;	&oelig;	&#339;
Ÿ	Uppercase Y, umlaut	&#159;	&Yuml;	&#376